Crime Prevention and Security Management

Series Editor
Martin Gill, Perpetuity Research, Tunbridge Wells, UK

It is widely recognized that we live in an increasingly unsafe society, but the study of security and crime prevention has lagged behind in its importance on the political agenda and has not matched the level of public concern. This exciting new series aims to address these issues looking at topics such as crime control, policing, security, theft, workplace violence and crime, fear of crime, civil disorder, white collar crime and anti-social behaviour. International in perspective, providing critically and theoretically-informed work, and edited by a leading scholar in the field, this series will advance new understandings of crime prevention and security management.

Aleksandras Dobryninas · Simonas Nikartas
Editors

Understanding Crime Control and Punishment in Lithuania

A Punitive Society?

palgrave
macmillan

Editors
Aleksandras Dobryninas
Faculty of Philosophy
Institute of Sociology and Social Work
Department of Criminology, Vilnius University
Vilnius, Lithuania

Simonas Nikartas
Faculty of Philosophy
Institute of Sociology and Social Work
Department of Criminology, Vilnius University
Vilnius, Lithuania

ISSN 2946-3513 ISSN 2946-3521 (electronic)
Crime Prevention and Security Management
ISBN 978-3-032-05537-8 ISBN 978-3-032-05538-5 (eBook)
https://doi.org/10.1007/978-3-032-05538-5

Cover credit: Aleksandras Dobryninas

This Palgrave Macmillan imprint is published by the registered company Springer Nature Switzerland AG
The registered company address is: Gewerbestrasse 11, 6330 Cham, Switzerland

Preface

The present volume emerges from the intricate mosaic of Lithuania's past and present—a society whose justice system reflects both historical resilience and contemporary challenges. Lithuania, a country at the crossroads of Eastern and Western Europe, has borne the weight of shifting political powers and economic transitions.

During the Soviet era, Lithuania's punitive system was heavily influenced by the broader Soviet criminal justice framework, which prioritised state control and repression over individual rights. The system was used as a tool for political control, targeting dissenters, intellectuals, and anyone perceived as a threat to Soviet authority. Many Lithuanians were deported to labour camps (Gulags) or executed. The legal and punitive systems in Lithuania were subordinate to Moscow. Soviet laws and policies took precedence over local regulations, leaving little room for autonomy. Punishments were severe, often disproportionate to the crimes committed, including long prison sentences, forced labour, and even capital punishment for political offences. The judicial process was often a formality, with predetermined outcomes, while defendants had limited rights.

After regaining independence in 1990, Lithuania faced the monumental task of redefining its justice system in line with democratic values. Yet, this process raised critical tensions: how does a society reconcile the necessity of control and accountability with the principles of freedom, fairness, and humanity inherent in democracy?

The relationship between punitiveness and democracy is a central thread running through this book. Democracies, which in theory strive to ensure justice systems are not instruments of oppression but rather tools for fairness, rehabilitation, and the maintenance of social harmony. However, as David Garland (2001) discusses in *The Culture of Control*, even democratic societies can adopt punitive measures in response to social anxieties, fears of disorder, and perceptions of risk. Lithuania's trajectory offers a fascinating case study of this dynamic, shaped by its history of authoritarianism and the challenges of transitioning to democracy.

Michel Foucault's (1975) insights from *Discipline and Punish* further illuminate the tension between surveillance-based control and the democratic ideal of individual freedom. Lithuania, during the Soviet era, saw punishment as an instrument of state power, used to enforce conformity. In post-independence Lithuania, the justice system began to shift towards aligning punishment with principles of accountability and respect for human rights. Yet, lingering elements of authoritarian control posed significant obstacles, creating a complex interplay between historical legacies and democratic aspirations.

Vincenzo Ruggiero's (2013) analysis of European penal systems in his *Punishment in Europe: A Critical Anatomy of Penal Systems* provides a valuable perspective for understanding these processes. Ruggiero emphasises how socio-economic inequalities and cultural contradictions often shape punitive practices within democracies. In Lithuania, economic struggles and systemic disparities have contributed to the persistence of punitive measures, particularly for vulnerable groups such as women, minors, and economically disadvantaged individuals. Ruggiero's framework helps us see how the justice system operates not just as a mechanism of law enforcement but as a reflection of broader societal tensions.

At the core of the present volume is an exploration which goes beyond legal frameworks and penal institutions. It delves into the lived human experiences of punishment. It also considers alternatives to punishment that have emerged in recent years. These alternatives reflect a growing recognition that traditional punitive measures, such as incarceration, are not always effective in reducing recidivism or addressing the root causes of crime. Lithuania's adoption of restorative justice practices, such as victim-offender mediation, has gained traction. These practices prioritise reconciliation, healing, and the restoration of relationships over retribution, offering a more humane approach to justice, aligning with democratic principles of participation and inclusion.

Beyond restorative practices, other alternatives include community-based sanctions and rehabilitative programs. Instead of incarceration, offenders may engage in community service or structured programs addressing issues like addiction, unemployment, or mental health. For women offenders, in particular, gender-sensitive interventions tailored to their unique circumstances, such as caregiving responsibilities or histories of abuse, are increasingly implemented. For minors, education-focused strategies and diversion programs emphasise skill-building and reintegration into society rather than detention.

Central to this book is therefore the human dimension of justice. What does punitiveness look like in a democratic society? How do individuals navigate systems of punishment that oscillate between control and compassion? Stories of young offenders finding a path forward through educational programs or women overcoming violence with support systems bring to light the human struggles that lie at the heart of Lithuania's justice system. This work moves beyond abstract criminological and legal concepts to the lived realities of punishment. What does it mean to be a woman dealing with violence or harassment, a drug addict living with their stigma, or a policymaker trying to reconcile the Soviet legacy with European ideals? These stories bring the punitive system to life, capturing its contradictions, vulnerabilities, and potential for change.

This book draws from broader theoretical frameworks, including a Durkheimian perspective on punishment as a social phenomenon shaped by concurrent social and cultural factors, Michel Foucault's insights into power and surveillance, David Garland's exploration of the cultural dynamics of control, and critical criminological analysis of punishment as a mechanism of inequality. Following Nils Christie's (1986) 'suitable victims', the concept of 'suitable punishable subjects' is introduced, namely individuals who are more prone to facing punishment within the criminal justice system or being viewed as deserving of punishment within society.

Yet these theories are not presented in isolation. They are applied with care, mapped onto the specific contours of Lithuania's justice system, where history and culture intertwine to create a distinctive penal identity. In Lithuania, the legacy of Soviet authoritarianism still casts long shadows, shaping not only institutions but also media and public perceptions of crime, justice, and punishment.

At the same time, this work investigates the quiet but powerful transformations taking place within the country. It reconstructs the process of abolishing the death penalty in Lithuania and impact of this decision on the broader international abolitionist policy. Restorative justice initiatives, community-based sanctions, and rehabilitative programs challenge the traditional punitive narrative, offering glimpses of hope. Such measures do not merely address crime; they seek to heal fractured relationships, rebuild trust, and restore dignity. These shifts reflect the resilience and humanity of a society striving to balance accountability with compassion.

However, the authors of the book do not turn a blind eye to the still-existing obstacles and challenges. Lithuania's prison system has faced criticism for its hierarchical structure, a remnant of Soviet times. This system is seen as fostering stigma and hindering reintegration into society. Another critical aspect is that Lithuania has a low incidence of parole compared to the EU average, which limits opportunities for prisoners to reintegrate into society. This has been linked to higher rates of recidivism. Former prisoners in Lithuania also face significant societal barriers, including discrimination in housing and employment. This stigma makes reintegration challenging and can lead to a cycle of reoffending.

This book has broader implications for scholars and practitioners alike. It serves as a bridge between theory and practice, offering insights for criminologists, legal scholars, sociologists, policymakers, and activists.

Written by a team of dedicated Lithuanian scholars from Vilnius University, who are well-known for their interdisciplinary and critical approach, this book without doubt presents a significant contribution to literature and expertise in criminology, criminal policy, and criminal justice. The authors of this book are not only advancing academic research but also applying their findings to shape criminal justice policies and crime prevention strategies in Lithuania, providing critical depth and situating Lithuania within the larger European and global context of justice systems in transition.

Ultimately, this book is not just about Lithuania. It is about the universal struggle to define the role of punishment in society and to reconcile the demands of justice with the needs of humanity. It invites readers to reflect on what it means to build a system that is not only fair but also restorative, not only bureaucratic but also compassionate.

Researchers and practitioners will find valuable insights into how punitive systems operate and adapt within diverse socio-political contexts. Moreover, by addressing alternatives to punishment, this book highlights the potential for a more compassionate justice system that reduces harm and fosters rehabilitation. Lithuania's evolving approaches offer lessons not only for its own society but for the global community grappling with the limitations of punitive policies and the search for effective alternatives. It challenges us to think critically about whether punitiveness can coexist with democratic values and how societies can pursue justice systems that uphold dignity, fairness, and humanity. Justice in a democracy, ultimately, is not measured merely by control but by the capacity to heal, empower, and uplift the lives it touches.

University of Utrecht Dina Siegel

References

Christie, N. (1986). The ideal victim. In *From crime policy to victim policy: Reorienting the justice system*, 17–30. London: Palgrave Macmillan UK.

Foucault, M. (1975). Discipline and punish. *A. Sheridan,Tr.,Paris,FR,Gallimard*.
Garland, D. (2001). *The culture of control: Crime and social order in contemporary society* (Vol. 77). Oxford University Press.
Ruggiero, V., & Ryan, M. (2013). *Punishment in Europe: A critical anatomy of penal systems*. Springer.

Acknowledgements

The book cover displays an interior view of the former Lukiškės prison. The editors express gratitude to Sigita Černevičiūtė, Goda Damaševičiūtė, and the "Lukiškių kalėjimo 2.0" team for their assistance in organizing the photography.

Series Editor Introduction

If punishment worked wouldn't crime prevention be so much easier? Assessing why it so often does not is a key feature of this book. It assesses punitiveness in Lithuania, a now democratic society (since 1990) but one that has lived in the shadow of a prior era where the Soviet system dominated, which, the editors describe "prioritised state control and repression over individual rights". The editors, Aleksandras Dobryninas and Simonas Nikartas have brought together a collection of papers that examines the reasons why punitiveness is popular and why alternatives often are not, and more broadly, of the relationship between punishment and democratic values. In short, they argue, "how does a society reconcile the necessity of control and accountability with the principles of freedom, fairness, and humanity inherent in democracy".

The book is divided into three parts, the first looking at the reasons for punitive attitudes in Lithuanian society. To pick some examples, we learn that although people often espouse a belief in rehabilitation, in reality they are driven by retribution, anger, and a desire for "just deserts" (Kristina Vanagaitė and Violeta Cimalanskaitė-Kazlauskienė). While another perspective based on 322 life histories develops the notion of "punishment from below" seeing punitiveness as a reaction to prior injustice thereby finding expression in everyday attitudes (Laima Žilinskienė).

In the second part the editors focus the narrative around "suitable punishable subjects" who are individuals who are more likely to face punishment and/or be viewed as more deserving of it. For example, the "inappropriate" lifestyle of the financially disadvantaged that marks them out as "punishable subjects." (Arūnas Poviliūnas and Arūnas Juška). And where the prosecution of online offenders is not focussed on the more serious offenders with their technical expertise but on those who exploit a victim's trust and then tends to be the poorer and previously convicted offenders (Maryja Šupa, Vytautas Kaktinas, and Eglė Stankevičiūtė). And women who are "doubly deviant in breaking the law but also prevailing perceptions of a caring role that is perceived as the norm" (Rimantė Gaičevskytė).

The final part of the book offers a comparative perspective and generates many interesting insights. A good example is the discussion about how some types of community penalties can adopt characteristics more closely associated with imprisonment. The chapter by Simonas Nikartas, Loreta Matačiūtė, and Neila Sventickytė which is based on interviews with those on probation is a case in point.

The powerful insights in this book have a much wider application beyond Lithuania of course. They invite a detailed analysis of what works and why some measures don't. The message that remedies rest on dealing with issues way beyond the remit of the criminal justice system and its practitioners is not new, but it is important. I am delighted we can include this book in the "Crime Prevention and Security Management Series". Happy reading!.

July 2025

Martin Gill
Series Editor

Contents

Editors and Contributors

About the Editors

Dr. Aleksandras Dobryninas is a Professor of Sociology and Chair of the Department of Criminology at the Institute of Sociology and Social Work, Faculty of Philosophy, Vilnius University, Lithuania. His research interests include the theoretical foundations of criminological knowledge, corruption, violent crime, media and crime, and public confidence in criminal justice institutions. In 2020–2021, he served as President of the European Society of Criminology.

Dr. Simonas Nikartas is an Associate Professor at the Department of Criminology, Institute of Sociology and Social Work, Faculty of Philosophy, Vilnius University, Lithuania. His research focuses on various aspects of criminal justice and crime prevention, with a particular emphasis in recent years on probation and community sanctions. He previously served as Head of the Probation Division at the Prison Department under the Ministry of Justice of the Republic of Lithuania.

Contributors

Jolanta Aleknevičienė Faculty of Philosophy, Institute of Sociology and Social Work, Department of Criminology, Vilnius University, Vilnius, Lithuania

Algimantas Čepas Faculty of Philosophy, Institute of Sociology and Social Work, Department of Criminology, Vilnius University, Vilnius, Lithuania

Violeta Cimalanskaitė-Kazlauskienė Faculty of Philosophy, Institute of Psychology, Vilnius University, Vilnius, Lithuania

Goda Damaševičiūtė Faculty of Philosophy, Institute of Sociology and Social Work, Department of Criminology, Vilnius University, Vilnius, Lithuania

Aleksandras Dobryninas Faculty of Philosophy, Institute of Sociology and Social Work, Department of Criminology, Vilnius University, Vilnius, Lithuania

Rimantė Gaičevskytė-Savickė Faculty of Philosophy, Institute of Sociology and Social Work, Department of Criminology, Vilnius, Lithuania

Arunas Juska East Carolina University, Greenville, USA

Vytautas Kaktinas Faculty of Philosophy, Institute of Sociology and Social Work, Department of Criminology, Vilnius University, Vilnius, Lithuania

Mindaugas Lankauskas Faculty of Philosophy, Institute of Sociology and Social Work, Department of Criminology, Vilnius University, Vilnius, Lithuania

Loreta Matačiūtė Faculty of Philosophy, Institute of Sociology and Social Work, Department of Criminology, Vilnius University, Vilnius, Lithuania

Simonas Nikartas Faculty of Philosophy, Institute of Sociology and Social Work, Department of Criminology, Vilnius University, Vilnius, Lithuania

Aušra Pocienė Faculty of Philosophy, Institute of Sociology and Social Work, Department of Criminology, Vilnius University, Vilnius, Lithuania

Arūnas Poviliūnas Faculty of Philosophy, Institute of Sociology and Social Work, Vilnius University, Vilnius, Lithuania

Eglė Stankevičiūtė Faculty of Philosophy, Institute of Sociology and Social Work, Department of Criminology, Vilnius University, Vilnius, Lithuania

Maryja Šupa Faculty of Philosophy, Institute of Sociology and Social Work, Department of Criminology, Vilnius University, Vilnius, Lithuania

Neila Sventickytė Faculty of Philosophy, Institute of Sociology and Social Work, Department of Criminology, Vilnius University, Vilnius, Lithuania

Kristina Vanagaitė Faculty of Philosophy, Institute of Psychology, Vilnius University, Vilnius, Lithuania

Jovita Žėkaitė-Maconko Faculty of Philosophy, Institute of Sociology and Social Work, Department of Criminology, Vilnius University, Vilnius, Lithuania

Laima Žilinskienė Faculty of Philosophy, Institute of Sociology and Social Work, Department of Criminology, Vilnius University, Vilnius, Lithuania

List of Figures

List of Tables

1

Lithuania as a Punitive Society: An Introduction

Aleksandras Dobryninas and Simonas Nikartas

The concept of a 'punitive society' has been analysed by various philosophers and criminologists, most notably Michel Foucault (1973/2015) and David Garland (2001). Foucault (2015) first introduced the term in his lecture series 'La société punitive', in which punishment is understood not only as a legal reaction but as a way of exercising power that permeates the entire structure of society. Garland (2001) discusses how late modern societies have become increasingly oriented towards risk management, security, and repressive criminal justice measures, which have led to the emergence of the so-called punitive turn.

A. Dobryninas · S. Nikartas (✉)
Faculty of Philosophy, Institute of Sociology and Social Work, Department of Criminology, Vilnius University, Vilnius, Lithuania
e-mail: simonas.nikartas@fsf.vu.lt

A. Dobryninas
e-mail: aleksandras.dobryninas@fsf.vu.lt

A. Dobryninas and S. Nikartas (eds.), *Understanding Crime Control and Punishment in Lithuania*, Crime Prevention and Security Management,
https://doi.org/10.1007/978-3-032-05538-5_1

In contemporary literature (e.g., see: Aebi et al., 2015; Cohen, 1985; Foucault, 1977; Phelps, 2017; Simon, 2007; Wacquant, 2009), punitiveness is reflected in the routine use of criminal law to manage social conflict, rather than as a last resort. In such societies, imprisonment becomes the norm, and criminal control extends into community sanctions characterised by surveillance and restriction. Scholars describe this as 'governing through crime,' where penal measures legitimise political authority. Disciplinary practices permeate institutions, shaping compliant individuals. As social welfare declines, punitive mechanisms intensify, particularly under 'punitive neoliberalism.' A culture of punishment—marked by zero-tolerance rhetoric, moral panic, and public support for harsh policies—emerges. Thus, punitive societies maintain order through expansive, culturally reinforced control systems and penal governance. Institutional punitiveness—expressed through control and disciplinary practices across various social domains—typically interacts with cultural factors such as citizens' values, everyday practices, and attitudes towards punishment.

The concept of a 'punitive society' has traditionally been associated with the United States, which is often noted for its comparatively harsh criminal justice policies among democratic nations. Although the term "punitive society" is rarely used in the European context, some countries in this region—especially those with a legacy of the communist regime—exhibit key features characteristic of these societies, such as strict criminal policies and limited attention to rehabilitation (see Krajewski, 2016, 2014; Slade & Light, 2015). However, scholarly attention to punitiveness in these countries remains limited, particularly with regard to penal control and public attitudes in post-communist European contexts. Rare publications (see also Slade & Kupatadze, 2017; Nikartas, 2020) link the idea of a punitive society with repressive criminal justice policy, historical traces of authoritarianism, and low trust in institutions. These factors converge with a logic of discipline and control embedded in both public discourse and institutional practice. In such societies, harsh punishments are not only legal responses but symbolic tools used to fulfil expectations related to order, retribution, and security. However, this distrust-based system often reinforces structural mistrust, creating a closed cycle of punitiveness and control.

As portrayed within criminological publications, the hallmarks of a punitive societal structure typically include the following characteristics.

Dominance of imprisonment. Imprisonment continues to be the primary punishment, even though alternative sanctions are expanding.

Expansion of social control through community sanctions. Probation, electronic monitoring, and house arrest frequently supplement, rather than replace, prison sentences.

Primacy of disciplinary and control logic. Instead of rehabilitation or restorative justice, the penal system prioritises monitoring, restrictions, and enforcing compliance.

Penal populism. Public expectations of punishment and order are met by political and institutional actors through punitive rhetoric and policies, thereby enhancing their perceived legitimacy.

Low institutional trust. Stricter penalties do not build public trust in authorities; instead, they often worsen it.

Extension of control into other social domains. Discipline extends beyond the criminal justice system, shaping education, healthcare, welfare, and employment through self-regulation, compliance, and the adoption of societal norms.

Legacy of authoritarianism. Communist-era norms and institutional logic significantly shaped current approaches to social control and the suppression of social issues.

This book's pages thoroughly examine the many facets of a punitive society as they specifically relate to Lithuania. What makes Lithuania stand out? From our perspective, Lithuania, a democratic nation within the European Union, serves as a stark example of a society with a punitive approach to justice, notably maintaining, for two decades, one of the highest incarceration rates within the entire European Union. For example, the incarceration rate in 2024 reached 156 individuals per 100,000 residents, according to data compiled by the World Prison Brief in 2024. Despite a decrease from 323.91 in 2012, according to data from Eurostat, this figure still ranks among the highest in Europe. Sakalauskas et al. (2020) found that the extended average prison sentence, roughly three years, substantially contributes to this issue; this represents a considerable length of time spent incarcerated. According to data from the Lithuanian Prison Service in 2024, a significant majority of prisoners in 2022, precisely 2041 out of 3730, were serving custodial sentences exceeding a five-year term (Lithuanian Prison Service, 2025).

In addition to other notable statistics, Lithuania has a significantly high number of people currently subject to community-based sanctions. Lithuania also ranks high in terms of the number of individuals under community sanctions. In 2023, there were 215.2 persons under probation supervision per 100,000 inhabitants (Lithuanian Probation Service, 2024)—significantly higher than the European average of 174.9 provided in the SPACE II report (2023). Furthermore, the probation system is heavily weighted towards methods of control and is plagued by a substantial number of revoked probations (see Nikartas & Paliauka, 2024; Nikartas et al., 2021).

Lithuania's punitive label encompasses more than just its high incarceration rate. A harsh public approach to punishment is apparent in the overabundance of corrections personnel, substandard prison conditions, and ongoing human rights violations (see Sakalauskas et al., 2020). Other factors include negative societal views, a focus on harsh punishments, and low public confidence in government, parliament, the courts, and the prison system. Lithuania's punitive social attitudes are partly a result of the Soviet era's cultural impact, according to Buzaitytė-Kašalynienė et al. (2024).

However, some Eastern European countries, such as Slovenia and Romania, demonstrate that a communist past does not automatically lead to a harsh penal system. Lithuanian penal policy has also been influenced by other cultural and social factors, which this book will examine in more detail.

Lithuania's struggle with its Soviet past provides a unique case study for this book's comprehensive analysis of punitiveness in a democratic European setting, filling a void in the existing research. It contributes to the ongoing research on punishment in Europe, especially in Eastern

European countries. These crucial criminological findings provide a valuable resource for policymakers seeking to replace punitive approaches with more effective, rights-based criminal justice strategies.

The Structure of the Book

In light of the previously mentioned problems, the book uses a thematic structure to examine the punitiveness phenomenon thoroughly. The topic covers punishment's theoretical and practical sides, including societal views and institutional practices. The book's chapters examine the Lithuanian case, exploring the social, political, cultural, and historical roots of 'punitiveness' and its varied forms across society.

The book's opening section examines Lithuania's punitive society's theoretical and empirical underpinnings, incorporating psychological, philosophical, political, and cultural perspectives.

Kristina Vanagaitė and Violeta Cimalanskaitė-Kazlauskienė, in their chapter 'Psychology of punishment: Why do we punish others?', analyse why people support harsh punishments and how such attitudes are formed. The authors thoroughly explain the psychological factors underlying punitiveness. They discuss the main functions of punishment—deterrence, social regulation, and retribution—and how they are reflected in individual decision-making and public discourse. Based on psychological theories and empirical research, they emphasise that although people often declare preventive or rehabilitative goals, dominant motivations are frequently driven by emotional retribution, anger, and expectations of 'just deserts'.

The authors also draw attention to the prevalence of authoritarian attitudes in Lithuanian society, the influence of historical experiences (e.g., the Soviet regime or violent upbringing), and social factors, such as gender, age, and education, which are linked to punitiveness. Furthermore, the chapter addresses public scepticism towards alternatives such as restorative justice or halfway houses, especially when applied in cases of serious crimes. A lack of institutional trust and persistent misconceptions, such as the belief that harsher penalties are more effective, hinder the development and acceptance of less harmful but empirically grounded punishment strategies.

Aušra Pocienė, in her chapter 'The Social and Cultural Context of Punitiveness in Lithuania', introduces the reader to Lithuanian society's social and cultural development from 1990 to 2023. The author explains how changes shaped public perceptions of crime and punishment during this period. In other words, she seeks to reveal the social and cultural factors that underlie manifestations of punitiveness in society.

In doing so, Aušra Pocienė links empirical data on Lithuanian society with the theories of Émile Durkheim, David Garland, and Robert Agnew. She shows that in the early years of independence, marked by social tension, unemployment, and rising crime, punitive attitudes were driven by emotion and a demand for retribution. In later years, with Lithuania's accession to the EU and NATO, improving economic conditions, and decreasing crime rates, the sense of security increased, and the collective consciousness began to shift, becoming less punitive and more oriented towards a rational and human rights-based perspective. Pocienė argues that in recent years, Lithuania has seen the emergence of a shift from retributive criminal policy to a restorative justice model, in which crime is seen as a social conflict to be resolved through dialogue and restored accountability, rather than through punishment alone.

The other three chapters in this section delve into the historical-cultural layers of punitiveness by analysing generational experiences.

In the chapter 'Lessons from the abolition of the death penalty in Lithuania: looking through a kaleidoscope of professional, political and public discourses', the author, Aleksandras Dobryninas, looks back on the process of abolition of the death penalty and its possible impact on the formation of anti-punitiveness mentality in Lithuania. A significant milestone in Lithuania's justice system was reached twenty-five years ago when the legal system officially abolished the death penalty, signifying a momentous shift in the country's approach to punishment and justice. In a message addressed to both its citizens and the global political arena, the Lithuanian state conveyed its unwavering commitment to maintaining a humane and civilised criminal justice system, ensuring complete adherence to all international human rights standards and obligations. The transition, however, proved to be a complicated process, far from straightforward or effortless, and its complexity defied any simple categorisation as a mere formal procedure.

Employing the social phenomenological and discursive theoretical frameworks established by prominent thinkers Alfred Schutz and Michel Foucault, the presentation will systematically analyse and meticulously reconstruct the intricate political timeline tracing the abolition of capital punishment in Lithuania. A thorough investigation into the multifaceted discussions surrounding the death penalty in Lithuania, this analysis delves into the professional, political, and public discourses, including professionals debates for and against its abolition or retention of the death penality, the formation of coalitions and conflicts among experts, politicians and the public, and the consequential impact of these interactions on the ultimate policy outcome. Moreover, this analysis undertakes a comprehensive assessment of this decision's potential effects, investigating its capacity to not only transform the international landscape of abolitionist policy but also to reduce, to a certain extent, the pervasive impact of penal populism on the criminal justice policies implemented in democratic societies.

In her chapter 'Punitive Thinking in Different Times and Generations', Laima Žilinskienė analyses how different historical periods' social, economic, and political conditions shaped people's relationships with punishment and social order. Drawing on a substantial body of empirical material—322 life histories—she applies the concept of 'punishment from below'. She reveals how conformist-innovative behaviour—adaptation through creative norm violations—became the prevailing response to systemic injustice both during the Soviet period and the post-1990 transformations following independence. Using theoretical frameworks such as Merton's anomie theory and Bourdieu's notion of 'delinquent habitus,' the author demonstrates that these adaptive strategies not only enabled survival but also functioned as symbolic resistance—a form of social punishment directed at those who created or upheld an unjust system. Such actions—stealing from collective farms, working off the books, tax evasion, or rule-bending—were not perceived as crimes but as moral responses to a system that failed to ensure dignified living conditions.

This dimension of punitiveness—as an emotional and cultural reaction to experienced injustice—emerges across different areas of life and helps to explain how the logic of punishment extends beyond the legal sphere, becoming embedded in everyday practices and attitudes. At the same time, the author's analysis helps illuminate current societal views on criminal behaviour. For example, it can be assumed that the historical experiences discussed by the author may interact with the high levels of societal tolerance for corruption, tax evasion, and financial misconduct revealed by sociological research.[1]

In the chapter 'Punitive Attitudes Toward Difference: The Drift of Bullying Perception in the 1980–2000 Generation', Goda Damaševičiūtė and Jovita Žėkaitė-Maconko analyse manifestations of punitive culture through the experiences of bullying reported by individuals born between 1980 and 2000 in Lithuania. Drawing on the analysis of 67 biographical interviews, the authors examine how the social, economic, and cultural changes that followed the restoration of independence shaped children's and adolescents' experiences with bullying, authority, and social relationships.

Using the frameworks of restorative justice and shame management theory, the authors reveal how weak adult authority, fragmented communities, and prevailing shame-based stigmatisation created conditions in which aggression became an accepted model of behaviour. Bullying is interpreted here as a form of punitive peer relationship, through physical, social, or emotional violence, power hierarchies were established, and children perceived as weak or 'different' were excluded. The authors

[1] For example, the 2018 *Lithuanian Corruption Map* survey commissioned by the Lithuanian Special Investigation Service revealed that the majority of respondents (63%) believe that a bribe helps to solve problems; 17% stated they would offer a bribe to resolve their own issues, and another 40% said it would depend on the circumstances (Special Investigation Service, 2018). Diržytė and Patapas (2018) found that 40% of Lithuanian residents believe it is justified not to pay taxes to a state that is unjust toward its citizens, and nearly 44% of respondents agreed that it is acceptable to justify people who give or receive money without paying taxes to the state.

argue that, within informal youth communities, punishment and humiliation functioned as tools of social control, while responsibility for bullying was often placed on the victim.

These insights contribute to a deeper understanding of contemporary expressions of punitiveness in society—many individuals currently involved in shaping and implementing criminal justice policy belong to the very generation analysed by the authors. It can be assumed that childhood exposure to a culture of bullying—characterised by dominance, humiliation, and victim-blaming- may have influenced current views on crime and punishment. Such experiences may contribute to legitimising punishment as the primary response to wrongdoing, downplaying the importance of reintegration, social support, and the need to address the structural roots of criminal behaviour.

The book's second part unveils the complexities surrounding the selectivity of the criminal justice system, targeting specific social groups. We employ the 'suitable punishable subjects' concept to delineate these groups. We draw parallels between this definition and the 'suitable victims' concept utilised in criminology and victimology research literature. Nils Christie (1986) introduced the idea of 'suitable victims' to describe groups of individuals who are more likely to be victimised due to their vulnerability or socially constructed deviance, and therefore perceived as legitimate victims. In a similar vein, we conceive 'suitable punishable subjects' as individuals who, by virtue of their social and economic characteristics, are more prone to facing punishment within the criminal justice system or being viewed as deserving of punishment within society.

These ideas are not new to criminological literature. In their 1939 book Punishment and Social Structure, Georg Rusche and Otto Kirchheimer argued that penal systems are deeply intertwined with economic conditions and social structure. They are often directed at the lower social strata, whose precarious status makes them more vulnerable and more easily punished. Similar dynamics, in the Lithuanian context, are explored in the chapter Disciplining the Poor: The Politics of Responsibilizing the Underclass in Lithuania by Arūnas Poviliūnas and Arūnas Juška.

Drawing on Loïc Wacquant's concept of the punitive state and the cultural studies tradition (Birmingham School), the authors show how, following political conflicts over social inequality, especially after the impeachment of President Rolandas Paksas, a disciplinary and individualising approach to poverty took hold in Lithuania. They analyse how poverty began to be interpreted as a matter of individual morality, and how public policy shifted towards punitive and corrective approaches, demanding work, responsible behaviour, and the demonstration of socially accepted values in exchange for support. According to the authors, this shift established a new regime of 'punitive responsibilisation', in which social assistance is based not on solidarity but on control, moral judgement, and preconceptions about the 'inappropriate' lifestyle of the poor. Their analysis corresponds closely to the notion of the poor as 'punishable subjects.' They show how socially excluded individuals are not only recipients of assistance but also morally suspect and constantly evaluated subjects whose behaviour must be observed, corrected, and disciplined.

This tendency to discipline the socially disadvantaged is also evident in criminal justice practice. Criminological literature reveals that the penal system too often criminalises 'poverty crimes' (e.g., theft, possession of drugs for personal use), which are frequently committed by individuals affected by social, economic, or addiction-related problems (Weis, 2021). By contrast, so-called 'white-collar crimes' (e.g., economic, corruption, or cybercrime) are punished far less frequently. Furthermore, even when white-collar crimes are prosecuted, the criminal justice system may selectively target weaker individuals.

A specific manifestation of this pattern is explored in the chapter 'Technology and Future Trajectories of Punitivity: Lessons Learned from Selective Persecution of Online Offenders in Lithuania' by Maryja Šupa, Vytautas Kaktinas, and Eglė Stankevičiūtė. Based on a case study of Lithuania, the authors show that while public discourse focuses on complex, transnational cybercrimes, actual court practice tends to prioritise minor fraud and deception based on social engineering—that is, exploiting people's trust rather than using technical knowledge. These crimes are most often committed by less-educated, previously convicted individuals. Due to their social and economic status, they are more likely to be subjected to criminal liability, even when the harm caused is far less than that of large-scale cybercrime. The authors demonstrate that such selective prosecution helps maintain an illusion of order and enhances control over those who are most visible and least capable of defending themselves. This supports the idea that criminal justice does not always target the greatest threats to society but often operates on a logic where the heaviest burden falls on those who are most accessible.

Another aspect of criminal justice selectiveness in targeting socially vulnerable individuals is revealed in Mindaugas Lankauskas' chapter on Lithuania's drug control policy. Analysing legal documents, statistical data, and public attitudes, the author shows how a harsh and repressive approach to drug use primarily affects people with addiction, who are more likely to receive prison sentences instead of treatment. These individuals, often incarcerated for possession of small quantities or low-level distribution, become the most visible targets of the penal system, despite their relatively minor harm to society compared to large-scale drug trafficking or white-collar crime. According to the author, this selective prosecution stems from prevailing societal stigma against drug users and is supported by laws that offer no real alternatives to incarceration. Such a policy not only marginalises individuals with addiction but also contributes to their criminalisation and labelling, thereby creating a closed cycle between addiction, imprisonment, and social exclusion.

Yet another form of selectivity—this time in the media—is revealed by Rimantė Gaičevskytė-Savickė, who analyses representations of women in crime news. Drawing on an analysis of Lithuania's largest news portal DELFI, the author shows how the media actively shapes the image of criminalised women through a patriarchal lens. A female offender is portrayed as 'doubly deviant'—violating not only the law but also dominant expectations of femininity, care, and motherhood. These portrayals are particularly pronounced in the context of violent or child-related crimes, where women's behaviour is often moralised, with emphasis on their appearance, family status, or supposed moral decline. While most women commit non-violent offences, the media focuses on exceptional, shocking cases, reinforcing stereotypes and societal bias against socially vulnerable women. This selective attention not only distorts the real picture of crime but can also influence public opinion and political decisions, ultimately contributing to the marginalisation and stigmatisation of certain groups. In this way, the media constructs the image of women as 'punishable subjects'—a gender seen, through stereotypical assumptions, as incapable of crime, making their offences, following Harold Garfinkel's concept of 'sacred crimes', transgressions not only of legal but also of sacralised moral norms in society.

The book's third part delves into the institutional facets of punitiveness. Compared to Western European countries, Lithuania's criminal justice institutions are relatively young and still in development. Lithuania's institutional punishment system is navigating a protracted transition, moving away from the Soviet-era ideology rooted in coercion and control towards one centred on re-socialisation and support. In this context, ongoing penal reforms are regularly initiated, with stated aims of enhancing the effectiveness of punishment and facilitating reintegration. By applying critical perspectives, this section focuses on reform efforts in prisons, probation, and victim support systems.

The first chapter of this section, 'Reform Again? Penal Reform as a Never-Ending Story', by Jolanta Aleknevičienė, analyses the trajectory of penal enforcement reforms in Lithuania from 2000 to the present, focusing on institutional changes in the prison system and their implementation. Drawing on an analysis of policy documents and expert interviews, the author reveals that although reforms are often framed in reintegration and human rights rhetoric, their practical implementation remains fragmented and insufficiently coherent. According to the author, shortcomings such as a lack of strategic planning, limited staff involvement, and insufficient evaluation of program effectiveness result in a situation where declared changes do not always translate into real institutional practice. This analysis helps explain why, despite formal ambitions to modernise the penal system, the logic of control and formalism continues to prevail, hindering systemic change.

In the second chapter, 'A Prison Without Bars: Prisonisation of Probation through Intensive Supervision in Lithuania', Simonas Nikartas, Loreta Matačiūtė, and Neila Sventickytė examine how community sanctions—particularly intensive supervision with electronic monitoring—adopt punitive characteristics typically associated with imprisonment.

Drawing on Goffman's and Sykes's concepts of discipline and control and qualitative research based on interviews with probation clients, the authors show that probation in Lithuania, rather than focusing on reintegration, replicates prison-like regimes. Intensive supervision restricts freedom of movement, creates a constant experience of surveillance, disrupts family ties, and stigmatises the offender in the eyes of others. These practices, the authors argue, amount to the prisonisation of probation—the adoption of imprisonment's logic of control within community-based penalties, thus extending punitiveness beyond prison walls.

Algimantas Čepas, in his chapter 'Crime Prevention and Victim Support: New Actors in the Field of Criminal Justice', examines the development of crime prevention and victim support policies in Lithuania. Highlighting two distinct trajectories—the historical influence of Soviet legacies on crime prevention and the EU-driven expansion of victim support—the author demonstrates how different external pressures have paradoxically led to similar outcomes: fragmented, weakly coordinated, and overly formalised systems. In crime prevention, a centralised control model and situational rather than social approaches still dominate. Victim support, while formally enshrined as a right, often remains limited to minimal assistance rather than addressing broader questions of justice and restoration. According to the author, both areas suffer from a deeply ingrained 'us versus them' mentality that reinforces excessive punitiveness and impedes effective reform.

In summary, through its analysis of Lithuania, this book offers a deeper understanding of punitiveness and its social, cultural, political, economic, and historical factors. The aim is to show that the logic of punishment and control mechanisms operates well beyond the formal boundaries of criminal justice. Here, punitiveness is understood not only as a tool of state power but also as a phenomenon deeply rooted in social structures and everyday culture, manifesting in public discourse, institutional practices, media representations, and individuals' moral judgements. The various forms of punitiveness explored—from stigmatising narratives and social reactions to probation and imprisonment practices—reveal how certain members of society become more visible, more heavily controlled, and more frequently viewed as 'punishable subjects.'

The reader is invited to reconsider the foundations of societal security, the construction of criminal images, and the implications for democratic quality, social cohesion, and human rights.

Although the empirical analysis focuses on Lithuania, the book's findings resonate in a broader international context. For Central and Eastern European countries, the book provides insight into shared structural challenges in post-authoritarian systems: the long-term legacy of repressive practices, limited confidence in reintegration approaches, and a persistent demand for 'order'. Meanwhile, the book offers an opportunity for Western societies to reflect on how punitiveness can expand even within democratic and socially progressive contexts, particularly through informal, symbolic, and institutionally 'neutral' yet stigmatising mechanisms. It calls for international dialogue on how punishment cultures operate across different societies and what can be done to ensure that justice is not only formal but also socially responsive.

References

Aebi, M. F., Delgrande, N., & Marguet, Y. (2015). Have community sanctions and measures widened the net of the European criminal justice systems? *Punishment & Society, 17*(5), 575–597.

Buzaitytė-Kašalynienė, J., Švedaitė-Sakalauskė, B., Kalpokas, V., & Sakalauskas, G. (2024). "Is juvenile delinquency in Lithuania increasing because of the bad influence of the west"? Punitive attitudes of the Lithuanian population towards juvenile offenders. *East European Politics and Societies, 38*(2), 411–431.

Christie, N. (1986). *The ideal victim. In: From crime policy to victim policy: Reorienting the justice system* (pp. 17–30). Palgrave Macmillan UK.

Cohen, S. (1985). *Visions of social control*. Polity Press.

Foucault, M. (1977). *Discipline and punish: The birth of the prison*. Allen Lane.

Foucault, M. (2015). *La société punitive: Cours au Collège de France (1972–1973).* Gallimard/Seuil.

Garland, D. (2001). *The culture of control*. Oxford University Press.

Krajewski, K. (2014). Different penal climates in Europe. *Kriminologijos studijos, 1*, 86–111.

Krajewski, K. (2016). Sentencing in Poland: Failed attempts to reduce punitiveness. In M. Tonry (Ed.), *Sentencing and punishment in Western countries since 2000. Crime and justice: A review of research* (Vol. 45). University of Chicago Press.

Lithuanian Prison Service. (2025). *Annual report for 2024*. Retrieved from May 11, 2025, from https://kalejimai.lrv.lt/lt/administracine-informacija/ataskaitos/metu/

Lithuanian Probation Service. (2024). *Annual report for 2024*. Retrieved from April 10, 2025, from https://probacija.lrv.lt/lt/apie-lietuvos-probacijos-tarnyba/statistika/metines-ataskaitos/

Nikartas, S. (2020). Privatisation of criminal justice in Eastern Europe. In *Criminal justice and privatisation* (pp. 215–230). Routledge.

Nikartas, S., & Paliauka, J. (2024). "I would work with a client, but I have to fill out papers": Understanding professional roles and role conflicts experienced by Lithuanian probation officers. *Probation Journal, 0*(0). https://doi.org/10.1177/02645505241267120

Nikartas, S., Vaičiūnienė, R., & Rinkevičiūtė, G. (2021). Probation officers' discretionary decisions in responding to probation violations: The case of Lithuania. *Probation Journal, 68*(1), 28–46.

Phelps, M. S. (2017). Mass probation: Toward a more robust theory of state variation in punishment. *Punishment & Society, 19*(1), 53–73.

Rusche, G., & Kirchheimer, O. (1939). *Punishment and social structure*. Columbia University Press.

Sakalauskas, G., Jarutienė, L., Kalpokas, V., & Vaičiūnienė, R. (Eds.). (2020). *Kalinimo sąlygos ir kalinių socialinės integracijos prielaidos*. Žara, Lietuvos teisės institutas.

Simon, J. (2007). *Governing through crime: How the war on crime transformed American democracy and created a culture of fear*. Oxford University Press.

Slade, G., & Kupatadze, A. (2017). Popular punitiveness? Punishment and attitudes to law in post-soviet Georgia. *Europe-Asia Studies, 69*(6), 879–896.

Slade, G., & Light, M. (2015). Crime and criminal justice after communism: Why study the post-soviet region? *Theoretical Criminology, 19*(2), 147–158.

Wacquant, L. (2001). The penalisation of poverty and the rise of neoliberalism. *European Journal on Criminal Policy and Research, 9*, 401–412.

Wacquant, L. (2009). *Punishing the poor: The neoliberal government of social insecurity*. Duke University Press.

Weis, V. V. (2021). Operationalizing injustice: Criminal selectivity as a tool for understanding (and changing) criminalization in Argentina. *Criminological Encounters, 4*(1), 13–30.

World Prison Brief. (2024). *Lithuania, prison population rate (per 100,000 of national population).* Retrieved from May 11, 2025, from https://www.prisonstudies.org/country/lithuania

Part I

Understanding punitiveness

2

Psychology of Punishment: Why Do we Punish Others?

Kristina Vanagaitė
and Violeta Cimalanskaitė-Kazlauskienė

Introduction

There are numerous situations in which individuals desire to punish others. When someone suffers unjust harm, such as assault or robbery, there is often a strong urge to penalise the offender (Carlsmith et al., 2002). From a psychological perspective, what drives this motivation and justifies such behaviour? This chapter focuses on the psychology of punishment, examining ordinary people's motives, emotions, and punitive attitudes. We will also explore various factors contributing to a propensity to impose harsher penalties in certain situations.

K. Vanagaitė (✉) · V. Cimalanskaitė-Kazlauskienė
Faculty of Philosophy, Institute of Psychology, Vilnius University, Vilnius, Lithuania
e-mail: kristina.vanagaite@fsf.vu.lt

V. Cimalanskaitė-Kazlauskienė
e-mail: violeta.cimalanskaite@fsf.vu.lt

A. Dobryninas and S. Nikartas (eds.), *Understanding Crime Control and Punishment in Lithuania*, Crime Prevention and Security Management,
https://doi.org/10.1007/978-3-032-05538-5_2

Studies conducted in Lithuania indicate a societal trend towards strengthening punishments. We can support this notion by surveys of Lithuanian residents over different periods, revealing a perception of current punishments as insufficiently severe. For instance, a 2009 survey by Spinter Research for the *Delfi* information portal found that only 2% of participants believed existing punishments were adequately severe, while 31% were convinced that harsher penalties were necessary (Spinter tyrimai, 2009). Furthermore, in 2010, surveys indicated that 74–77% of police officers and 44–59% of the public felt penalties for juveniles and adults were too lenient (Vileikienė, 2010). Recent research showed that about half of the Lithuanian population supports stricter punishment for minors when they are seen as more responsible for their actions (Buzaitytė-Kašalynienė et al., 2023).

It is crucial to note that the desire for harsher punishment encompasses not only a wish to penalise more lawbreakers but also concerns about the intensity and duration of these penalties (e.g., perceptions that prisons or parole are "too easy" and support for longer sentences or the death penalty) (Maruna & King, 2009). Given that public opinion on punishment can significantly influence justice policy decisions, this chapter aims to uncover the nuances behind the formation of attitudes favouring harsher penalties.

Reasons of Punishment

In contemporary law enforcement, the objectives of punishment include deterrence and crime prevention. However, one prevalent rationale for imposing punishment is the belief in "just deserts," or that individuals deserve punishment commensurate with their moral transgressions. Within the just deserts theory framework, moral outrage and the intrinsic motivation to punish are directly proportional to the severity of the transgression (Carlsmith et al., 2002). In other words, the greater the harm done, the stronger the motive to punish the perpetrator (Carlsmith et al., 2002).

How do people understand the purpose of punishment? The public perceives punishment as serving two primary objectives: instrumental (or utilitarian) goals and retribution (Carlsmith et al., 2002; Vidmar, 2001). Instrumental goals link punishment to future benefits, such as reducing the likelihood of recidivism. They seek to deter both the perpetrator and potential offenders from rule-breaking. In contrast, retributive justice concerns the offence's moral nature. In this case, the goals of retribution are not centred on crime prevention but on delivering retribution. This approach is anchored in the belief that offenders deserve punishment proportional to their crimes. Research indicates that although individuals may outwardly support deterrence as a goal of punishment, the predominant motivation tends to align more closely with principles of just deserts and retribution (e.g., Carlsmith et al., 2002).

Thus, scientists point to the desire for retribution as a primary motivator behind punitive actions (Gerber & Jackson, 2013; Osgood, 2017). Two aspects of the desire for retribution can be distinguished (Bone & Raihani, 2015). The first aspect involves re-establishing justice by achieving proportional reparation for the harm inflicted (retribution as just deserts). Here, two elements are important: restoring justice (retribution driven by the inclination to balance the outcomes and redress the disparities caused by the crime) and compensating the damage inflicted, by the proportionality principle. This implies that offenders should not derive any benefit from their illicit actions.

The second aspect of retribution is to take revenge on the violator and cause him suffering (retribution as revenge). This dimension encompasses not only the restoration of balance but also the intent to cause suffering as retribution. The act of revenge seeks to counterbalance power dynamics (Vidmar, 2001) and restore the victim‘s self-esteem (Miller, 2001). Crimes disrupt power equality and can damage the victim's self-worth by contravening personal autonomy and will (Orth, 2004). Individuals express strength and power through revenge to prevent unjust and illegal behaviour (Miller, 2001).

Moreover, some scholars suggest that "direct motor of vengeful desire is pain: the pain of insult or harm or loss, of having been slighted, of having been subjected to another person's power or whim, or of humiliation" (Frijda, 1994, p. 279). In this context, "pain" encompasses both physical and psychological dimensions. Based on this perspective, revenge is posited as a mechanism for mitigating psychological discomfort (or pain) (Frijda, 1994). "Perhaps all vengeful acts are attempts to escape pain; it may be regarded as the basic pushing power" (Frijda, 1994, p. 279). Nonetheless, research indicates that any relief gained through acts of revenge is fleeting, and long-term vengeful feelings are unaffected by the severity of the perpetrator's punishment (Orth, 2004).

The motivation of people's behaviour can be explained based on attribution theory. It is indicated that people tend to impose a harsher punishment when the cause of the crime is perceived as more internal (e.g. determined by factors related to the person himself, like disposition), controllable (e.g. intentional, done on purpose) and stable (conditioned by constant factors, so it is likely that it may repeat itself in the future). Conversely, individuals are more lenient in their judgements when the causes of crime are perceived as more external (e.g., due to situational factors such as the environment), uncontrollable (e.g., an unintentional act), and unstable (e.g., due to temporal factors, so it is likely, that it may not happen again in the future) (Weiner, 2006). Thus, it is likely that if a person believes that the crime was committed intentionally, they may think that the person who committed the crime is responsible for the crime. Such an opinion can increase anger, decrease sympathy for the person who committed the crime, and arouse the desire for retribution. It can be said that anger can enhance perceptions of intent and causal control behind harmful behaviours and increase punitiveness towards the perpetrator (Ask & Pina, 2011). This assumption is supported by research results showing that individuals report experiencing strong feelings of anger, disgust, and contempt in response to being harmed by an offence, and these emotions cause a desire for revenge (Darley & Pittman, 2003; Yoshimura, 2007).

Punishment and Emotions

It is reasonable to say that the emotions experienced by people are one of the most important factors considered when trying to understand the motives behind punishment. Given that most violent crimes often arouse a strong emotional response that arguably influences punishment preferences, it is important to take a closer look at the connections between negative emotions and harsher punishment.

Vidmar (2001), analysing the connections between emotions and punishment, proposes a six-stage social psychological retributive justice model. According to the model, violations of perceived rules or norms trigger negative emotional reactions, leading to a desire for punishment both from the victim's perspective and that of society. Anger, a central component of revenge motivation, is pivotal in this process.

So, arousal of retributive motives arise from: 1) there is a perceived rule or norm violation; 2) the rule violator's intention is perceived as blameworthy; 3) the combination of (1) and (2) threatens or harms values related to the perceiver's personal self, status, or internalised group values; 4) the negative emotion of anger is aroused; 5) the cognitions and aroused emotions stimulate reactions against the violator; 6) during or following punishment the anger dissipates, cognitions return towards homeostasis, and the rule or norm is perceived to be vindicated (Vidmar, 2001).

Thus, anger often leads to revenge on a person for their aggressive behaviour (Jackson et al., 2019). At the same time, liking fosters prosocial behaviour (often helping) and reduces antisocial behaviour (such as punishment) (Weiner, 2006). Studies indicate that anger towards crime significantly predicts punitive attitudes, with heightened anger correlating with a tendency to impose harsher penalties (Johnson, 2009).

However, anger is not the only emotion which may cause a desire for revenge. Anticipations of the pleasure derived from revenge also influence decisions favouring retaliatory actions (Jackson et al., 2019). Thus, the revenge is posited to ameliorate the negative mood engendered by norm violations (Carlsmith et al., 2008; Jackson et al., 2019). In other words, the revenge should give some degree of satisfaction. Neuroscientific research supports this, demonstrating activation of neurological reward centres during retaliatory aggression (Chester & DeWall, 2015; De Quervain et al., 2004). However, Gollwitzer and his colleagues (2011) found that for victims to experience satisfaction, offenders must perceive revenge as punitive, indicating that revenge alone might not inherently satisfy victims. This means that revenge itself does not necessarily bring satisfaction to victims. Furthermore, in some instances, revenge outcomes may contradict expectations, possibly exacerbating negative emotions and prolonging rumination over the transgression (e.g. Carlsmith et al., 2008). Eadeh and his colleagues (2017) summarised that revenge can trigger both positive and negative emotional reactions (bittersweet model of revenge). These findings suggest a complex relationship between anticipated satisfaction from revenge and punitive attitudes.

In addition, it is important to mention why anger towards the offender can be felt not only by the victims of the crime, but also by those who have no direct experience of encountering crimes. Psychologists note that compassion for victims is a "natural justice"reaction that may have origins in our sociobiological nature. Witnesses of harm may empathise with victims and feel angered by the situation (Vidmar, 2001). Likewise, the reaction of outsiders to harm done to others can be interpreted based on a violation of a social contract. A sense of justice arises from the internalised rules during the socialisation process, which ensures well-run group interaction. When those rules are violated, the resulting threat in the group fosters feelings of hostility towards the rule breaker (Vidmar, 2001). Also, in this case, the media can play a significant role by presenting crime and punishment in emotionally charged narratives, often highlighting sympathy for victims and moral disgust towards offenders (Karstedt, 2002). This can encourage the public's anger and intensify the desire for harsh punishment.

Perceived Sense of Security and Fear of Crime

Researchers investigating the relationship between emotions and punitive measures examine not only anger but also the emotion of fear. A common question is whether a greater fear of crime leads individuals to support more severe punishments.

Analysing the relationship between fear of crime and attitudes to punishment, research results are conflicting, and it is not entirely clear whether greater fear leads to the public favouring harsher punishments

(Johnson, 2009). Although some authors note that the more fearful individuals are of crime, the more they express punitive attitudes compared to less fearful individuals (Brookman & Wiener, 2017; Dowler, 2003), while other researchers find no such relationship (Kleck & Jackson, 2017). Nevertheless, it emphasised that crime policies are explicitly based on expressing collective emotions of fear and anger about crime (Karstedt, 2002).

In 1997, the results of an international comparative victimological study conducted in Lithuania showed that Lithuanian residents were almost twice as likely to be victims of crime as the average European population and even three and a half times more often than Scandinavian residents. According to a 2001 survey of residents of the Lithuanian capital, the level of fear of crime had increased, reaching 64% (Babachinaitė, 2006). However, when we compare a longer period, we see that people's sense of security gradually increased: in 2006, 54% of surveyed Lithuanian residents indicated that they felt safe, and in 2022, 87% (Vileikienė & Gelčytė, 2022). In addition, if in 2006 only 34% Lithuanian residents indicated that they have a low risk of becoming a victim of crime, and in 2022—as much as 75% residents believed that the risk of becoming a victim of crime in their area of residence is low (Vileikienė & Gelčytė, 2022).

Surveys of the residents of Lithuania were also conducted, in which the residents' perceived safety was assessed, revealing a trend that men feel safer in their place of residence compared to women (Vileikienė & Gelčytė, 2022). Since greater fear may lead to a preference for harsher punishment, the question is, would women punish more harshly? The researchers note that individual fear of crime is indeed a significant predictor of punishment attitudes for women, but not for men. A possible explanation is that punishment expresses people's desire to control events outside their control. Compared to men, women may feel more powerless in relation to individual victimisation and are therefore more likely to rely on criminal punishment to control events that are outside of their locus of control (Armborst, 2017; Dodd, 2018). In 2009, the results of a survey of Lithuanian residents conducted by "Spinter research" on behalf of *Delfi* information portal showed that women, 46 years old and older respondents, residents with lower incomes and lower education were more likely to believe that punishments in Lithuania are not sufficiently severe. Women were also more likely to support chemical castration of pedophiles (Spinter tyrimai, 2009). On the other hand, the results of a study conducted in Lithuania during the pandemic showed that men and women had a very similar assessment of the severity of responsibility for violating prohibitions and restrictions and were inclined to agree that the punishment applied to persons who do not comply with the requirements of self-isolation should be more severe, rather than milder (Valickas et al., 2021). Thus, considering the research results' ambiguity, deciding whether women tend to punish more severely is not easy. Further research is needed to support or disprove this assumption.

Brookman and Wiener (2017) also point out that support for harsher punishments may be related to people's fear of becoming a victim of crime themselves. This fear can be reinforced by brutal crimes that are widely reported in the media (therefore, the population's perceived sense of security can be significantly reduced during this period). It should be noted that the public is generally poorly informed about crime rates and the types of crimes committed, and obtains this inaccurate information from the media. Therefore, detailed media coverage of various criminal acts can create the impression that crime is increasing in the country, which in turn increases fear and insecurity even more (Brookman & Wiener, 2017). This effect can be illustrated by the following case of a brutal crime committed in 2013 in the vicinity of the town of Dembava:

> Two young men under the influence of alcohol and drugs saw a girl at a bus stop while driving around the city and offered her a ride. The underage girl who got into the car was taken to the forest, raped, and later burned alive in the trunk of the car. Kidnapped and locked in the trunk of the car, the girl called the General Assistance Centre 10 times asking for help, but the equipment did not show the victim's mobile phone number. Without it, the institution staff could not determine the caller's location. An hour later, the rescuers received a report about a car burning in the forest. After arriving at the scene and extinguishing the fire, a burnt body was found in the car's trunk (Delfi, 2014).

This brutally committed crime shocked the entire population of Lithuania, as a result of which there was even a discussion in society that it would be worthwhile to return the death penalty. It can be said that this case, which was widely reported in the media, could increase the feeling of insecurity and mistrust of law enforcement institutions, cause strong anger towards the perpetrators, and strengthen the desire for retribution.

Punitive Attitudes

People's punitive attitudes might involve the support of harsher penal punishments and can have real consequences on the functioning of the criminal justice system and crime prevention policies (Jennings et al., 2017). For example, populist politicians, when making decisions, might be more guided by the opinions and emotional reactions of the public. Therefore, it is essential not only to explain punitive attitudes but also to evaluate the structure of the concept (Trajtenberg et al., 2024).

What are the "punitive attitudes"? There are many definitions where punitive attitudes are "attitudes toward sanctioning or punishment", "attitudes", "sentiments" and "style of reaction to crime" (Trajtenberg et al., 2024). Lack of clarity on the concept of punitive attitudes poses some problems: for example, when we want to measure these punitive attitudes, very different indicators have been used. Some studies include measures of citizens' support for specific stiffer penal sanctions or sentencing policies (e.g. the preference for the death penalty, long-term or life prison sentences). Other researchers focus on prison conditions and the pains suffered by inmates, asking respondents whether prisons should have harsher conditions, lack of access to privileges or even degrading circumstances. Some studies include punishment goals in their measurement scales and typically define respondents' punitiveness as a rejection of rehabilitation and psychological treatment, and/or support for retributive justice, among other factors (Armborst, 2017). Different ways of measuring punitive attitudes show the complexity of public attitudes towards punishment. Moreover, when evaluating punitive attitudes, researchers try to consider three areas: the areas of affect (feelings towards offenders), cognition (explanations of the causes of offending), and action (measures for the reduction of offences) (Buzaitytė-Kašalynienė et al., 2023).

Authoritarian Attitudes and Punitiveness

Lithuanian society underwent dramatic changes in the past thirty years, following its departure from the Soviet Union and its accession to the European Union. These changes led to various reforms and problems (including increased crime, population insecurity, etc.). Whether the Soviet past could have played a role in the formation and maintenance of penal provisions is difficult to say, since there are few such studies. However, research comparing East and West Germany shows that post-communist society tends to be more authoritarian than one having longer liberal democracy traditions (Buzaitytė-Kašalynienė et al., 2023). Considering the fact that authoritarian attitudes predict punitiveness, we can assume that the cultural context can condition the desire of Lithuanian society to punish more severely. Found that elderly persons, who have lived longer under the Soviet occupation, have more authority than young adults, who were born in independent Lithuania (Grigutytė & Rukšaitė, 2016). About half of the parents surveyed have an authoritarian, highly conservative approach to parenting (Buzaitytė-Kašalynienė et al., 2023). The idea that authoritarian parenting is common in Lithuania is supported by the results of some studies showing that 42% of the children in Lithuania reported experiencing parental emotional and/or physical abuse during the last year (Sebre et al., 2004). The prevalence of any different types of childhood sexual abuse experience before the age of 18 was 15.9% in Lithuania. The majority of child sexual abuse is committed in a family context, including relatives (stepfathers, siblings) and individuals well known to the child or family (Žukauskienė et al., 2023).

Attention from authorities and lawmakers in Lithuania regarding the use of corporal punishment and other forms of violence against children was notably heightened in 2017, following the tragic death of a four-year-old boy within his family. The public outcry over this incident prompted the reform of the child rights protection system, commonly referred to as the "Matukas Reform." One significant outcome of this reform was the amendment of the Law on Fundamentals of Protection of the Rights of the Child, which instituted a prohibition on all forms of violence against children (Republic of Lithuania Law on the Fundamentals of Child Rights Protection, 2018). Despite these strengthened regulations and the prohibition of all kinds of violence, the issue of corporal punishment against children persists as a significant concern in Lithuania.

According to the State Child Rights Protection and The Adoption Agency, the number of reported cases of potential violence against children increased by 24% in 2023 compared to 2022 (State Child Rights Protection and The Adoption Agency, 2024b). This suggests that over 3000 children may have experienced violence within their families during 2023 (State Child Rights Protection and The Adoption Agency, 2024b). Furthermore, the agency highlights that a substantial segment of the Lithuanian population tends to justify violence against children, viewing it as a parenting measure. This perspective was evident in a public opinion survey conducted by Spinter Research at the end of 2023 (State Child Rights Protection and The Adoption Agency, 2024a). For instance, in 2021, when participants were asked about whether corporal punishment for child disobedience or misconduct constitutes violence, 59% were either ambivalent or regarded it as a parenting measure (State Child Rights Protection and The Adoption Agency, 2024a). By 2023, this proportion had reduced to 53%, reflecting a slight shift in public attitudes (State Child Rights Protection and The Adoption Agency, 2024a).

Accordingly, the consequences of authoritarian regimes have a fundamental impact on every person. It is also commonly viewed as a cultural trauma. Studies of the consequences of the authoritarian regime and cultural trauma in Lithuania reveal that the violence perpetrated by state institutions and the persecution of citizens have disrupted the formation of their relationship with authority, both internal and external (Gudaitė, 2016). Considering these traumatic experiences, authority is perceived as punishing, controlling, and persecuting. In personal relationships, it encourages domestic violence. In relations with the state, it breeds mistrust and resistance. This is also confirmed by the results of the study conducted in Lithuania, which show a tendency that the surveyed participants of the 18–25-year-old age group trust law enforcement institutions more and have a less negative attitude towards law enforcement officers, compared to older participants (Valickas et al., 2013). These studies might explain why punitive attitudes are more common among older Lithuanians (Buzaitytė-Kašalynienė et al., 2023; Grigutytė & Rukšaitė, 2016).

Trust or distrust in authority can help to explain the factors that influence punitive attitudes towards sentencing. One relevant approach in this context is the "Crime-distrust" model, which proposes that such attitudes are shaped by two related perceptions: that crime rates are increasing in a way that threatens the public's way of life, and that the government and the courts are not sufficiently capable of protecting society from this threat (Brookman & Wiener, 2017).

This model distinguishes two important constructs: crime salience (perceived danger of crime and fear of crime) and institutional distrust. We have already mentioned that the fear of crime can encourage people to approve harsher sentences. However, when it comes to people's desire to punish more strictly, not only the fear of crimes, but also the mistrust of the courts is important. Although the research results are ambiguous, some show the relationship between the public's distrust in the courts and punitive attitudes (Brookman & Wiener, 2017).

Public opinion polls in Lithuania indicate a general lack of trust in the national court system. For instance, surveys by Vilmorus revealed that only 16% of the Lithuanian population trusted the courts in 2000. This trust increased to nearly 24% in 2004 but subsequently declined to approximately 14% in 2010 (see Valickas et al., 2013). However, a survey commissioned by the Ministry of the Interior of the Republic of Lithuania and the Police Department under the Ministry of the Interior of the Republic of Lithuania indicates an improvement in public perception of the courts beginning in 2013, with nearly half of the respondents rating the courts positively by 2022 (see Vileikienė & Gelčytė, 2022).

One potential explanation for these fluctuations in public opinion is the influence of media portrayals of the judiciary, in addition to direct interactions with law enforcement. For example, in 2014, an analysis of publications from popular news portals *Delfi* and *Lietuvos Rytas* related to a high-profile pedophilia scandal (referred to as the "Garliava story") revealed a predominance of negative assessments of judges. These sources frequently criticised judicial decisions, openly questioning the integrity and objectivity of the judges (Valickas ir Jarutienė, 2014). This suggests that the negative depiction of judges during the pedophilia scandal may have fuelled public distrust, shaping a negative perception of both judges and the broader law enforcement system (Valickas & Jarutienė, 2014).

When examining punitive attitudes, it is essential to address *false beliefs*. Misconceptions can be harmful as they may lead to incorrect interpretations and decision-making errors. Such beliefs can be seen as a distinct form of misperception, often upheld despite a lack of specific evidence. An example is the "tough-on-crime" belief, which posits that harsher punishments are the most appropriate way to deal with offenders (Shaw & Woodworth, 2013). This belief emphasises retribution over rehabilitation, despite research indicating that longer imprisonment can exacerbate criminal behaviour. Individuals advocating for stricter punishments may lack understanding of behaviour correction and rehabilitation. They may exhibit certain personality traits, such as authoritarian tendencies or retributive attitudes, compared to those endorsing less punitive systems. Research demonstrates that acquiring empirical knowledge in legal psychology can reduce false beliefs about punishment and foster less punitive attitudes (Kääriäinen, 2019; Shaw & Woodworth, 2013). Furthermore, it is noted that less educated individuals tend to rely more on media information when assessing punishments, potentially making them more punitive in both beliefs and sentencing behaviour (Kääriäinen, 2019).

To illustrate how misconceptions relate to beliefs, we will briefly discuss a 2022 study in Lithuania that examined public perception of quarantine restrictions, responsibilities, and penalties for noncompliance during different COVID-19 waves. The study revealed that during the first wave, respondents were more inclined to advocate for criminal liability, rather than warnings or fines, for noncompliance with regulations. However, their opinions shifted later, with many advocating for lighter penalties. The findings across the different COVID-19 waves also indicated a significant positive correlation between support for criminal liability for self-isolation rule violations and the severity of punishment desired. Respondents supporting criminal liability also favoured severe penalties, such as imprisonment (Valickas et al., 2023).

It can be added that during the first COVID-19 wave, respondents were undecided about the fairness of imposing harsher penalties for pandemic-related violations, but this perspective evolved. By the second and fourth waves, participants increasingly questioned the fairness of stricter penalties, ultimately viewing severe punishments as unjust during the fourth wave. This shift may have been influenced by increased information availability and reduced uncertainty in later pandemic waves. However, the initial public stress experienced during the pandemic also likely impacted punitive attitudes. The study indicates that stress levels were highest during the first wave compared to subsequent waves (Valickas et al., 2023).

The study's results highlight how a lack of information and negative emotions can drive individuals to favour harsher punishments. It is also likely that at the beginning of the pandemic, people relied on the information represented in the media, which emphasised the threat and dangers of the virus, which, in turn, may have induced fear, leading to a preference for stricter penalties.

To understand why individuals may exhibit punitive attitudes, it is crucial to discuss the concept of "*a belief in redeemability*." Researchers suggest that public reactions to crime are influenced by their opinions and trust in offenders' ability to change their behaviour. In other words, a dimension of stability versus instability can be added to attribution theory. This dimension ranges from the belief that "once a criminal, always a criminal" to the belief that offenders can rehabilitate and improve their lives, known as a "belief in redeemability" (Maruna & King, 2009). Research indicates that those who believe in the potential for change in offenders are more likely to support more lenient punishments and endorse reentry programs and services (Maruna & King, 2009; Ouellette et al., 2017).

The halfway house is a widely recognised reentry program utilised in Lithuania. This community-based correctional program provides reentry services through residential facilities for inmates (Wong et al., 2018). Although definitions and services may vary by country, halfway houses typically offer temporary community-based housing supervised by correctional officers (Seiter & Kadela, 2003). Usually, halfway houses include occupational activities (such as employment and education) and correctional and self-improvement programs (Wong et al., 2018). Research supports the effectiveness of halfway houses as a correctional strategy for successful reentry (e., Routh, 2015; Wong et al., 2018).

In Lithuania, halfway houses operate as specialised units within prisons (Uscila, 2022). Uscila (2022) notes that one indicator of their effectiveness is the low rate of convicts returning to a semi-closed or closed prison regime. Between 2016 and 2021, only 43 of approximately 400 offenders were returned to prisons from halfway houses (Uscila, 2022), suggesting that most successfully adhered to their reentry plans.

Despite evidence supporting the efficiency of halfway houses, these programs are often criticised for perceived risks to public safety and receive weak public—and consequently, political—support (Costanza et al., 2015). This reflects a public reluctance to accept halfway houses in residential areas, exemplified by the "not in my backyard" movement. Analysing halfway house practices in Lithuania, Uscila (2022) highlights community resistance, particularly when these facilities are near residential areas or public institutions like schools and kindergartens.

As an illustration of negative public attitudes, we will briefly discuss opening a halfway house in 2023, widely reported in Lithuanian media (e.g., 15 min.lt, Kauno diena.lt). Following the announcement of a new halfway house in Domeikava eldership, Kaunas district, residents protested and submitted a petition to express their opposition. Media reports revealed community concerns over the penitentiary system's ability to ensure supervision, the safety of nearby schools and kindergartens, and perceived threats to seniors and other residents.

While research specifically exploring negative attitudes towards halfway houses in Lithuania is scant, studies from other countries identify several key factors influencing such attitudes. Firstly, belief in the redeemability of convicts is an important predictor of public support for reentry programming (Ouellette et al., 2017). Secondly, retributive values significantly shape attitudes towards prisoner reentry initiatives (Garland et al., 2011). Lastly, some researchers note that economic self-interest influences support for reentry programs (Garland et al., 2011).

Attitudes to Alternatives to Punishment

While traditional criminal justice punishments have been applied for centuries, research shows that imprisonment is often costly and ineffective (e.g., Cook & Haynes, 2020; Karp & Frank, 2016; Loeffler & Nagin, 2022). Imprisonment may increase the risk of reoffending (Cook & Haynes, 2020) and can sometimes be incorrectly imposed (Karp & Frank, 2016). Traditional punishments are also ineffective in alleviating the strong negative experiences suffered by crime victims, as the punishment of offenders does not always provide a sense of closure or renewed safety. This has led researchers and criminal justice practitioners to explore more effective alternatives to traditional measures. Thus, in the latter half of the twentieth century, restorative justice interventions gained significant attention and development in Western countries (Braithwaite, 1999; Gavrielides, 2014).

The primary objective of restorative justice is to restore and compensate for the harm caused by crime (Gavrielides, 2014). All parties involved in the restorative justice process typically include the victim, the offender, and a community or societal representative (Gavrielides, 2014). Restorative justice also emphasises repairing emotional and relational harm through facilitated stakeholder dialogue (Paul, 2021). Restorative justice interventions aim to satisfy the interests of the victim (right to compensation), the offender (right to a fair and reasonable process), and the public (prevention of further violations and adequate response to the offence) (Michailovič et al., 2014).

Research indicates that restorative measures reduce reoffending rates (Bergseth & Bouffard, 2013; Kennedy et al., 2019; Sherman et al., 2014) and enhance satisfaction and perceived procedural justice for both victims and offenders, compared to traditional criminal justice measures (Fulham et al., 2023). However, the effectiveness of restorative justice measures can vary depending on the nature of the crime, the circumstances of the interventions, and other factors (Fulham et al., 2023).

Despite inconsistencies in research findings, existing knowledge suggests that restorative justice measures can help reduce reoffending and thus enhance public safety in some cases. Nonetheless, the application of restorative justice in both Lithuanian and international contexts remains limited and faces various challenges (Brooks, 2015; Reches, 2010).

The success of alternatives to prosecution and punishment, such as restorative justice, depends on public support (Moss et al., 2019). Research shows that attitudes towards restorative justice are influenced by various factors (e.g., Ahlin et al., 2015; Roberts & Stalans, 2004). It is established that public members who are better informed about restorative justice measures and their effectiveness tend to hold less punitive attitudes and are more favourable towards such approaches (Ahlin et al., 2015; Roberts & Stalans, 2004). Kaminskiene and co-authors (2023) investigated judicial mediation obstacles in Lithuania, revealing that a lack of public awareness about restorative justice is a reason for the stagnation in the development of judicial mediation. Some judges-mediators who participated in a qualitative study also reported a lack of publicity regarding judicial mediation (Kaminskienė et al., 2023).

Another significant factor influencing public attitudes towards restorative justice is the severity of the crime (Gromet & Darley, 2006; Roberts & Stalans, 2004). In other words, public support for restorative measures decreases as the severity of the crime increases. The more serious the offence, particularly violent or sexual crimes, the more the public demands severe punishments (Roberts & Stalans, 2004). The Criminal Code of the Republic of Lithuania (Article 38(1)) reflects this attitude, ruling out reconciliation as a relief from criminal liability for serious and very serious offences (Criminal Code of the Republic of Lithuania, 2000).

Studies suggest that an intuitive response to intentional crimes is retribution (Carlsmith, 2006; Goldberg et al., 1999; Osgood, 2017; Reches, 2010). In other words, people's decisions about crime punishment are more often influenced by retributive rather than utilitarian or deterrent motives, even if they claim to be concerned with the latter (Carlsmith, 2006). This indicates an intrinsic desire for proportional punishment. Researchers note that where people support restorative justice (e.g., in minor crimes), they view these measures as sufficient retribution (see Reches, 2010). This understanding may help explain why public attitudes towards restorative justice correlate with offence severity.

Additionally, public views on restorative justice are influenced by beliefs about offenders'ability to change (redeemability) and decision-making competence. Research shows that those who believe offenders can fundamentally change are more supportive of restorative justice and rehabilitation (Moss et al., 2019; Paul, 2021; Weimann-Saks et al., 2022). Weimann-Saks and colleagues (2022) found that beliefs about offenders' ability to change mediate attitudes towards restorative justice, particularly in offences deemed irredeemable, like sexual and violent crimes.

Likewise, beliefs about decision-making competence, or the ability to understand and make appropriate decisions, are related both to offender restoration and information-gathering goals. If the public doubts offenders' ability to make sound decisions, they may question their capacity to comprehend their wrongdoing and learn from it. Studies show that the more people view offenders as redeemable and competent decision-makers, the more effective and appropriate they find restorative processes, and the more they support such measures (Paul, 2021).

Concluding Remarks

In this chapter, we aimed to address the question of why individuals tend to punish others. Our investigation drew upon research conducted internationally and within Lithuania and various psychological theories. We also aimed to identify both common factors and those specific to the Lithuanian public that influence attitudes towards punishment.

In summarising the discussed aspects, several key aspects of attitudes towards punishment emerge. First, research indicates that people generally have an intuitive inclination towards retribution, even when they outwardly support utilitarian and deterrent approaches. Secondly, the tendency of the Lithuanian population to impose stricter punishments can partly be attributed to authoritarian attitudes as a lingering post-Soviet influence. As a result, severe punishments are seen not only as satisfying a natural desire for retribution but also as "appropriate" measures for behaviour correction (or parenting measures).

Another crucial factor influencing punitive attitudes is the fear of crime and the anger provoked by criminal acts. Both fear and anger have been observed to drive support for harsher penalties. Furthermore, studies show that knowledge about crime and severe punishments' (in-) effectiveness significantly affects attitudes towards punishment. In other words, misconceptions may lead individuals to rely on media portrayals of crime, which are often sensationalised, and endorse more severe punishments. The lack of knowledge also fosters false beliefs and stereotypes, which can hinder consideration of alternative punishment forms, such as reentry programs or restorative justice interventions.

Finally, we note that the application of alternative punitive measures like restorative justice is not sufficiently developed, despite substantial research supporting their effectiveness in reducing reoffending and enhancing satisfaction with the justice process and perceived procedural justice. Researchers agree that public support is critical for successfully implementing restorative justice or other less severe, more rehabilitative punishment forms. Studies indicate that the public is more likely to accept restorative justice interventions under specific conditions, such as in cases of minor offences. Moreover, existing knowledge suggests that public attitudes towards restorative justice are connected to entrenched concepts of retribution, beliefs in offenders' capacity for change, and the level of public awareness about the benefits of restorative justice for public safety.

Overall, our findings suggest that education about the origins of crime and the (in)effectiveness of various penalties might be a crucial measure for reducing public punitive attitudes and increasing support for less severe but rehabilitative or restorative justice methods. Therefore, if society aspires to be less punitive, enhancing public education about punishment is essential.

References

Ahlin, E. M., Gibbs, J. C., Kavanaugh, P. R., & Lee, J. (2015). Support for restorative justice in a sample of U.S. university students. *International Journal of Offender Therapy and Comparative Criminology, 61*(2), 229–245. Retrieved from May 9, 2025, from https://doi.org/10.1177/0306624X15596386.

Armborst, A. (2017). How fear of crime affects punitive attitudes. *European Journal on Criminal Policy and Research, 23*, 461–481. Retrieved from May 9, 2025, from https://doi.org/10.1007/s10610-017-9342-5

Ask, K., & Pina, A. (2011). On being angry and punitive: How anger alters perception of criminal intent. *Social Psychological and Personality Science, 2* (5), 494–499. Retrieved from May 9, 2025, from https://doi.org/10.1177/1948550611398415

Babachinaitė, G. (2006). Saugumo jausmo ir nusikaltimų baimės raida Lietuvoje. *Jurisprudencija, 79*, 25–30.

Bergseth, K. J., & Bouffard, J. A. (2013). Examining the effectiveness of a restorative justice program for various types of juvenile offenders. *International Journal of Offender Therapy and Comparative Criminology, 57*(9), 1054–1075. Retrieved from May 9, 2025, from https://doi.org/10.1177/0306624X12453551

Bone, J. E., & Raihani, N. J. (2015). Human punishment is motivated by both a desire for revenge and a desire for equality. *Evolution and Human Behaviour, 36*(4), 323–330.

Braithwaite, J. (1999). Restorative justice: Assessing optimistic and pessimistic accounts. *Crime and Justice, 25*, 1–127. Retrieved from May 9, 2025, from http://www.jstor.org/stable/1147608

Brookman, R.P., & Wiener, K.K. (2017). Predicting punitive attitudes to sentencing: Does the public's perceptions of crime and indigenous Australians matter? *Australian & New Zealand Journal of Criminology, 50*(1) 56–76. Retrieved from May 9, 2025, from https://doi.org/10.1177/0004865815620702

Brooks, T. (2015). Punitive restoration: Rehabilitating restorative justice. *Raisons politiques (En ligne), 59*(3), 73–89. Retrieved from May 9, 2025, from https://doi.org/10.3917/rai.059.0073.

Buzaitė-Kašalynienė, J., Švedaitė-Sakalauskė, B., Kalpokas, V., & Sakalauskas, G. (2023). Is juvenile delinquency in Lithuania increasing because of the bad influence of the west. *East European Politics and Societies and Cultures, 38*, 411–431. Retrieved from May 9, 2025, from https://doi.org/10.1177/08883254231194274

Carlsmith, K. M. (2006). The roles of retribution and utility in determining punishment. *Journal of Experimental Social Psychology, 42*(4), 437–451.

Carlsmith, K. M., Darley, J. M., & Robinson, P. H. (2002). Why do we punish? Deterrence and just deserts as motives for punishment. *Journal of Personality and Social Psychology, 83*(2), 284–299.

Carlsmith, K. M., Wilson, T. D., & Gilbert, D. T. (2008). The paradoxical consequences of revenge. *Journal of Personality and Social Psychology, 95*(6), 1316–1324. https://doi.org/10.1037/a0012165

Chester, D. S., & DeWall, C. N. (2015). The pleasure of revenge: Retaliatory aggression arises from a neural imbalance toward reward. *Social Cognitive and Affective Neuroscience, 11*(7), 1173–1182. https://doi.org/10.1093/scan/nsv082

Cook, A., & Haynes, S. H. (2020). Imprisonment pains, reentry strains, and perceived likelihood of reoffending. *Criminal Justice Studies, 34*(1), 16–32. Retrieved from May 9, 2025, from https://doi.org/10.1080/1478601X.2020.1771332

Costanza, S. E., Cox, S. M., & Kilburn, J. C. (2015). The impact of Halfway houses on parole success and recidivism. *Journal of Sociological Research, 6*(2), 1–39. https://doi.org/10.5296/jsr.v6i2.8038

Criminal Code of the Republic of Lithuania. 2000. *Valstybės žinios*, No. 89–2741. Consolidated version from 14 June 2024 to 31 October 2024.

Darley, J. M., & Pittman, T. S. (2003). The psychology of compensatory and retributive justice. *Personality and Social Psychology Review, 7*(4), 324–336. https://doi.org/10.1207/s15327957pspr0704

De Quervain, D. J. F. (2004). The neural basis of altruistic punishment. *Science, 305*(5688), 1254–1258. https://doi.org/10.1126/science.1100735

Delfi. (2014). *Automobilio bagažinėje sudegintos septyniolikmetės budeliai išgirdo, ko verti*, *Delfi*, 3 December. Retrieved from May 16, 2025, from https://www.delfi.lt/news/daily/crime/automobilio-bagazineje-sudegintos-septyniolikmetes-budeliai-isgirdo-ko-verti-66572048

Dodd, S. (2018). The punitive woman? Gender differences in public attitudes toward parole among an Australian sample. *International Journal of Offender Therapy and Comparative Criminology, 62*(10), 3006–3022. https://doi.org/10.1177/0306624X17739560

Dowler, K. (2003). Media consumption and public attitudes toward crime and justice: The relationship between fear of crime, punitive attitudes, and perceived police effectiveness. *Journal of Criminal Justice and Popular Culture, 10*, 109–126.

Eadeh, F. R., Peak, S. A., & Lambert, A. J. (2017). The bittersweet taste of revenge: On the negative and positive consequences of retaliation. *Journal of Experimental Social Psychology, 68*, 27–39. https://doi.org/10.1016/j.jesp.2016.04.00

Frijda, N. H. (1994). The lex talionis: On vengeance. In T. H. M. van Goozen, N. E. Van de Poll, & J. A. Sergeant (Eds.), *Emotions: Essays on emotion theory* (pp. 263–289). Erlbaum.

Fulham, L., Blais, J., Rugge, T., & Schultheis, E. A. (2023). The effectiveness of restorative justice programs: A meta-analysis of recidivism and other relevant outcomes. *Criminology & Criminal Justice, 0*(0). Retrieved from May 9, 2025, from https://doi.org/10.1177/17488958231215228.

Garland, B., Wodahl, E., & Schuhmann, R. (2011). Value conflict and public opinion toward prisoner Reentry initiatives. *Criminal Justice Policy Review, 24*(1), 27–48. https://doi.org/10.1177/0887403411424081

Gavrielides, T. (2014). Reconciling the notions of restorative justice and imprisonment. *The Prison Journal, 94*(4), 479–505. https://doi.org/10.1177/0032885514548010

Gerber, M. M., & Jackson, J. (2013). Retribution as revenge and retribution as just deserts. *Social Justice Research, 26*, 61–80. https://doi.org/10.1007/s11211-012-0174-7

Goldberg, J. H., Lerner, J. S., & Tetlock, P. E. (1999). Rage and reason: The psychology of the intuitive prosecutor. *European Journal of Social Psychology, 29*(5–6), 781–795. Retrieved from May 9, 2025, from https://psycnet.apa.org/record/1999-03560-014

Gollwitzer, M., Meder, M., & Schmitt, M. (2011). What gives victims satisfaction when they seek revenge. *European Journal of Social Psychology, 41*(3), 364–374. https://doi.org/10.1002/ejsp.782

Grigutytė, N., & Rukšaitė, G. (2016). Lithuanian historical heritage: Relation with authority and psychological well-being. *2nd international conference on health and Health Psychology*, 274–284. https://doi.org/10.15405/epsbs.2016.07.02.27

Gromet, D. M., & Darley, J. M. (2006). Restoration and retribution: How including retributive components affects the acceptability of restorative justice procedures. *Social Justice Research, 19*(4), 395–432. https://doi.org/10.1007/s11211-006-0023-7

Gudaitė, G. (2016). Santykis su autoritetu ir asmeninės galios pajauta. Vilniaus universiteto leidykla. ISBN: 9786094597329.

Jackson, J. C., Choi, V. K., & Gelfand, M. J. (2019). Revenge: A multilevel review and synthesis. *Annual Review of Psychology, 70*(1), 319–345. https://doi.org/10.1146/annurev-psych-010418-103305

Jennings, W., Farrall, S., Gray, E., & Hay, C. (2017). Penal populism and the public thermostat: Crime, public punitiveness, and public policy. *Governance, 30*(3), 463–481. https://doi.org/10.1111/gove.12214

Johnson, D. (2009). Anger about crime and support for punitive criminal justice policies. *Punishment & Society, 11*(1), 51–66. https://doi.org/10.1177/1462474508098132

Kääriäinen, J. (2019). Knowledge, punitive attitudes and punitive gap: Finnish findings. *European Journal on Criminal Policy and Research, 25*, 409–425. https://doi.org/10.1007/s10610-018-9384-3

Kaminskienė, N., Tvaronavičienė, A., & Žemaitytė, I. (2023). Teisminės mediacijos Lietuvoje raida ir galimos tobulinimo kryptys: teisėjų požiūrio tyrimas. Jurisprudencija, 30(1), 209–237. ISSN 2029-2058 (online).

Karp, D. R., & Frank, O. (2016). Anxiously awaiting the future of restorative justice in the United States. *Victims & Offenders, 11*(1), 50–70. https://doi.org/10.1080/15564886.2015.1107796

Karstedt, S. (2002). Emotions and criminal justice. *Theoretical Criminology, 6*(3), 299–317. https://doi.org/10.1177/136248060200600304

Kennedy, J. L. D., Tuliao, A. P., Flower, K. N., Tibbs, J. J., & McChargue, D. E. (2019). Long-term effectiveness of a brief restorative justice intervention. *International Journal of Offender Therapy and Comparative Criminology, 63*(1), 3–17. https://doi.org/10.1177/0306624X18779202

Kleck, G., & Jackson, D. B. (2017). Does crime cause punitiveness. *Crime & Delinquency, 63*(12), 1572–1599. https://doi.org/10.1177/0011128716638503

Loeffler, C., & Nagin, D. S. (2022). The impact of incarceration on recidivism. *Annual Review of Criminology, 5*, 133–152. https://doi.org/10.1146/annurev-criminol-030920-112506

Maruna, S., & King, A. (2009). Once a criminal, always a criminal? Redeemability and the psychology of punitive public attitudes. *European Journal of Criminal Justice Research, 15*, 7–24. https://doi.org/10.1007/s10610-008-9088-1.

Michailovič, I., Bikelis, S., Čepas, A., Dobrynina, M., Simaitis, R., Šneideris, D., Ūselė, L., & Venckevičienė, J. (2014). *Atkuriamojo teisingumo perspektyvos Lietuvoje*. Vilnius.

Miller, D. T. (2001). Disrespect and the experience of injustice. *Annual Review of Psychology, 52*(1), 527–553. https://doi.org/10.1146/annurev.psych.52

Moss, S. A., Lee, E., Berman, A., & Rung, D. (2019). When do people value rehabilitation and restorative justice over the punishment of offenders. *Victims & Offenders, 14*(1), 32–51. https://doi.org/10.1080/15564886.2018.1539688

Orth, U. (2004). Does perpetrator punishment satisfy victims' feelings of revenge. *Aggressive Behaviour, 30*, 62–70. https://doi.org/10.1002/ab.20003

Osgood, J. M. (2017). Is revenge about retributive justice, deterring harm, or both. *Social and personality psychology Compass, 11(1), Article e12296*. https://doi.org/10.1111/spc3.12296

Ouellette, H. M., Applegate, B. K., & Vuk, M. (2017). The public's stance on prisoner reentry: Policy support and personal acceptance. *American Journal of Criminal Justice, 42*(4), 768–789. https://doi.org/10.1007/s12103-016-9382-2

Paul, G. D. (2021). The influence of belief in offender redeemability and decision-making competence on receptivity to restorative justice. *Negotiation and Conflict Management Research, 14*(1), 1–20. https://doi.org/10.34891/hap6-y266

Reches, R. (2010). Psichologinio pasipriešinimo atkuriamajam teisingumui problema. *Socialinių mokslų studijos, 2*(6), 357–374.

Republic of Lithuania Law on the Fundamentals of Child Rights Protection. (2018). *State Gazette*, 1996-04-12, No. 33–807. Consolidated version. Retrieved from May 9, 2025.

Roberts, J. V., & Stalans, L. J. (2004). Restorative sentencing: Exploring the views of the public. *Social Justice Research, 17*(3), 315–334. https://doi.org/10.1023/b:sore.0000041296

Routh, D., & Hamilton, Z. (2015). Work release as a transition: Positioning success via the Halfway House. *Journal of Offender Rehabilitation, 54*(4), 239–255. https://doi.org/10.1080/10509674.2015.1024909

Sebre, S., Sprugevica, I., Novotni, A., Bonevski, D., Pakalniskiene, V., Popescu, D., Turchina, T., Friedrich, W., & Lewis, O. (2004). Cross-cultural comparisons of child-reported emotional and physical abuse: Rates, risk factors and psychosocial symptoms. *Child Abuse & Neglect, 28*, 113–127. https://doi.org/10.1016/j.chiabu.2003.06.004

Seiter, R. P., & Kadela, K. R. (2003). Prisoner Reentry: What works, what does not, and what is promising. *Crime & Delinquency, 49*(3), 360–388. https://doi.org/10.1177/0011128703049003

Shaw, J., & Woodworth, M. (2013). Are the misinformed more punitive? Beliefs and misconceptions in forensic psychology. *Psychology, Crime & Law, 19*, 687–706. https://doi.org/10.1080/1068316X.2013.793335

Sherman, L. W., Strang, H., Mayo-Wilson, E., Woods, D. J., & Ariel, B. (2014). Are restorative justice conferences effective in reducing repeat offending? Findings from a Campbell systematic review. *Journal of Quantitative Criminology, 31*(1), 1–24. https://doi.org/10.1007/s10940-014-9222-9

Spinter tyrimai. (2009, November 16). *Dauguma gyventojų—už pedofilų kastraciją ir griežtesnes bausmes.* Retrieved from May 9, 2025, from https://spinter.lt/dauguma-gyventoju-uz-pedofilu-kastracija-ir-grieztesnes-bausmes/

State Child Rights Protection and The Adoption Agency (2024a, February 8). A study by child rights defenders revealed how many children in Lithuania may experience violence. Retrieved from May 9, 2025, from https://vaikoteises.lrv.lt/lt/naujienos/vaiko-teisiu-gyneju-atliktas-tyrimas-atskleide-kiek-vaiku-lietuvoje-gali-patirti-smurta/

State Child Rights Protection and The Adoption Agency (2024b, March 12). Child rights defenders: as the number of reports increased significantly last year, children needed help every 9 minutes. Retrieved from May 9, 2025, from https://vaikoteises.lrv.lt/lt/naujienos/vaiko-teisiu-gynejai-praeju siais-metais-zenkliai-isaugus-gautu-pranesimu-skaiciui-vaikams-pagalbos-pri reike-kas-9-minutes/

Trajtenberg, N., Ezquerra, P., & Williams, M. (2024). Lock them up and throw away the key: An evaluation of the structure of punitive attitudes. *Psychiatry, Psychology and Law, 0*, 1–27. https://doi.org/10.1080/13218719.2023.229 6476

Uscila, R. (2022). Nuteistųjų pusiaukelės namų taikymo praktika Lietuvoje. *Kriminalistika ir teismo ekspertologija: mokslas, studijos,* praktika, 18, 170–178. Retrieved from May 9, 2025, from https://cris.mruni.eu/cris/handle/007/18563

Valickas, G., & Jarutienė, L. (2014). Pedofilijos skandalo metu informaciniame žinių portale Delfi ir dienraštyje Lietuvos rytas pateikto teisėjų įvaizdžio ypatumai. *Teisė, 92*, 19–33. ISSN 1392-1274.

Valickas, G., Justickis, V., Vanagaitė, K., & Voropaj, K. (2013). *Procedūrinis teisingumas ir žmonių pasitikėjimas teisėsaugos pareigūnais bei institucijomis.* Vilniaus universiteto leidykla. p. 388. ISBN 978–609–459-193-8.

Valickas, G., Vanagaitė, K., & Švedas, G. (2023). Pirmos, antros ir ketvirtos COVID-19 pandemijos bangų metu Lietuvoje taikytų ribojimų ir draudimų vertinimas. *Teisė, 127*, 8–24. https://doi.org/10.15388/Teise.2023.127.1

Valickas, G., Vanagaitė, K., Švedas, G., & Barysė, D. (2021). COVID-19 pandemijos pirmos bangos metu Lietuvoje taikytų ribojimų ir draudimų vertinimas. *Teisė, 121*, 8–26. https://doi.org/10.15388/Teise.2021.121.1

Vidmar, N. (2001). Retribution and revenge. Edited by S. Sanders & V.E. Hamilton, Handbook of justice research in law, (p. 31–63). Kluwer Academic/Plenum Publishers. ISBN 0–306–46340-7.

Vileikienė, E. (2010). Lietuvos gyventojų ir policijos pareigūnų požiūris į linkusius nusikalsti nepilnamečius. *Socialinis darbas, 9*, 45–53.

Vileikienė, E., Gelčytė, M. (2022). Ataskaita apie viešojo saugumo būklę Lietuvoje 2005–2022 m. LR Vidaus reikalų ministerija. Retrieved from May 9, 2025, from https://vrm.lrv.lt/media/viesa/saugykla/2023/12/kzl9XHsw-Cc.pdf

Weimann-Saks, D., Peleg-Koriat, I., & Halperin, E. (2022). Incremental beliefs and public attitudes toward restorative justice: The cases of sexual, violent and property offenses. *Journal of Offender Rehabilitation, 61*(4), 169–187. Retrieved from May 9, 2025, from https://doi.org/10.1080/10509674.2022.2062518.

Weiner, B. (2006). *Social motivation, justice, and the moral emotions: An attributional approach*. Lawrence Erlbaum Associates. ISBN 0–8058–5526-2.

Wong, J. S., Bouchard, J., Gushue, K., & Lee, C. (2018). Halfway out: An examination of the effects of Halfway houses on criminal recidivism. *International Journal of Offender Therapy and Comparative Criminology, 63*(7), 1018–1037. https://doi.org/10.1177/0306624x18811964

Yoshimura, S. (2007). Goals and emotional outcomes of revenge activities in interpersonal relationships. *Journal of Social and Personal Relationships, 24*(1), 87–98. https://doi.org/10.1177/0265407507072592

Žukauskienė, R., Bakaitytė, A., Kaniušonytė, G., Segal, A., Ustinavičiūtė-Klenauskė, L., & Santtila, P. (2023). The lifetime prevalence of child sexual abuse assessed in young adults in Lithuania. *Child Abuse & Neglect, 138*, 1–12. https://doi.org/10.1016/j.chiabu.2023.106061.

3

The Social and Cultural Context of Punitiveness in Lithuania

Aušra Pocienė

Introduction

On 11 March 1990,Lithuania regained its independence and rejoined the family of democracies. This was a radical change because after spending five decades in the socialist-communist regime of the Soviet Union behind the Iron Curtain, the country has now radically changed direction. "Go west" became the new slogan, and integration into Western structures became the goal. From that moment on, more than three decades of political, economic, and social transformations began, generating new sources of insecurity and threats, leading to a corresponding level of crime and forming the basis for societal reactions to them. In the early 1990s, a large part of Society, which had been brought up and socialised under the Soviet system and ideology, was

A. Pocienė (✉)
Faculty of Philosophy, Institute of Sociology and Social Work, Department of Criminology, Vilnius University, Vilnius, Lithuania
e-mail: ausra.pociene@fsf.vu.lt

A. Dobryninas and S. Nikartas (eds.), *Understanding Crime Control and Punishment in Lithuania*, Crime Prevention and Security Management,
https://doi.org/10.1007/978-3-032-05538-5_3

confronted with a reality it had never experienced before. The transition from a planned to a market economy, the creation of the first businesses, the manifestations of "wild capitalism," competition, and personal responsibility for one's destiny became the new reality.

This chapter seeks to answer two questions. The first is the socio-cultural context in Lithuania during the years of independence and how it may have led to violations of social norms or even crimes. The second question, which follows from the first, is what the reactions of Society were to the criminogenic situation and how socio-cultural factors might shape these reactions.

Sociological Perspectives on Crime and Punishment: A Framework for Interpreting the Lithuanian Context

The socio-cultural context in Lithuania between 1990 and 2023 is outlined, and a macro-sociological approach is used, employing Emil Durkheim's theory of crime and punishment, David Garland's concept of the culture of control, and Robert Agnew's General Strain Theory to answer these questions. These three sociological theories can be a tool for understanding how the Lithuanian socio-cultural context generated the specific criminogenic situation and in what context the response to it - punishment - was formed.

Emile Durkheim on Crime, Punishment, and Penal Evolution

The 19th-century French sociologist Emile Durkheim viewed crime as a social fact. According to him, all crimes have common features: firstly, they violate the moral sentiments of a group (community, Society); secondly, they are normal phenomena because they exist in all societies and occur under the existing social conditions; and thirdly, they have many functions in a society: the drawing of boundaries, the activation of a defensive feeling towards the perpetrator and assuring the solidarity. Just like crime, punishment is a normal social fact. It arises as a consequence of an action (crime) initiated by the offender. Through punishment, one can know what constitutes a crime in a specific society (Breathnach, 2002). The concept of collective consciousness is central to Durkheim's interpretations of punishment. Collective consciousness is a metaphor for the totality of collective sentiments, not the arithmetical sum of individual consciousnesses, but a separate reality sui generis. The real essence of the crime is not the act committed, but the violation of these collective sentiments. The need for retribution–punishment arises from violating collective sentiments. The idea is that the more sensitive the sentiment that is violated, the more tumultuous the automatic reaction, and the harsher the punishments demanded by the members of Society for the offender. Thus, to explain the penal attitudes in Lithuania, the following questions can be raised based on Durkheim's theory: What sensitised the collective consciousness of the Lithuanian population in these decades, and why has this reaction been particularly harsh or moderate in certain periods?

However, Durkheim not only provided a static interpretation of crime and punishment but also explained the evolution of punishment throughout history in his The Two Laws of Penal Evolution. He linked the evolution of punishment to the development of Society. Examining punishment practices in different eras and socio-cultural contexts, he concluded that "the intensity of punishment is greater to the extent that societies belong to a less advanced type, and the central power has a more absolute character" (Durkheim, 1969). The more primitive the society and the more power is concentrated in one hand (the ruler, the monarch, the authoritarian), the more absolute it is. Conversely, more diffuse power (in democratic societies) has less or no absolutism. As societies evolve from a primitive to an advanced type, the penalties for crimes are reduced in their intensity. Thus, the absolutism of power leads to harsh penalties and vice versa. Signs marking that punishments become more moderate are the decrease in the number of offences subject to capital punishment and the abolition of various forms of corporal punishment. According to the classics, in primitive communities of mechanical solidarity, punishment had a religious connotation because the offender was committing a crime against collective sacred things. Here, punishment was more fed by collective sentiments and manifested itself with great force ("religio criminality"). By contrast, in the modern Society of Organic Solidarity, crimes against human beings have become the basis of criminal law ("human criminality"). Thus, according to the classic, in modern societies, punishments become more controlled, less emotional, less harsh, and less brutal.

David Garland on Punishment and the Culture of Control

However, Durkheim's evolutionary theory of punishment has not withstood the criticism of time. Not all modern states are characterised by moderate penal policies. Many of them in the twentieth century have demonstrated leaps of punitiveness. This was noted by one of Durkheim's followers and critics, the American criminologist David Garland. Applying the rules of the sociological method, he shows how changes in the social, economic, and cultural life of the United States and Great Britain in the mid-20th century led to a sharp increase in crime (Graland, 1990). In other words, he analysed how a series of social facts (suburbanisation, increasing consumerism, changes in household structure, increasing labour market entry) led to the emergence of another social fact (high crime) (Garland, 2002, pp. 81-89). He applied these rules to interpret penal policy as well. In his book "The Culture of Control: Crime and Social Order in Contemporary Society" (Garland, 2002), the penologist distinguishes two periods in the United States and Great Britain: before and after 1970. The 1970s are unique in that they were followed by a change from the previous moderate welfare penal policy, based on the principle of rehabilitation/correction, to a harsh, expressive neoconservative penal policy, based on the principles of retribution and detention (Garland, 2002, pp. 96-102). While Garland associated the moderate penal policy with low crime rates, low risk of victimisation, and a high level of social welfare, respectively, he attributed the harsh retributive policy to the high crime rate, the high fear of crime in Society, and the ineffective crime control measures. Moreover, although he found the desire to solve the problem of crime with harsh punishments illogical, he had a sociological explanation for this increase in punitiveness. Garland described the modern "penalty" as "the broad range of laws, processes, discourses and institutions" that come together to criminalise and punish behaviour (Garland, 2002, p. 10).

Macro-sociological Approach to Strain-generated Crime and Punitive Attitude by Robert Agnew

The beginning of Lithuania's independence was fraught with social tensions. The question of the extent to which these tensions can generate crime is not new in academic discourse. The US sociologist Robert Agnew, one of the authors and developers of the macrosocial General Strain Theory (GST), has examined the strains that lead to crime (Agnew, 2001). The theory distinguishes between two types of strains: objective and subjective. Objective strains are events or conditions that are disliked by the majority of the members of a given group. Such events and conditions can range from physical violence to a lack of food or housing. Subjective strains are events or conditions disliked by the people who experience them. In other words, subjective strain is when a person experiences something he/she does not like. Research shows that people have different subjective perceptions of their experiences. For example, acceptance of the death of a family member can vary significantly between people depending on other circumstances. The acceptance depends on individual factors (e.g., irritability), personal and social resources (self-confidence, autonomy, social support from others), goals/values/identities, and a series of life circumstances. There are many types of stressors, but the stressors that lead to crime, according to Agnew, must (1) be seen as unjust, (2) be seen as high in magnitude, (3) be associated with low social control, and (4) create some pressure or incentive to engage in criminal coping (Agnew, 2001,319).

Reframing the General Strain Theory, it can be presumed that the socio-economic context in Lithuania has inevitably influenced the prevalence of deviance and crime. The first years of independence were characterised by strains that not all members of society managed to cope with adequately and which manifested themselves in destructive behaviours such as alcoholism, suicide, violence, and, consequently, criminal behaviour. On the contrary, the subsequent increase in social well-being (see below) reduced insecurity, which correlated with decreased crime.

GST explains not only the spread of deviant behaviour and crime as a response to stress. It also explains why society members react more severely to crime and seek harsher punishments in a state of insecurity and tension. This is the way they express their inner strains. In other words, high levels of strain and feelings of injustice can not only lead to crime but can also lead to harsher punishment for criminals. Conversely, a society that feels secure is calm, not defensive, and reacts more moderately to the situation.

Social Transformations and Sources of Strain in the Early Years of Independence

Building on the sociological perspectives discussed above, and treating crime as a social fact, it is essential to explore the broader social context in which it occurs. In this section, attention is turned to the situation in Lithuania during the first decade of independence, focusing on the social tensions and conditions that coexisted with rising crime rates.

The restructuring of the economic system was marked by growing unemployment. When Lithuania left the Soviet Union, many sectors of the economy became redundant. The closure of large industries, which had previously served the broad market, began. It had a devastating effect on big cities, but especially on the regions. For example, from 1998 to 2001, the unemployment rate grew from 13% to 17%. The process has resulted in structural unemployment, creating a serious challenge for the population. Perhaps most significantly, the responsibility for finding a job has shifted to the individual, unlike in the former Soviet Union, where the "caring state" assumed this role and unemployment was not officially recognised as a social issue.

Rural areas faced particular challenges. Whereas fifty years ago, as Lithuania was annexed to the Soviet Union, after the nationalisation of land, farmers were forced into collective farms (kolkhozy), now the reverse process has begun: the dismantling of the kolkhozes and the privatisation of land. The population did not immediately adapt to these changes. Rural areas have experienced ageing and depopulation, with young people moving to the cities or emigrating abroad. A typical rural image of that time was abandoned buildings of former collective farms, barren fields, and poor village life. Alcoholism prevailed.

The Lithuanian inhabitants used different strategies to adapt to the new time. Some who did not lose their jobs and lived on a modest salary chose a conformist or ritualistic path. Others radically changed their lives and decided to set up their businesses. Some emigrated to the West in "search of a better life". Notably, there was some confusion and underestimation of social status among occupational groups. For example, highly skilled professionals such as doctors, university professors, civil servants, and others have been working for low wages due to the economic downturn, which has reduced the prestige of these professions.[1]

Emigration to the West was one of the strategies of adaptation. In 1990, 23.592 people emigrated from Lithuania after the opening of the borders.[2] In 1992-31,972. The trend continued until 2001, with around 25,000 emigrants per year. It is estimated that more than 900 thousand people left the country between 1990 and 2016, or almost a quarter of the population. Although in the early 1990s, there were also emigrants who left for their ethnic homelands (Jews, Russians), later economic emigration to Western Europe and the United States prevailed.

Until 2004, Lithuanian citizens did not have the right to work in Western European countries. This led to short-term emigration for unqualified seasonal farm work. Usually, it was illegal work. This context also generated new risks. Fraudulent job offers lured inhabitants, especially from socially vulnerable groups. Deceived by fake "agencies" to

[1] Some of them, however, have decided to change their occupations and take up less skilled, less prestigious, but better-paid jobs. For example teachers, started working in constructions or selling goods in market places.

[2] All statistical data presented in this chapter is taken from the data of the State Data Agency and the Official Lithuanian Criminal Register. Not all data have been collected since 1990. Some of the statistical studies were performed only once or twice. State Data Agency, official statistics portal https://osp.stat.gov.lt/. Accessed 18 Oct 2024.

organise a work trip, they not only lost money and did not get a job, but also lost their documents and even became victims of human trafficking. "You will be sold as a doll" – this social advertisement preventively targets young girls who may become victims of human trafficking after being lured by so-called "modelling agencies." Ironically, one unfortunate "positive" outcome of mass emigration was that many individuals with criminal backgrounds also left the country. As a result, criminal activity was somewhat displaced abroad, which unfortunately harmed Lithuania's international image.

Another way to adapt to new situations is to start one's own business. Although small and medium-sized businesses were already beginning in the late Soviet era, when the first cooperatives were being created, the processes accelerated after the 1990s. In this context, one type of business aptly illustrates how the changed geopolitical context has opened up new opportunities and created risks simultaneously. This is a trade-in for used cars from Western Europe. After the Soviet-era shortages, demand for Western cars surged. Lithuania gradually became the used car depot of Western Europe, with Soviet vehicles rapidly replaced by Western models. Within a decade, the number of cars doubled: in 1990, there were nearly 493,000 registered vehicles; by 1995, the number had risen to 685,000, and by 2000, it had exceeded one million. Large used car markets emerged in Lithuania, serving not only domestic buyers but also attracting customers from across Eastern Europe. This thriving trade provided fertile ground for entrepreneurship. However, the phenomenon had a darker side. Car thefts increased significantly, with stolen vehicles often transported abroad or held for ransom. Moreover, car traders were frequently subjected to extortion. To operate safely, they were compelled to make regular payments to organised criminal groups in exchange for protection, a practice colloquially referred to as paying for a "roof."

Another defining feature of the first decade of independence was the emergence of organised criminal groups. The conditions for their rise were more than favourable: a social stratum of young men excluded from conventional paths to achieving socially approved goals, the rapid growth of private business activity, and a weak, still-developing law enforcement system all contributed to a fertile environment for organised crime. By 1993, it is estimated that around one hundred such groups were operating in Lithuania.[3] They primarily concentrated in major cities and their surrounding districts. Many of these organisations evolved from smaller criminal groups initially formed around shared interests or neighbourhood ties.

The first "activity" of such groups was the aforementioned racketeering of businessmen. After 1993, once they had accumulated initial capital through criminal means, many of these groups began to legalise their operations, often integrating into legitimate business sectors. After the laws on privatising state property had been adopted, mass privatisation of state property began. With the available money, the criminal groups privatised many former state facilities. It is not a secret that they used threats and coercion to do it at the lowest cost. At first, they established themselves in the most profitable branches of the economy, such as trade in oil products, alcohol, or tobacco. They also established commercial banks and engaged in other commercial activities. The gangs used violence and coercion not only for the racketeering of business people but also in conflicts with other criminal groups. The public knew about these criminal organisations, their methods, and the murders from the tabloid media, which covered such events extensively at the time.[4]

Apart from conformist–or, conversely, criminal–attempts to adapt to the new reality, a segment of society failed to do so. For these individuals, resignation became the dominant response, often culminating in self-destruction. The widespread prevalence of alcoholism and suicide serves to illustrate this social despair. Alcohol consumption has become a way for some people to deal with strains in a state of uncertainty. As scholars note (Goštautas, 1998), abundant alcohol consumption, for which Lithuania is still being mentioned today, increased consistently

---

[3] The most famous groups of that time: "Vilniaus Brigada", "Daktarai", "Žaliakalnio", "Gaidjurgio", "Princų", "Tulpinių", "Kavioro", "Baublių". It must be noticed that the leader of "Vilniaus Brigada," Boris Dekanidzė, was sentenced to the death penalty and executed in 1995. It was the last execution after which the death penalty in Lithuanian was terminated in 1996 and abolished in 1998.

[4] Organized crime groups have been operating and continue to operate now. However, their scale has diminished. Many leaders of former groups are now serving prison sentences or have passed away. The profiles of current organized groups have changed; they have become international. Unlike at the beginning of the period, the topic of organized crime no longer captures public attention.

after the 1990s. In 2000, it reached 7,8 litres per inhabitant of the country. Later, this number grew (Karpuškienė et al., 2019). According to the World Health Organisation, in 2010, Lithuania consumed the world's highest amount of pure alcohol per year per adult population. The consequences of alcoholism were felt not only by consumers but also by their families: lack of income, violence, and neglect of children - this was the daily routine. Rural areas, where the problem of unemployment was especially acute, faced alcoholism in particular. Alcohol use often ends in violence against oneself.

With the beginning of independence, the number of suicides began to increase. According to the data from the Department of Statistics[5] in 1990, there were 26.2 suicides per 100,000 inhabitants, and in 2001, it was already 43.9. From 1990 to 2000, 13 thousand people committed suicide. Males dominated (82%). Suicides were more prevalent in rural than in urban areas. In 2000, the mortality rate from suicides was 3.8% of all deaths. Moreover, it was one of the highest indicators in Europe and the world at that time. Moreover, although we are facing a consistent decline in suicides since the 2000s, the first decade was challenging in this regard.

Perhaps one of the most apparent indicators showing that society is in a state of tension is the murder rate. In the first years after regaining independence, a sharp growth in murders was observed. In 1991, 260 murders were committed in Lithuania; in 1994, they doubled to 523 and reached the limit of 0.9% of the overall crime structure (whereas today, in 2023, murders account for about 0.2% of all criminal acts). Since 1994, murders have begun to decline gradually, and the trend continues to this day. Criminologists who studied the phenomenon of murders in Lithuania assumed that such a trend would continue due to the improvement in the socioeconomic situation (Čepas et al., 2014). Their predictions came true: the country's socioeconomic indicators were improving (see section below), and homicide rates were falling. However, the authors also emphasised that there is no direct correlation between murder rates and socioeconomic status. Rather, the number of murders should be viewed as one of several indicators of overall social well-being,

[5] Former title of the State Data Agency.

alongside alcohol consumption, income inequality, suicide rates, unemployment, and other factors (see Čepas et al., 2014). Accordingly, the rise in homicides during the early years of independence can be interpreted as a manifestation of social disorganisation.

An overview of the first decades would be incomplete without addressing one issue that has become normalised and widely taken for granted: corruption. In the Soviet Union, a "blat culture" (Russian: блат) that originated from Russian culture was pervasive. This form of corruption consisted of a system of informal agreements, exchanges of services, personal connections, Party contacts, and black-market deals used to achieve desired outcomes or gain advantage. For ordinary citizens, it functioned as a practical means of accessing scarce resources, such as goods, job positions, or other opportunities, within the context of a deficit-driven economy. Therefore, this culture was highly normalised at the beginning of independence. It was a culture of corruption that permeated the entire body of society, from state institutions to ordinary citizens.

However, corruption control was one of the main conditions for Lithuania's candidacy and later becoming a member of the European Union.

Have put much effort into ensuring these requirements: diagnosing the problem,[6] adjusting the legal framework and establishing responsible institutions[7] (Monitoring the EU Accession Process, 2002). In this way, the issue of corruption was actualised and became a topic of public discourse. Scientific research, public reporting of results, developing anti-corruption procedures, and growing law enforcement attention helped bring corruption into public view and establish it as a major social issue. However, it is important to emphasise that this shift did not occur because the public suddenly realised that what was previously considered "normal" was in fact deviant or even criminal behaviour, undermining the foundations of state stability. Rather, it was — and continues to be — the result of long-term public awareness and education efforts.

[6] The quantitative survey "The Lithuanian Map of Corruption" has been started, that is periodically repeated up to now.

[7] In 1997 the Special Investigation Service (STT) under the Ministry of the Interior has been established.

Economic Growth as the Premise for a Better Life After 2004

Political events undoubtedly determined economic and social changes after 2004. In March 2004, Lithuania became a member of NATO; in May 2004, it joined the European Union; and in December 2007, it joined the Schengen area. The aftermath of these events significantly affected the life choices and well-being of Lithuanian residents. Membership in NATO and the European Union paved the way for Lithuanian security: geopolitical, economic, and social. Since that time, Lithuania has experienced an improvement in its economic situation; the growth of GDP per capita illustrates it: in 1995, GDP per capita, at current prices, was 552 US dollars, in 2004–1444 US dollars, in 2008–3279 US dollars, in 2014–3709 US dollars and in 2024 already 6427 US dollars. The EU's common market, economic support, and investments led to faster economic development and, at the same time, an increase in the quality of life.

Changes in the unemployment rate also illustrate life improvements. It has diminished in comparison to the early years of independence. For example, in 2007, the unemployment rate was 4%. This year was also exceptional because significant investments from the EU structural funds were received, and the economy and wages grew. Another increase in unemployment in 2010 was determined by the global bank crisis, which Lithuania coped with quite well, and unemployment was again relatively low (in 2018, 6%)[8]. It is worth mentioning that Lithuania, now in 2024, faces the opposite problem - the lack of a labour force in the unskilled sector. That indicates social well-being when the population is unwilling to work for low wages.

As for emigration, after 2004, it acquired a mainly economic character. Three rises were observed: in 2005, 57885 Lithuanian citizens emigrated, in 2010, 83157, and in 2015, 50333. The first wave was conditioned by the opportunity to work legally in EU countries. At that time, Lithuania's living standard was lower than the EU average. Unlike before, there was long-term emigration: whole families or the main breadwinners (father

[8] For comparison, in 2023 m., unemployment was 7 %.

or mother) left the country. A new form - a family with parents abroad - was formed (Juozeliūnienė et al., 2008). The second 2010 wave was a reaction to the global banking crisis. The third 2015 wave (experts interpret it differently) was when a large part of the citizens of Russia, Ukraine, and Belarus returned to their countries due to the tightened rules of residence in Lithuania.[9]

Thus, in the early 2004s, while Lithuania was still catching up with the old European countries regarding economic indicators, high emigration prevailed.[10] Since 2018, emigration has been stable, and a decreasing trend has been observed. In 2022, 23021 inhabitants emigrated from Lithuania.[11] The reverse process is currently being observed: Lithuanians return to their homeland. The return is not only due to patriotic motives but also because the standard of living and opportunities have almost caught up with those of the developed EU countries.

Statistical data also reflect the growth of well-being. According to the Lithuanian State Data Agency, between 2014 and 2021, the poverty rate declined across several key indicators. The proportion of residents unable to participate regularly in leisure activities fell from 17% to 4%. Similarly, those who could not afford to leave home for at least one week per year, whether to stay in a secondary residence or with friends or relatives, decreased from 17% to 5%. The share of individuals unable to replace even part of their worn clothing dropped from 10% to 3%, and the percentage of those unable to invite friends to socialise or share a meal declined from 8% to 2%.

Of course, it must be recognised that these are general macro-level data. Lithuania still has many problems: poverty and social exclusion of some social groups, income inequality, emerging marginalised

[9] As for the third wave of emigration from Lithuania in 2015, according to experts, only a part consisted of economic emigrants from Lithuania. A significant increase in emigration was related to the departure of citizens of Russia, Ukraine, and Belarus, whose departure was encouraged by the tightening of provisions on the issuance of temporary residence permits to foreigners in Lithuania. They are associated with the institutions' desire to control illegal migration more effectively, in particular by restricting legal but fictitious activities.

[10] Emigrants substantially contributed to Lithuania's economic growth: the money earned abroad was sent to families in Lithuania or otherwise invested here.

[11] One of the reasons for this emigration may be the threat posed by the war launched by Russia against Ukraine.

groups, and others. However, this does not negate that overall social and economic well-being has significantly increased compared to the early 1990s. Their level of happiness best illustrates the well-being and life satisfaction of Lithuanian residents. According to European Value survey data (Savicka & Žiliukaitė, 2023), since 1990, the share of the population who felt very happy or just happy has increased steadily. Taken as a whole, the share of the lucky ones grew: in 1990, 48 %; in 1999, 62 %; in 2008, 65 %; and in 2017, 73 %.

The level of happiness implicitly includes many factors, including a sense of safety. Thus, assuming that after 2004, the prerequisites for an economically safer life were found in Lithuania, it is worth examining how the criminogenic situation responded to these economic changes. Even more important in the topic we are considering is how safe the residents of Lithuania were and how safe they felt from crimes.

Crime Trends in 1990–2023 and Sources of Information About Crime

Regarding the level of crimes in Lithuania (Fig. 3.1), two trends are recorded during the period: a sharp increase in the number of crimes until 2004 and their consistent decline with some fluctuations until now.

The trends are echoed by relative indicators. In 1990, there were 1003 criminal offences per hundred thousand inhabitants; in 2004, this indicator more than doubled to 2766, then in 2023, it decreased to 1566 criminal offences. In this decreasing trend, 2013 stands out with 2864 criminal offences per hundred thousand inhabitants and 84,715 registered criminal acts. This is because the Law on Protection against Domestic Violence came into force[12]. Due to this, many cases of domestic violence, which had been latent until then, began to be registered. Despite this exception, the overall decrease in the number of offences since 2004 in Lithuania has been observed. It repeats some

[12] Following the adoption of this law, since 2012, a sharp increase in registered criminal acts under Article 140 of the Criminal Code, Causing physical pain or slight harm to health, and Article 145, Threatening to kill or seriously harm a person's health, has been observed.

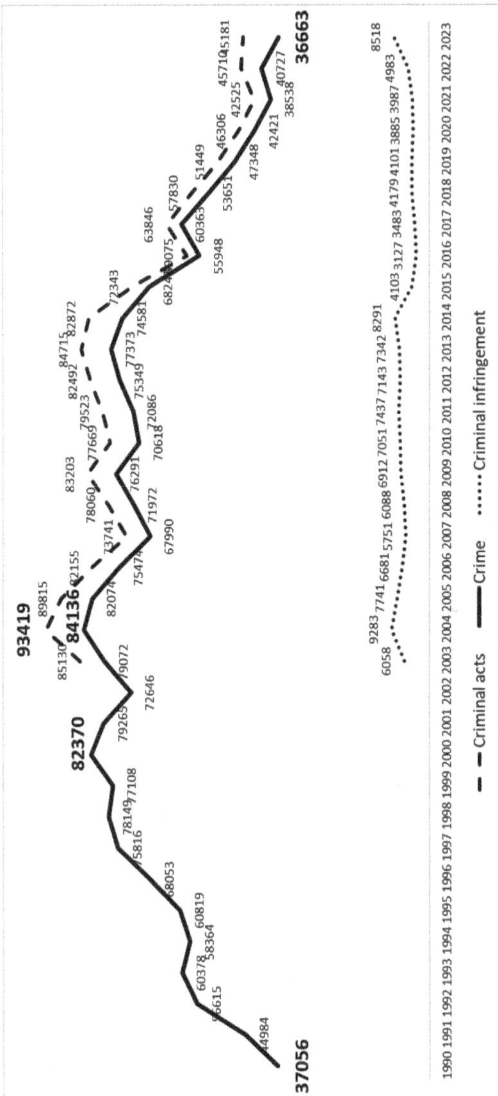

Fig. 3.1 Crime indicators in Lithuania 1990–2023

trends in North America and Europe (Aebi et al., 2010), (Pociene et al., 2023), (Payne & Piquero, 2020).

A more informative picture of criminal acts after 2004 is revealed by the 2005–2023 report of the Ministry of the Interior of the Republic of Lithuania. The drop in crime rates is observed in many categories, such as:

- Robbery (Art. 180 of CC) (-93 %);
- Thefts from residential premises (-90 %);
- Theft from vehicles (-88 %);
- Intentional murders (Art. 129-131 of CC) (-81 %),
- Violations of public order (Art. CC) (-75 %);
- Theft (Art. 178 of the CC): (-75 %);
- Violations of road traffic safety rules (Art. 281 of CC) (-74 %).
- Theft of vehicles (-71 %);
- Causing serious health disorders (Art. 135-137 of CC) (-65 %);
- Rapes (Art. 149 of CC) (-65 %);
- Destruction or damage to property (Art. 187 of CC) (-50 %);
- Fraud (Art. 182 of CC) (-12 %);

However, there was a clear increase in crime in the following three areas:

- Causing physical pain and slight impairment of health (Art. 140 of CC) (+449%),
- Crimes by e-mail for the security of data and information systems (Art. 196–198 of the CC) (+3439%)
- Possession of drug substances (Art. 259–268 of CC) (+116%)[13].

These trends can be explained by the aforementioned stricter treatment of domestic violence, as more cases were registered. The increase in cybercrime is a natural consequence of the E-society when lawbreakers are increasingly active online. The increase in crimes related to the possession of drug substances can be explained by an increase in the

[13] Growth in criminal acts related to illegal drug possession: 2004 - 1551, 2012 - 2963, 2018 - 3151, 2023 - 3921 criminal acts.

phenomenon itself, by the increased attention of law enforcement, and by the increasingly frequent coverage of these acts in the media.

Thus, it can be concluded that the number of registered criminal acts halved between 2004 and 2023. Notably, the declining delinquency among young people mirrors the trends observed in adult crime. In 2004, 4,232 juveniles committed criminal acts, whereas in 2022 the number had decreased almost sevenfold to 631. Regarding latent delinquency, criminological research (ISRD) also indicates a downward trend (see Pocienė et al., 2023; Justickaja et al., 2015).

In our context, the crime rate is important in several aspects. First, it shows the real threat of the population becoming a victim of crime. Secondly, we can question how ordinary citizens perceive this threat. Thirdly, they should know what sources of information they use to learn about crimes. National surveys show that from the first decade of independence until now, information sources about crimes have changed significantly (Table 3.1). In 2003, residents mostly learned about crimes from national TV channels, radio, national press, experience of friends and acquaintances, regional press, and personal experience. However, almost two decades later, in 2021, the list of sources is redistributed. Now, the dominant sources are national TV channels and the internet. Such sources as the national press, radio, personal experience, and experience of friends are far behind them. So, it can be stated that today, the internet and social networks play an important role in informing citizens about crimes.[14]

Keeping in mind that in the early 1990s, traditional means of mass media were the main sources of information about crime, it should be noted that they tended to exaggerate the criminogenic situation (Dobryninas, 2001, p. 76). Even more, at that time, so-called "tabloids" or the yellow press played their role, successfully selling the topic of crimes to the audience. Older residents certainly remember the extremely popular yellow press newspaper "Akistata," which described crimes in great detail. Notably, not only the tabloids but also national dailies and commercial TV news channels had a separate "Crime" section alongside

[14] The representative survey of Lithuanian residents was conducted in August–November 2021. The survey was conducted by the market and public opinion research company Spinter Research.

Table 3.1. Sources of information about crime

	2003(%)	2021(%)
National TV channels	89	62
Radio	83	29
National press	80	22
Experience of friends, acquaintances	72	33
Regional press	69	
Personal experience	64	34
Special literature, seminars, conferences	21	
Internet	20	61
Social networks	-	33
Law enforcement authorities/ institutions	-	20
Public events in open spaces	-	12

daily news, sports, and weather. At the time, public trust in the media was also high—71% believed that criminal justice issues were presented objectively. Two decades later, this situation changed significantly: trust dropped to just 30%.

Sense of Safety, Punitive Attitudes and Trust in Institutions

Awareness of crime is to some extent linked to whether people feel fear of it and how safe they perceive their environment to be. The sense of safety, however, goes beyond the fear of crime and is connected to the psychological concept of anxiety (Dobryninas & Gaidys, 2004). Anxiety can stem from a variety of sources, with fear being one of its manifestations. In the context of this topic, the most relevant form of fear is the fear of becoming a victim of crime. This fear can, in turn, fuel the demand for punishment, as society seeks to defend itself against perceived aggressors.

In 2004, Lithuanian researchers studied the population's fear of crime (Dobryninas & Gaidys, 2004). They found that at that time, the population felt strong anxiety about the following: increasing crime in general – 48 %, the increase of drug addiction – 50 %, aggressive behavior of young people – 41 %, corruption – 39 %, the spread of

AIDS - 33%, the spread of terrorism – 29 %. Paradoxically, rural residents felt a greater fear of crime than urban residents, although their actual risk of victimisation was lower. Another important observation: at that time, Lithuanian residents were even more concerned about their health and economic well-being than about the issues listed above. This indicates that life was highly stressful, as worries about personal well-being outweighed concerns about crime, even though crime was at its peak during that period.

A kind of disappointment with one's country was also observed at that time (Dobryninas & Gaidys, 2004). Significant parts of the population believed that their rights were poorly ensured in a number of areas: the rights of crime victims, the protection of women from domestic violence, the right to a fair trial, and the child's right to be free from violence and coercion. But (and this must be underlined) the rights of the imprisoned persons, according to the inhabitants, were fairly well ensured. So, the prevailing perception was that criminals were better off than victims of crime or society as a whole. Here, we can see a kind of antagonism between the victims of crime and the perpetrators. This antagonism is one of the explanations why a significant part of the population supported harsh punishments. A significant part of society considers fixed-term imprisonment to be the most effective means of crime control and supports long-term imprisonment (Dobryninas & Gaidys, 2004, p. 41). Even six years later, after the death penalty was abolished in 1998, the population, especially the older and less educated residents, considered it an appropriate punishment. The majority of the public was inclined to punish severely. Paradoxically, residents who had no experience of victimisation were inclined to punish sentenced people more severely than victimised ones. The need for severe punishments correlated with the perceived dangerousness of the crime: hooliganism and thefts were assessed more moderately, while bodily injury, rape, and murder - more severely. For serious crimes, residents require long prison terms, life imprisonment, or even the death penalty.

In twenty years, the situation regarding the fear of crime has changed significantly in Lithuania. In 2023, according to data, 88 % of Lithuanian residents felt safe. 74 % believed that the probability of becoming a victim of crime is low, and 79 % believed that the criminogenic situation in Lithuania is good. It is true that the feeling of safety was correlated with sociodemographic characteristics: older residents had a worse assessment of the criminogenic situation and, therefore, felt less safe, although their risk of victimisation was the lowest. In twenty years, the list of the biggest perceived threats has also changed: Fraud 62 %, Drug users or drug dealers 60 %, Drunk/intoxicated persons 58 %, and Domestic violence 43 %. The leitmotif of the drug threat is not new, but today, this fear is more inspired by media reports than the actual situation. However, there is a reason to worry about domestic violence. It is worth noting that most murders in Lithuania still take place in a close environment. Special attention was drawn to this problem in 2014 after a lethal incident in which a child died due to constant parental abuse and violence. Not only was greater public attention drawn to the problem, but changes to the criminal law were also adopted.

In twenty years, in addition to the increase in the sense of safety, another significant change has occurred - residents are increasingly involved in ensuring their own safety and security.[15] In the period from 2006 to 2023, from 63 % to 96 %, the population's concern for their own safety and their property increased. This indicates the strengthening of civil society, where residents themselves take responsibility for their own security. However, when it comes to the state institutions directly responsible for the administration of justice, the situation is poor. They have been more distrusted than trusted since the 1990s (Dobryninas et al., 2012). In 2024, only 29 % of residents trusted the prosecutor's office, and courts, even less, only 26 %[16]. However, the police stand out in this context: according to the Eurobarometer, from 2007 to 2024, trust in the police in Lithuania increased more than twice, from 35 % to 81 %[17]. How can we explain such different assessments? In addition

---

[15] For example: storing personal data, armored and lockable stairwell doors, property insurance, not walking alone after dark, cooperating with neighbors, and installing security systems in the house.

[16] The representative survey of Lithuanian residents was conducted in September 2024. The survey was conducted by the market and public opinion research company Vilmorus.

[17] A similar jump occurred only in the Czech Republic (from 41 to 76%). If in 2007 Lithuania did not reach the EU average (64%) and was among the top three countries, together with Bulgaria (33%) and Slovakia (34%), where the police were least trusted, then in 2024 it already exceeded the EU average (72%) and is among the six countries with the highest percentage

to the fact that the Lithuanian police made great efforts to improve its image, it can also be noted that it is the only institution that the residents see most often and have the most contact with, while the work of the prosecutor's office and the courts is invisible and often incomprehensible to them.

Shifts in Public Morality

Emile Durkheim has stated that to recognise what "crime" is in society, we should observe what the collective consciousness reacts to. It is closely related to the value system of the society. As Žiliukaitė et al. (2016) argue based on their research, in the first decade after the restoration of independence, Lithuanian society was marked by moral uncertainty and relativism—many believed that the boundary between good and evil depended on the context. Over time, an increasing number of people began to adopt moral absolutism, seeking clear moral reference points amid normative and social disorder. This shift was driven by societal anomie and a religious revival (see Žiliukaitė et al., 2016).

Later, moral contextualism also began to emerge more clearly—an approach that recognises the existence of clear moral rules but allows for exceptions in particular circumstances. This view was especially common among younger generations. For example, while joyriding or bribery was strongly condemned, more lenient attitudes were observed towards minor offences such as tax evasion or riding public transport without a ticket. Sociologists interpreted these trends as signs of societal modernisation (see Žiliukaitė et al., 2016).

In the second decade, no clear trajectory of change in moral attitudes was observed. Moral pluralism increased, and the differences between relativists, absolutists, and contextualists became less distinct. Although generational change may have contributed to greater tolerance, sociologists emphasised that this process was not irreversible—public morality

of trust, together with the Scandinavian countries: Finland (95%), Sweden (91%), Denmark (90%), the Netherlands (87%) and Luxembourg (85%).

could strengthen again as governance and law enforcement improved (Žiliukaitė et al., 2016, p. 189).

At the same time, Lithuania's civil society remained weak by European standards. Low interpersonal trust, limited solidarity, and low civic engagement were linked to the social atomisation and privatisation of public life rooted in the Soviet era. Deeply embedded individualism and mistrust—forms of historical adaptation to an authoritarian system—undermined collective values such as cooperation and responsibility. Thus, increased tolerance for breaches of civic morality may reflect not so much modernisation, but rather a continuation of social and political alienation (see Žiliukaitė et al., 2016).

How strong is civil society in Lithuania today? There are a number of indicators showing it has strengthened. Residents are increasingly inclined to cooperate; they care more about societal rather than private interests, and they use civic tools more often to defend those interests. For example, in 2019 and 2024, referendums were organised to preserve dual citizenship for Lithuanians living outside Lithuania. Residents are increasingly mobilising on individual issues: rallies, writing petitions, joining associations, etc., for the representation of their interests. In particular, the features of civil society became evident in 2022, when Russia's war against Ukraine started. Many support actions were organised. Residents react more and more actively to violations of public morality and do not tolerate previously normalised problems, such as the shadow economy, domestic violence, bullying, sexual harassment, mobbing, etc. Also, as mentioned above, civil society is increasingly involved in ensuring security.

Concluding Remarks

During more than three decades of independence, Lithuanian society has changed. From an atomised individualist, trying to deal with the tension caused by economic deprivation, having no experience of community and therefore putting personal interests first, towards closer social solidarity, a society based on community relations. The rise of economic and, at the same time, social well-being, the increasing sense of safety, and the decreasing fear of crimes create the conditions to calm down and move from an aggressive, emotionally defensive position to a more moderate, rational mind and listening-based approach to crimes and the persons who committed them. Of course, the process is not finite. It continues to this day. If, in the early 1990s, the collective consciousness primarily reacted to gross violations of norms (violence and coercion) generated by the era, then, after the latter had decreased, in a state of relative peace, collective sentiments became more subtle and sensitive to violations of more lenient social and moral norms. An increasingly sensitive reaction to such offences as domestic violence, physical punishment of children, sexual harassment, petty corruption, etc., shows that human rights violations that were previously considered "normal" are becoming increasingly intolerable.

Such a prevailing perception allows us to move from a repressive criminal policy, where severe punishments for the evil committed must cause suffering to the criminal and threaten society, towards one where crimes are perceived as social conflicts and transferred from the criminal to the civil law area. Here, social conflicts are seen in the context in which they arose, and a wide arsenal of non-criminal but social control measures is used to resolve them. This is how we move from criminal to restorative justice: not to punish and threaten, but to restore the damaged order of things.

Back in the 18th century, Cesare Beccaria stated that the size of the punishments should correspond to the situation of the nation itself. More sensitive and stronger impressions should be applied to rough nations, those that were just wild: "It takes the force of thunder to lay down an untamed lion because rifle shots only irritate him" (Bekaria, 1992, p. 64). Therefore, a rhetorical question can be raised here: What does our culture of punishment say about our state?

References

Aebi, M. F., & Linde, A. (2010). Is There a Crime Drop in Western Europe. *European Journal on Criminal Policy and Research, 16*(4), 251–277. https://doi.org/10.1007/s10610-010-9130-y

Agnew, R. (2001). Building on the Foundation of General Strain Theory: Specifying the Types of Strain Most Likely to Lead to Crime and Delinquency. *Journal of Research in Crime and Delinquency, 38*(4), 319–361. https://doi.org/10.1177/0022427801038004001

Bekarija, Č. (1992). *Apie nusikaltimus ir bausmes.* Mintis.

Breathnach, S. (2002). *Emile Durkheim on Crime and Punishment (An Exegesis).* Universal Publishers.

Čepas, A., Dobrynina, M., Dobryninas, A., Kalpokas, V., Mickevič, A., Navickas, V., Nikartas, S., Šneideris, D., Valickas, G., & Vanagaitė, K. (2018). *Nužudymai Lietuvoje.* Justitia.

Dobryninas, A. & Gaidys, V. (2004). *Is the Lithuanian society safe? Lithuanian population's victimisation experience and attitudes towards criminal justice and public safety.* UAB Petro Ofsetas.

Dobryninas, A. (2001). *Virtual reality of crime.* Eugrimas.

Dobryninas, A., Drakšienė, A., Gaidys, V., Vileikienė, E., & Žilinskienė, L. (2012). *Pasitikėjimo Lietuvos teisėsauga profiliai.* Vilniaus universiteto leidykla.

Durkheim, E. (1969). Two laws of penal evolution. *University of Cincinnati Law Review, 38*, 32–55.

Durkheim, E. (2001). *Sociologijos metodo taisyklės.* Vaga.

Garland, D. (2002). *The Culture of Control: crime and social order in contemporary society.* The University of Chicago Press.

Garland, D. (1990). *Punishment and Modern society: a study in social theory.* Oxford University Press.

Goštautas, A. (1998). *Vyrų gyvenimo stiliaus ypatumų ryšys su mirtimi per 20 metų. Sociologija: praeitis ir dabartis.* Mokslinės konferencijos pranešimų medžiaga. 2 kn., Kauno technologijos universitetas. Kaunas: Technologija, 1998, p. 233–236.

Information Technology and Communications Department under the Ministry of the Interior (n.d) *Official register of criminal offences in Lithuania.* (Retrieved from 25 November 2024). https://ird.lt/lt/paslaugos/tvarkomu-valdomu-registru-ir-informaciniu-sistemu-paslaugos/nusikalstamu-veiku-zinybinio-registro-nvzr-atviri-duomenys-paslaugos. Payne, J. L.; Piquero, A. R. (2020).

International Self-Report Delinquency Study (n.d). *ISRD*. (Retrieved from 16 May 2025). https://isrdstudy.org/

Juozeliūnienė, I., Kanapienienė, L., & Kazlauskaitė, A. (2008). Atotolio šeima: nauja užduotis šeimos sociologijai. *Sociologija. Mintis ir veiksmas, 21*, 119–133. https://doi.org/10.15388/SocMintVei.2008.1.6051

Justickaja, S., Aleknevičienė, J., Kalpokas, V., Giedraitytė-Mačiulienė, R., Mickevič, A., Žilinskienė, L. & Žėkas, T. (2015) *Jaunimo delinkvencinis elgesys ir nepilnamečių justicijos politika Lietuvoje: tendencijos ir lyginamieji aspektai*. Kolektyvinė monografija. Vilnius: Justitia. (Retrieved from16 May 2025). https://teise.org/wp-content/uploads/2016/06/JAUNIMO_DELINK_ELGESYS.pdf

Karpuškienė, V., Rastenienė, A., & Leipuonius, A. (2019). Alkoholio vartojimo įpročiai, aplinka ir pasekmės Lietuvoje. *Socialinė teorija, empirija, politika ir praktika, 18*, 59–73. https://doi.org/10.15388/STEPP.2019.4

Monitoring the EU Accession Process. (2002). *Coruption and Anti-corruption policy*. Open Society Institute. EU Accession monitoring program.

Payne, J., Piquero, A. R. & Halim, S. (2022). *Developmental criminology and the crime decline: A comparative analysis of the criminal careers of two New South Wales birth cohorts*. Cambridge University Press. (Retrieved from 16 May 2025). doi:https://doi.org/10.1017/9781108882149

Pocienė, A., Aleknevičienė, J. & Kalpokas, V. (2023). 'Jaunuolių delinkventinis elgesys Lietuvoje: ką atskleidžia naujas delinkvencijos ir viktimcijos tyrimas?', *Filosofija. Sociologija*, 34(4, Priedas), pp. [nenurodyta]. (Retrieved from 16 May 2025). doi:https://doi.org/10.6001/fil-soc.2023.34.4. Priedas.Special-Issue.4.

Sakalauskas, G., Dobrynina, M., Justickaja, S., Kalpokas, V., Mališauskaitė-Simanaitienė, S., Nikartas, S., Pocienė, A., & Zaksaitė, S. (2011). *Registruotas ir latentinis nusikalstamumas Lietuvoje: tendencijos, lyginamieji aspektai ir aplinkos veiksniai*. Lietuvos teisės institutas.

Savicka, A. & Žiliukaitė, R. (2023) Laimės dinamika Lietuvoje kartų kaitos perspektyvoje, *Filosofija. Sociologija*, 34(4). Vilnius: Lietuvos mokslų akademijos leidykla. State data agency, official statistics portal. Retrieved from 25 Nov 2024. https://osp.stat.gov.lt/

Žiliukaitė, R., Poviliūnas, A., & Savickas, A. (2016). *Lietuvos visuomenės vertybių kaita per dvidešimt nepriklausomybės metų*. Vilniaus universiteto leidykla.

4

Lessons from the Abolition of the Death Penaltyin Lithuania: Looking Through a Kaleidoscope of Professional, Political, and Public Discourses

Aleksandras Dobryninas

Introduction

In recent decades, European capital punishment policies have been shaped by complex interactions between public opinion trends, professional debates, and political decision-making processes. These discourses reflect broader shifts in societal values, governance approaches, and international norms, making the death penalty a unique policy domain where moral, legal, and pragmatic factors converge. While today Europe has achieved near-universal abolition (with exception of Belarus), underpinned mainly by human rights frameworks and supranational pressures, it is worth to focus on how public, professional, and political discourses interact and influence capital punishment policies in these regions,

A. Dobryninas (✉)
Faculty of Philosophy, Institute of Sociology and Social Work, Department of Criminology, Vilnius University, Vilnius, Lithuania
e-mail: aleksandras.dobryninas@fsf.vu.lt

A. Dobryninas and S. Nikartas (eds.), *Understanding Crime Control and Punishment in Lithuania*, Crime Prevention and Security Management,
https://doi.org/10.1007/978-3-032-05538-5_4

emphasising the ideological, institutional, and societal contexts that shape these trends.

Studies of European abolition efforts show the centrality of supranational institutions like the Council of Europe and the European Court of Human Rights in embedding abolition within human rights frameworks, often in defiance of retentionist public opinion (Fawn, 2001; Yorke, 2010). In Europe, abolition proceeded primarily as a top-down process, with lawmakers relying on strategic framing to justify abolition in contexts where public majorities opposed it (Fawn, 2001). Professional discourse plays a pivotal role in this dynamic. Ideological underpinnings in Europe, such as framing capital punishment as antithetical to human dignity, informed legislative and institutional actions to prioritise abolition as a marker of democratisation and modern governance (Fijalkowski, 2011; Neumayer, 2008). Comparative studies further reveal that structural differences in governance and decision-making processes account for divergent abolition pathways. In contrast, Europe's centralised and normative frameworks foster cohesive abolitionist policies; the U.S., for example, remains reliant on fragmented, state-specific efforts to limit capital punishment (Ogletree & Sarat, 2009).

These findings collectively underscore the interplay between moral, pragmatic, and institutional dimensions in shaping the trajectory of the death penalty. Public opinion, while a key variable, is mediated by political will, media framing, and the role of professional expertise in constructing arguments for or against abolition.

Lithuania became an abolitionist country in 1998 and, like many post- communist countries of the European continent, perfectly fit those mentioned above "top-down" abolitionist process. However, the way to abolish the death penalty in the country was not as straightforward as one might expect. Democratically elected politicians suddenly released that on the integration to the European democratic institutions and commitment to implement political and civic rights is not a formal process and should consider not only international political and legal requirements, but also has to reflect national peculiarities and circumstances, e.g., political ratings, crime situation and public attitude towards criminal justice policy, including the question of necessity of the death penalty.

The current chapter does not intend to completely reconstruct the abolishment of the death penalty in Lithuania.[1] Instead, it tries to concentrate on one of its core elements: the relationship between political culture, legal systems, and public discourse in the governance of abolitionist policy, and attempts to make communication and decisions more relevant to the expectations of the members of societies. Moreover, this analysis undertakes a comprehensive assessment of this decision's potential effects, investigating its capacity to not only transform the international landscape of abolitionist policy but also to reduce, to a certain extent, the pervasive impact of penal populism on the criminal justice policies implemented in democratic societies.[2]

Criminological Discourses and Penal Policy

Speaking about the role of public opinion in the death penalty debates, R. Hood noted: "Many countries also cite 'public opinion' as one of the significant reasons for retaining the death penalty. However, many have abolished it and consistently resisted attempts to reinstate it, despite widespread support for capital punishment. There is a need to distinguish such popular support from well-informed opinion. Public opinion polls can prove to be a misleading indicator" (Hood, 1989, p. 167). These remarks are highly correlated with another prominent scholar, A. Schutz, who, evaluating the role of social knowledge in the democratic process of society, wrote: "A certain tendency to misinterpret democracy as a political institution in which the opinion of the uninformed man on the street must predominate increases the danger. Therefore, it is the duty and privilege of the well-informed citizen in a democratic society to make his private opinion prevail over the public opinion of the man on the street" (Schutz, 1976, p. 134).

The"well-informed citizen" is a key concept in Schutz's phenomenological stratification of social knowledge. According to him different

[1] A more thorough analysis is outlined in (Dobryninas, 2004).

[2] The author also expresses gratitude to Dr. Sigita Černevičiūtė for sharing crucial historical information on the abolition of the death penalty in Lithuania after regaining independence.

subject-specific competence of expertise allows for the construction of three different ideal types, which can be identified (in order of decline of competence) as "expert" (professional knowledge), "well-informed citizen" (intermediate knowledge) and "man from the street" (everyday knowledge) (Schutz, 1976). However, "professionals" could be no less dangerous for the political process in a democratic society than the above-mentioned "men from the street". While "man from the street" is oriented in stereotypical and emotional experience, "professional" pays its price for possessing expert competence, living in an anonymous, objective and detached world of the "true" knowledge. "Well-informed citizen" is a sweet spot in this distribution of social knowledge – he has enough competence not to be unlearned, but on the other hand, he is far from breaking the bond with the living world.

Based on this classification, one can speak of the corresponding social epistemic groups of "experts", "well-informed citizens" and "people from the streets", who not only have a specific understanding and vision of certain social issues, but can also produce their own speech or discourses about these issues Employing M. Foucault's idea about discourse as "empowered speaking" (Foucault, 1981), these three discourses can be effectively applied to analysing various social communication and interaction aspects. Notably, these ideas allowed the construction of the theory of criminological discourses (Dobryninas et al., 2014), which helps to comprehend the peculiarities of the reception of criminal justice issues in society.

In one way, the goals and problems of criminal justice are understood by professionals–criminologists, legal specialists, experts of law enforcement institutions, and in another way–by ordinary people, who usually learn about these problems from newspapers or television programs. There is another attitude of those who shape and implement criminal policy–national and regional politicians, administrators, and executors. The listed forms of knowledge are not entirely static and isolated: it changes, interacts with each other, determines and modifies each other. They have institutional and structural supports, reference groups, specific forms of expression, and linguistic nuances. To understand how criminal justice is perceived and maintained in society, it is necessary to consider these elements and those close to them. A similar principle can be applied to the penal policy, particularly to society's reception of the death penalty abolition policy.

The Political Context of the Abolition of the Death Penalty in Lithuania

The death penalty is a sharply debated topic in Lithuania, subject to considerable discussion within political, academic, and media spheres. Historically, the death penalty in Lithuania was applied for various serious crimes, and most commonly for murder. During the interwar years, Lithuania commonly imposed the death penalty for premeditated killings (Černevičiūtė ir Kaubrys, 2014). This repressive policy persisted in Lithuania under Soviet rule, beginning with the 1940 occupation (Indrišionis, 2016). Following its 1990 independence, Lithuania underwent a substantial transformation, aligning itself with Western values of liberal democracy, human rights, and the rule of law. Capital punishment was effectively limited to premeditated murder, resulting in a drastic reduction of cases, and no executions have taken place since the autumn of 1995.

However, while mitigating penal policy was an initial intention of the new democratic Lithuanian government, the request to abolish the death penalty came from international organisations. Becoming a member of the Council of Europe in 1993, Lithuania, eo ipso, was obliged to sign Protocol No. 6 to the European Convention on the Protection of Human Rights and Fundamental Freedoms, aiming to abolish the death penalty. On June 28 1996 Parliamentary Assembly of the Council of Europe in its Resolution stated: "Given the irrefutable arguments against the imposition of capital punishment, the Assembly furthermore urges Lithuania to institute a moratorium on executions without delay" (Parliamentary Assembly of the Council of Europe, 1996). Lithuanian response was pretty fast: in order to speed up abolitionist policy, on July 25 1996 President of the Republic of Lithuania proposed to Lithuanian Parliament (Seimas) to suspend the enforcement of death penalty in Lithuania until the acceptance of new Criminal Code. As the reason for his recommendation, the President pointed to two factors–the correspondence of such a decision to Lithuanian international engagements and the inefficiency of capital punishment as a means, preventing the growth of violent crime (including murder cases). Unfortunately, members of Seimas were more preoccupied with the upcoming parliament's election in October 1996 than with the politically risky issue of the abolishment of the death penalty. They decided not to pay serious attention to the President's letter.

The question of the death penalty was postponed until next year, when on April 27 1997, in Pärnu (Estonia), a Lithuanian parliamentarian delegation, together with their colleagues from two other Baltic countries–Latvia and Estonia–accepted The Baltic Assembly Resolution on the Abolishment of the Death Penalty. This document expresses the significance of human rights issues and recommends that the parliaments and governments of the three Baltic States prepare for the ratification of Protocol No. 6 to the Council of Europe Convention for the Protection of Human Rights and Fundamental Freedoms as an important step towards integration into European and international structures. At the same time, the authors of the Resolution emphasised three conditions for abolishing the death penalty in all Baltic States. These conditions are decreasing the crime rate, implementing life imprisonment instead of capital punishment in legal acts, and reforming prisons.

Two months later, members prepared the draft of The Resolution on the Abolishment of the Death Penalty. This document is written in light of the previous Baltic Assembly Resolution. It suggests suspending the enforcement of the death penalty in Lithuania until the ratification of Protocol No.6. The Lithuanian Seimas, during its session on June 24, 1997, started the discussion of this Resolution. However, the discussion was postponed to 1988 after a group of members of the Seimas sent a request to the Constitutional Court concerning the constitutionality of the death penalty. Factually, the responsibility for the decision to abolish or to keep the death penalty was transferred from the parliamentarian rooms to the court hall. Although such a political move is known in the history of adoptionism (Hungary case), it was unexpected, considering that most European countries, including close political and cultural neighbour Poland, abolished the death penalty using a parliamentary mechanism.

On December 09, 1998, the Constitutional Court of the Republic of Lithuania decided that the death penalty conflicts with the Constitution of Lithuania. On this basis, the Criminal Code was amended on December 21, 1998, and the death penalty was abolished. On June 22, 1999, the Lithuanian Parliament (Seimas) ratified the Protocol No. 6 to the European Convention on the Protection of Human Rights and Fundamental Freedoms. Without the death penalty sanction, the new Criminal Code of the Republic of Lithuania was adopted on September 26, 2000 (entered into force on 01.05.2003) and is in force today.

Death Penalty Abolition in Lithuania: Expert, Public, and Political Perspectives

The initial abolition of the death penalty in Lithuania is consistent with prevailing political trends; a move towards democracy, entry into the Council of Europe, and the increasing number of abolitionist nations in the area all suggest a higher chance of abolition, a correlation noted in Neumayer's (2008) or McCarthy and Brunton-Smith (2024) researches. In Lithuania, the abolition of the death penalty signified not only a significant step towards upholding human rights but also represents a crucial element in Lithuania's further integration into the European Union, causing the alignment of its criminal law provisions with those of the European Community, thus ensuring legal harmony across the Union (Drakšas, 2002).

One is compelled to question why Lithuania deviated from the common practice among its regional peers of directly abolishing capital punishment through legislative action; instead, they chose the more complex and indirect method of a Constitutional Court ruling, prompting further inquiry into the rationale behind their decision. The potential answer relates to the unique and combined influence of professional, public, and political discussions concerning the abolition of capital punishment within Lithuanian society.

The Constitutional Court's abolishment of the death penalty in Lithuania was met with immediate resistance from some politicians, who sharply criticised the decision as being contrary to public opinion and irrelevant to the crime situation in the country (see: Drakšas, 2002). Discussions among legal professionals, criminologists, and specialised NGO members overwhelmingly supported abolishing capital punishment. In academic publications (Dobryninas, 1996; Babchinaitė, 1998; Jovaišas, 1997, etc.), philosophical, historical, political, legal, and criminological aspects of the death penalty phenomenon in society were presented, and opinions were expressed on the possibility of abolishing the death penalty. In rare publications (e.g., Vaišvila, 1997), the death penalty is presented as an inevitable means against brutal crimes and defended in its deterrence nature.

The most interesting aspect was the typical situation among Lithuanian political elites: academicians with expertise in constitutional and criminal law often held leading positions in the Lithuanian Parliament (Seimas), the Lithuanian government (such as the Ministry of Justice), or influential non-governmental organisations like the Lithuanian Centre for Human Rights. In this context, it is not surprising that Dr. Stasys Stačiokas, the Chairperson of the Seimas' Law and Justice Committee and leading expert in constitutional law, was one of the key proponents of the appeal to the Constitutional Court regarding the compatibility of the death penalty with the Lithuanian Constitution. At the same time, two judges from the Constitutional Court, Dr. V. Pavilonis and Dr. J. Prapiestis, both well-known experts in penal law, were responsible for preparing this case. The Constitutional Court invited representatives from various professional, academic, and non-governmental institutions to participate in the hearing. These included the European Law Department, the Law Institute, the Lithuanian Law Society, the Lithuanian Law Academy, the Lithuanian Human Rights Center, the Lithuanian Human Rights Association, the Vilnius University Faculty of Philosophy, Seimas Committees, the Prosecutor General's Office, Traditional Confession Centers, the Lithuanian Political Prisoners' Association, and the Lithuanian Medical Union, among others. As expected, most of these representatives expressed a strong abolitionist stance (Konstitucinis Teismas, 1998).

Analysis of professional, political, and public discourses on criminal justice in Lithuania reveals strong overlapping between the two first discourses' types–professional and political (Dobryninas et al., 2014). An analysis of Lithuania's political landscape in the 1990s highlights that the lack of a stable political system and well-defined ideological boundaries during its transition to democracy contributed to the emergence of populism (Ulinskaitė & Pukelis, 2025). High crime rates, especially murder, and public support for capital punishment–factors widely recognised as fueling pro-death penalty views (Hood & Hoyle, 2008)–were strikingly apparent in Lithuania. The murder cases in Lithuania after the reestablishment of independence in 1990 dramatically grew from 260 until its maximum 523 in 1994, and left a very high level in the time of intensive public discussion on the fate of the death penalty in 1997–1998 (Čepas et al., 2018). An opposite trend emerged in public opinion regarding the abolition of capital punishment; in 1990, 27 per cent of the population supported abolition, but this figure declined to 18.3 per cent by 1997 (Dobryninas, 2004). Retentionist politicians commonly employed these factors to bolster their arguments for the death penalty in public discussions. For example, in 1996, two of the seven parliamentarian parties' leaders, who were asked by a journalist from the Lithuanian daily "Respublika" about their attitude to the Lithuanian President's idea to sustain the death penalty, were against it, mentioning crime problems in Lithuania (Skērytė, 1996). Simultaneously, a government-produced report for English-speaking audiences highlighted concerns that Lithuania's strong historical and political ties to capital punishment and significant public support could seriously impede abolition (The Lithuanian policy on the death penalty, 1996).

Another important aspect of discourses on the death penalty interplay was the role of the Lithuanian media in supporting or denying the abolishment of the death penalty. Observing the content of publications on this issue in popular newspapers during that period, such as *Lietuvos rytas*, *Respublica* or *Lietuvos aidas*, one could find an impartial role, where supporters and critics of the death penalty were not restricted from expressing their opinions. However, informational campaigns organised by human rights and civic nongovernmental organisations, especially in 1998, had a "framing" (Etman, 1993) effect and oriented to reduce massive support for the death penalty in Lithuanian society.

Conversely, one could argue that the media may inadvertently reinforce retentionists' perceptions due to the overrepresentation of crime in society. However, this viewpoint is not completely supported by findings from a comprehensive study conducted in Lithuania between 1977 and 1999, which examined how mass media—specifically print and television—construct a "virtual reality of crime." The study also explored how public perceptions of the crime situation could influence democratic criminal justice policies in Lithuania. Indeed, on the one hand, data reveals a rapid rise in crime-related media publications and presentations, driven by public demand and worsening crime rates, often at the expense of professional standards. Sensationalism, rights violations, and stereotyping in the crime presentation were common. Despite the extensive coverage, the media's portrayal of crime had a limited effect on individuals' actions or their political perceptions of reality in Lithuania (Dobryninas, 2001). These findings suggest that, although violent crimes were overrepresented and the actual crime situation was sensationalised, Lithuanian mass media at the time largely fulfilled a traditional "mirroring" role (Klapper, 1961). This reinforced the prevailing perceptions of crime in society, which, to put it mildly, were far from satisfactory.

From Retentionist's Public Support to Abolitionist's Well-Informed Opinion

In democratic societies, the decision to retain or abolish the death penalty ultimately rests with political leaders. Their responsibility is to translate ambiguous public sentiment into clear policies. As a result, political decisions often reflect the tension between public opinion and expert analysis. Criminological studies increasingly show that the death penalty is ineffective, unjust, and morally questionable. However, public beliefs—especially in post-communist countries experiencing social upheaval—often support harsh punitive measures. Lithuanian politicians advocating for abolition face a dilemma: they can either align with European human rights standards at the risk of unpopularity or cater to public fears for political gain. Consequently, public opinion remains a key factor in policy discussions.

It is worth mentioning that miscommunication between professionals, politicians and the public has become a primary stimulus for initiating the project "Death penalty in Lithuania: from Retentionists' public support to abolitionists' well-informed opinion" (coordinators A. Dobryninas, S. Katuoka); the Council of Europe financially supported the project. One of the project's main goals was to analyse the main factors forming retention ideology in Lithuania and plan practical means to enforce abolitionists' ideas in various social groups.

The project's first stage was organising and analysing the results of the national surveys on the death penalty that had been run in March–May 1997 in Lithuania. Unlike previous national surveys on the death penalty, this new survey features a different design and methodology. It consists of two surveys that used the same questionnaires: one targeting the general public and the other focusing on the elite, which includes representatives from the Seimas, political parties, heads of State Departments, lawyers, business executives, and others.

Another unique aspect of this survey is the way the questions were constructed. Instead of directly asking respondents whether they support abolishing or retaining the death penalty in Lithuania, the questions were framed in a "conditioned" manner. This approach aimed to evaluate respondents' legal, political, and moral perspectives on the issue of capital punishment. While it may not have transformed ordinary respondents into "well-informed" citizens, it did encourage them to think more deeply about the subject. In other words, these questions are provocative and require minimal deliberation and understanding of the problem.

The survey results (see Dobryninas, 2004) were extensively discussed in Lithuania and submitted to the Constitutional Court as supplementary materials during the hearing on the constitutionality of the death penalty. The findings indicated that there were potentially many more abolitionists in Lithuania than traditional public opinion polls, which posed unconditional and straightforward questions about the death penalty, suggested. Additionally, the survey revealed that the Lithuanian elite held a more abolitionist stance than the general public. This elite group could play a more active role in the movement to abolish the death penalty without fearing that their involvement would significantly harm their popularity among voters. In other words, the research demonstrated that it is possible to decrease the number of supporters for the death penalty if the general public and the elite widely accept the information provided by abolitionists.

The second stage of the project integrated educational and research activities through seminar discussions on the death penalty, involving 15 target groups. Thirteen of these groups comprised criminal justice professionals, including police officers, investigators, prosecutors, judges, and Ministry of Interior officials. The remaining two groups included university professors, teachers, and pedagogy students. Each group, comprising 15 to 20 participants, was introduced to capital punishment's historical, legal, moral, political, and international dimensions. Open discussions were encouraged throughout the seminars. To assess shifts in opinion, participants completed identical questionnaires before and after the seminars, addressing legal, ethical, and policy aspects of the death penalty. A comparative analysis of their responses aimed to evaluate the impact of the seminars on their perspectives.

The results (see: Dobryninas & Katuoka, 1999) showed that participants in influential societal positions are often not well-informed about various aspects of the death penalty. Most identified mass media as their primary source of information, suggesting that professionally prepared materials are not deemed acceptable. However, it can be argued that this social group is open to abolitionist arguments and could potentially become a well-informed cohort. To achieve this, there is a need for professional literature, academic courses, and other relevant abolitionist materials in the Lithuanian language. The educational aspect of the abolitionist policy in Lithuania remains paramount. This aspect cannot be overlooked, even after Lithuania abolished the death penalty. Without well-informed public support for the abolitionist idea, it would be challenging to expect widespread acceptance of this decision in Lithuanian society, potentially leading to political tensions. Such tensions could adversely affect the democratic process in Lithuania.

The final results of this stage of the project were presented at the conference titled "The Abolition of the Death Penalty in Lithuania: Present and Prospects," held on September 17, 1998, in Vilnius, just a few months before the Lithuanian Constitutional Court officially abolished the death penalty. These results were also shared extensively in public discussions, seminars, and media, both nationally and internationally.

Discussion and Conclusions

After regaining independence in 1990, Lithuania shifted significantly towards the Western ideals of liberal democracy, justice, fairness, humanity, and human rights. While the country drastically reduced the application of the death penalty in its criminal code compared to previous policies, it continued to impose it solely for the crime of murder. Although instances of its application were rare, the use of the death penalty in Lithuania became a topic of intense discussion among experts, politicians, and the general public. In this context, it is important to highlight several key aspects of this debate, particularly the process of abolishing the death penalty, which was legally achieved in 1999 with the signing of Protocol No. 6 to the Convention for the Protection of Human Rights and Fundamental Freedoms, adopted in Rome on November 4, 1950.

First, following the re-establishment of Lithuanian independence, the first ten years witnessed a disturbingly high number of homicides; this trend was especially pronounced between 1991 and 1995, a period characterised by a dramatic surge in violent killings. In the second place, there was a notable change in public sentiment during this period, as evidenced by a significant rise in the percentage of citizens who supported capital punishment. A further critical consideration is the significant international pressure, including sanctions and diplomatic isolation, being exerted on the nation to both sign Protocol No. 6 and to eliminate the death penalty ultimately. Fourth, a massive abolitionist awareness campaign was launched, spearheaded by national and international NGOs, using various media to spread their message far and wide. Fifth-the effective promotion of sociological and criminological studies highlighted the potential for a significant change in public opinion regarding abolition if the government could assure society of the secure isolation or effective resocialisation of dangerous murderers. Furthermore, the pivotal decision to abolish capital punishment in Lithuania stemmed from the Lithuanian Constitutional Court's ruling that it violated the nation's constitution. The court's resolution highlighted the incompatibility of the death penalty with fundamental constitutional articles.

Following the abolition of the death penalty in Lithuania, there has been a marked decline in both the public discourse surrounding capital punishment and the academic research conducted on related societal attitudes, with Lithuanian researchers rarely investigating these views. A nationally representative sociological survey, for instance, conducted in 2013 by the public opinion company Spinter, revealed that a considerable portion of the surveyed population, 48.3 per cent to be exact, expressed a desire for the reinstatement of the death penalty (Samoškaitė, 2013).

A 2013 sociological survey, part of the "Homicide in Lithuania: a criminological approach" project (Čepas et al., 2018), provides a nuanced perspective on public attitudes towards homicide punishment. The public primarily focuses on more brutal punishments to fight murder, but the death penalty is not favoured as a solution for all cases. Like other international studies, participants clearly distinguished between homicide and its punishments. In cases of brutal murder, such as one involving a victim who was mercilessly beaten, respondents favoured the harshest punishments more often; 30% chose the death penalty and 40% selected life imprisonment. The results showed a slight bias towards leniency for teenage killers. While 23% supported life imprisonment and 10% the death penalty, these numbers increased to 32% and 16% respectively for those convicted of killing adults.

A 2020 survey on EU citizens' values (Values and Identities of EU citizens, 2021) revealed that 37% of respondents from Lithuania expressed support for the death penalty. This is significantly higher than the EU average of 16%, indicating a concerning trend. However, previous surveys have shown a decline in support for the death penalty in Lithuania. This suggests that the Lithuanian case aligns with the common hypothesis that in countries where the death penalty has been abolished, there is a continued decrease in the number of supporters for it (see Hood & Hoyle, 2008).

The successful abolition of the death penalty in Lithuania, along with the lack of serious attempts to reinstate it, raises important questions about the maturity and humanity of the country's penal policies concerning severe punishment, including capital punishment. At least three critical questions require further academic investigation and thorough explanation.

First, while acknowledging the strong and effective involvement of the Council of Europe in the abolitionist process in Lithuania, it seems that the potential role of the European Court of Human Rights has been somewhat overlooked. Although this topic is beyond the current discussion, existing studies (Fijalkowski, 2011; Hood & Hoyle, 2008) indicate that further exploration could illuminate the development of professional human rights rhetoric. This rhetoric has significantly influenced discussions and decision-making processes, particularly at the level of the Constitutional Court, during the abolition of the death penalty in Lithuania.

Lithuania was neither the first nor the last country in Europe to use its Constitutional Court to validate the abolition of the death penalty (Hodgkinson, 2004). However, one might question whether this approach is efficient, especially without strong support from the Council of Europe. In this context, examining the extent to which European human rights standards are valid and acceptable to constitutional courts outside of Europe is important. For instance, can these courts unconditionally agree that the death penalty violates the fundamental human right to life? The recent decision by Taiwan's Constitutional Court regarding the death penalty[3] may not be the case. This topic could lead to extensive academic discussions.

[3] See: Summary of TCC Judgment 113-Hsien-Pan-8 (2024) 【The Constitutionality of the Death Penalty Case】 (https://cons.judicial.gov.tw/en/docdata.aspx?fid=5535&id=355776 accesed 1 June, 2025);

The author wishes to thank Ms. Chuanfen Chang (張娟芬), chairperson of the Taiwanese Alliance to End the Death Penalty (TAEDP), for providing information about this case.

The third and final observation closely relates to the previous point and raises important philosophical and moral questions. Can the abolition of the death penalty be viewed as a moral victory over the punitive tendencies inherited from our historical past? Does the punitive mentality in Lithuanian penal ideology and practice truly vanish with the elimination of the death penalty? The situation regarding life imprisonment, which has replaced the death penalty in the new Lithuanian Criminal Code, is not encouraging. International studies indicate that, in 2016, the largest segment of the prison population was made up of inmates sentenced for intentional homicides, accounting for 27.6% of the total. This figure is significantly higher than the average of 13.1% for the surveyed European countries and ranks second only to Albania, which had a rate of 33.2% (Aebi et al., 2017).

These critical questions are waiting for further research and discussions. However on the current stage, assessing the Lithuanian experience in abolishing policy, one, probably can agree that intensive and productive communication among professional, political, and public representatives was essential for mitigating the effects of "top-down" abolition policies; this fostered a horizontal, credible dialogue that successfully integrated experts, well-informed citizens, and the broader public.

References

Aebi, M.F., Tiago, M.M., Berger-Kolopp, L. & Burkhardt, C. (2017). *SPACE I – Council of Europe Annual Penal Statistics: Prison populations. Survey 2016*. Strasbourg: Council of Europe.

Babchinaitė, G. (1998). Viešoji nuomonė ir mirties bausmė: Prevencijos strategija. *Jurisprudencija, 10*(2), 64–68.

Baltic Assembly. (1997). Resolution 10: Resolution on the Abolishment of the Death Penalty.

Čepas, A., Dobryninas, A. & Valickas, G. (eds.) (2018). *Nužudymai Lietuvoje*. Vilnius: Justitia.

Černevičiūtė, S. & Kaubrys, S. (2014). Kartuvių kilpa, kulka ir dujų kamera: mirties bausmė Lietuvoje 1918–1940 metais. Vilnius: Gimtasis žodis.

Dobryninas, A. (1996). Mirties bausmė Lietuvoje: tarp teisinės semantikos ir politinės pragmatikos. In: Lomanienė, N. (ed.) (1996). *Žmogaus teisės Lietuvoje: teoriniai ir praktiniai aspektai*. Vilnius, pp. 68–81.

Dobryninas, A. & Katuoka, S. (1999). *Mirties bausmė Lietuvoje: teisiniai ir sociologiniai aspektai*. Vilnius: Lietuvos žmogaus teisių centras.

Dobryninas, A. (2001). *Virtual Reality of Crime*. Vilnius: Eugrimas.

Dobryninas, A. (2004). The Experience of Lithuanian Road to Abolition. In: Hodgkinson, P. and Schabas, W. (eds.) (2004). *Capital Punishment: Strategies for Abolition*. Cambridge: Cambridge University Press, pp. 233–252.

Dobryninas, A., Česnienė, I., Dobrynina, M., Giedraitis, V., & Merkevičius, R. (2014). *Perception of Criminal Justice in Society*. Vilnius University.

Drakšas, R. (2002). Mirties bausmė: situacija ir perspektyvos. Vilnius: Eugrimas.

Entman, R. M. (1993). Framing: Toward clarification of a fractured paradigm. *Journal of Communication, 43*(4), 51–58.

Fawn, R. (2001). Death Penalty as Democratisation: Is the Council of Europe Hanging Itself? *Democratisation, 8*(2), 69–96.

Fijalkowski, A. (2011). European Policy on the Death Penalty. In: Sarat, A. and Martschukat, J. (eds.) (2011). *Is the Death Penalty Dying? European and American Perspectives*, pp. 268–291.

Foucault, M. (1981). The Order of Discourse. In: Young, R. (ed.) (1981). *Untying the Text: A Post-Structuralist Reader*. Boston: Routledge and Kegan Paul, pp. 51–78.

Hodgkinson, P. (2004). Capital Punishment: Improve It or Remove It? In: Hodgkinson, P. and Schabas, W. (eds.) (2004). *Capital Punishment: Strategies for Abolition*. Cambridge: Cambridge University Press, pp. 1–35.

Hood, R. (1989). *The Death Penalty: A Worldwide Perspective*. Clarendon Press.

Hood, R., & Hoyle, C. (2008). *The Death Penalty: A Worldwide Perspective* (4th ed.). Oxford University Press.

Indrišionis, D. (2016). Mirties bausmė Lietuvos SSR 1950–1990 m.: teisiniai pagrindai ir periodizacija. *Genocidas ir rezistencija*, 1(39), pp. 65–80.

Jovaišas, K. (1997). Mirties bausmė: Teisėtas atpildas ar valstybės sankcionuota žmogžudystė? *Teisės Problemos, 1*, 15–29.

Klapper, J.T. (1961). *The Effect of Mass Communication*. The Free Press of Glencoe.

Konstitucinis Teismas (1998). Nutarimas „Dėl Lietuvos Respublikos baudžiamojo kodekso 105 straipsnio sankcijoje numatytos mirties bausmės atitikimo Lietuvos Respublikos Konstitucijai“, 1998 m. gruodžio 9 d. *Valstybės žinios*, 109–3004.

McCarthy, D., & Brunton-Smith, I. (2024). Attitudes towards the death penalty: An assessment of individual and country-level differences. *European Journal of Criminology, 21*(1), 116–139.

Neumayer, E. (2008). Death penalty: The political foundations of the global trend toward abolition. *Human Rights Review, 9*(2), 241–268.

Ogletree, C. J., & Sarat, A. (Eds.). (2009). *The Road to Abolition? The Future of Capital Punishment in the United States.* New York University Press.

Parliamentary Assembly of the Council of Europe. (1996). *Resolution 1097.* Council of Europe.

Schutz, A. (1976). The Well-Informed Citizen. In: Schutz, A. (1976). *Collected Papers II: Studies in Social Theory.* The Hague: Martinus Nijhoff, pp. 120–135.

Skėrytė, J. (1996). Mirties bausmė: į pagalbą prezidentui. *Respublika,* 11 June.

Samoškaitė, E. (2013). Apklausa: kokie žmonės pritaria mirties bausmei? *Delfi,* 4 July.

Ulinskaitė, J. & Pukelis, L. (2025). Analysis of the populist discourse of the Lithuanian political parties. *Intersections. East European Journal of Society and Politics,* 10(4), pp. 59–81.

Vaišvila, A. (1997). Bausmės problema teisinėje valstybėje: Mirties bausmės aporija. *Teisės Problemos, 1,* 30–65.

Values and Identities of EU citizens. (2021). *Special Eurobarometer 508.* European Commission.

Yorke, J. (2010). Inhuman Punishment and Abolition of the Death Penalty in the Council of Europe. *European Public Law, 16*(1), 77–103.

5

Punitive Thinking in Different Times and Generations

Laima Žilinskienė

Introduction

In the classical Bekarian sense, the members of a society agree to adhere to a set of common and binding rules. The question that arises is whether all members of a society concur on the rules and how to adhere to them. Without consensus, those who do not adhere to these norms may resort to self-correction, guided by their conceptions of justice. From a macro perspective, the objective of punishment is to correct behaviour. According to Carvalho (2017), society is regarded as a "punished entity" to maintain social order. In essence, the objective of punishment is to reestablish a particular social order by underscoring the advantages of compliance and by rendering the practice of punishment appealing. In this sense, the act of punishment, or the punishment of society, is realised

L. Žilinskienė (✉)
Faculty of Philosophy, Institute of Sociology and Social Work, Department of Criminology, Vilnius University, Vilnius, Lithuania
e-mail: laima.zilinskiene@fsf.vu.lt

A. Dobryninas and S. Nikartas (eds.), *Understanding Crime Control and Punishment in Lithuania*, Crime Prevention and Security Management,
https://doi.org/10.1007/978-3-032-05538-5_5

each time. This dynamic has ramifications for the propagation of penal logic beyond the confines of the penal sphere. Punishment operates at the personal, symbolic, political, and structural levels, influencing behaviour and feelings of insecurity in various aspects of life.

It is important to note that punishment is not only directed towards restoring social order, but also towards the associated power dynamics. However, the act of punishment can also provoke a counter-response, which can be characterised as attitudes towards punishment. Carvalho (2017) identified this concept as the punitive dimension. In this case, the punitive dimension is associated with the lived experiences of hostility directed towards the individual, which can stimulate a reaction not only towards the punishment-imposing authorities but also towards the architects of the rules and norms that underpin the system.

These phenomena can be conceptualised as emotional and affective processes that influence an individual's perception of the external environment and shape their responses to events and circumstances. Feelings and experiences of insecurity, vulnerability, fear, and frustration form the basis of punitive attitudes and encourage the individual to "act decisively," according to Costelloe et al. (2009). In this scenario, the individual engaging in the wrongful act occupies the "right" position, while those with the authority to impose punishment are positioned in the "wrong" position. Those in the "right" position are endowed with the prerogative to act in a manner that safeguards their interests. According to Fassin (2018), the sentiment of injustice can incite resentment and a retaliatory response, known as retribution, as the individual deemed deserving of punishment perceives a sense of moral rectitude. In such instances, hostility is not directed towards those who perpetrate crimes and are thus deserving of retribution; rather, it is directed towards the architects of the rules, norms, and punishments that have been established.

The conceptualisation of punishment from the macro, meso, and micro levels is referred to as the Onion model (Kury et al., 2004). At the macro level, the political discourse on punishment is addressed. The meso level focuses on judicial punitiveness, and the micro level addresses the human need to punish, depending on beliefs, perceptions, and values. This proclivity, as posited by Garland (2002), Sparks (2012), and Carvalho and Chamberlen (2018), finds its genesis particularly during periods of social vulnerability. However, the macro perspective also influences the societal inclination to impose retribution. According to Christie (1977), there is a consistent tendency in modern society to attribute the meaning of crime to "increasingly undesirable behaviours" and to punish such behaviours with imprisonment. In this context, as asserted by Mathiesen (1990), the penal system is designed to address the "bottom" of society rather than the "top" echelons. This phenomenon occurs because the fundamental purpose of punishment is not to maintain order in itself, but rather to preserve a specific order (Bauman, 2000). Punishment, understood through the lenses of different levels of punishment (macro, mezzo, and micro), is multifaceted due to its inherently ambiguous nature. On the one hand, it confirms disorder, thereby creating crime as something intrinsic and requiring constant management. On the other hand, it is argued symbolically that this disorder is not the result of society's structural inequalities and power imbalances. Rather, it is attributed to the dangerous actions and behaviours of criminals. This symbolic aspect demonstrates that punishment is not only necessary but also useful and desirable. This function of punishment is a critical factor contributing to the appeal and widespread use of punishment practices and institutions. Concurrently, it functions as a pivotal catalyst in the propagation of penal logic, transcending the confines of the criminal sphere and permeating diverse domains such as welfare, education, health, and migration.

Accordingly, applying punishment transcends the confines of a criminal law-oriented system. Rather, it necessitates a multifaceted approach that encompasses monitoring its propagation to other domains of social life. Additionally, it involves the observation of societal members' responses to the architects of rules and norms, as well as the enforcers of these norms. This aspect enables us to paraphrase Mathiesen's statement that the "bottom" of society strikes at the "top" using the means at their disposal.

This phenomenon can be characterised as a society that punishes. Suppose the architects of penal policy wield significant influence over the punitive society. In that case, the latter is Carvalho's classification of individuals whose behaviour does not conform to the norms and rules of a given historical period. This is not due to a lack of effort and malice, but rather due to a lack of resources, without which they cannot and do not have the resources to "live up to the norm." In this regard, a punitive society is characterised by its distinct logic of social punishment, which is tailored to a specific social order and exerts considerable influence on individuals' lives. Disobedience to "order," as Bauman (2000) contends, manifests in human behaviour against the architects of rules and norms. Those who adhere to this philosophy of punishment deliberately opt to transgress established rules in order to address matters that are of paramount importance to them or that they perceive as not aligning with their legitimate expectations. The punitive aspect of the punishing society reveals punitive practices in which members feel wronged and unable to secure the necessary means of life. In this regard, punitive societies can be identified as emotional and cultural practices driven by forces that lack the authority to construct punishment policies (Garland, 2002), signifying a backlash against rules and norms that defend such policies.

This chapter seeks to demonstrate that a comprehensive comprehension of punishment as a social phenomenon necessitates its delineation within a broader context than that of state punishment and criminal justice institutions. It aims to extend the purview of punishment beyond the realm of crime, thereby unveiling the various societal facets that engage in the act of punishment across different historical periods.

Such conceptualisation endeavours to furnish a more comprehensive perspective on punishment as a pervasive social phenomenon intertwined with broader societal trends. As Fassin (2018) has noted, societies employ various methods to punish those they deem deserving of retribution.

Theoretical Framework and Methodology

Historical contexts are characterised by distinct logics of norms and rules, which are designed to adapt and manage members of society in optimal ways. Adaptation transpires through practices that are not merely performed, but are active, acquired, and socially shaped. According to Bauman (2000), the concept of "order" (norm) is manifested in human behaviour. Conversely, social circumstances and conditions influence the acting subject, who is compelled to construct a view of the world. According to Srubar (2016:17), this process of self-programming involves the selection of available courses of action and encompasses both realised and potential possibilities, which are influenced by historical and cultural contexts. According to Bourdieu (2004), habitus is a product of history that produces individual and collective practices according to the schemas created by history. This notion underscores the notion that habitus exerts a governing influence on behaviour, while concurrently allowing for the emergence of creative deviations. This creativity manifests through behaviours that defy established norms and rules, showcasing attitudes towards the architects of the prevailing order. In Bourdieu's conceptual framework, this phenomenon is termed "delinquent habitus", signifying the capacity for unconventional and potentially subversive actions that defy established norms and conventions.

Individuals seek unique answers to the social and political issues that are relevant to them and which provide them with a corresponding emotional character. They possess unique "truths" about society and its social architecture and seek to redefine and understand their place in this architectural map. When individuals cannot achieve a secure societal position, they often protest against the prevailing system. This protest is driven by the desire to ensure a better life or survival for themselves or their family. In such cases, individuals often act according to prevailing norms and rules, while at the same time seeking "creative" solutions to enhance their well-being. This deliberate defiance of the established order can be interpreted as a form of punishment from the bottom up.

The Mertonian theoretical approach (1938) is employed to elucidate the bottom-up punishment, emphasising the particularities and contexts of the Conformistic innovative behavioural pattern in disparate historical periods. Conformistic innovative behaviour is defined as pursuing societal goals through legitimate means while simultaneously achieving personal objectives by engaging in behaviours not aligned with conventional standards or legal frameworks. According to Merton (1938), individuals can react to stress in different ways. These varied responses to stress and differing access levels to resources and means give rise to distinct patterns of "undesirable" deviant behaviour. Atkinson's (2020) work posits that individuals' behaviours are shaped not only by the force of external social structures but also by their lived experience. This theoretical framework allows for the elucidation of the factors that motivate individuals to adopt conformist innovative behaviours and the interpretations attributed to them by those who enforce social norms.

The analysis of societal bottom-up punishment is predicated on life story interviews collected within the framework of the national research projects: The Memory of the Soviet Era in the Life Stories of Lithuania: The Relationship between Public and Private Discourses (2010–2012); The Late Soviet Era in Life Stories: The First Generation of the Soviet Era (born between 1945 and 1960) (2015); The Last Generation of the Soviet Era in the Context of Changing Modernity (2017–2019). This sociological study focuses on individuals born between 1970 and 1980; Life Courses of 1980–2000 Cohorts, Behavioural Strategies and their Contexts (2021–2024). A total of 332 life stories are in the collection through these projects.

The samples were identified through biographical methods, and interviewees were selected to represent a range of social and economic characteristics (gender, age, place of residence, and educational level). Utilising the life stories and family histories methodology (Bertaux, 1981; Thompson & Bornat, 2000) enables the exploration of the events that have transpired throughout the respondent's life course up to the interview. The biographical approach enables the study of a social actor within a specific social structure during a defined historical period. Following the approaches outlined by Bertaux and Thompson (1993) and Miller (2000), the project implementers conducted the interviews, enabling the analysis of the socialisation of different generations, their behavioural models, intergenerational relationships, lifestyles, and identities. The empirical material gathered allows for the discovery of links between punishment and individual life narratives (Hallsworth, 2004; Millburn et al., 2013).

The empirical material also allows for exploring the relationship between the meanings of punishment and worldviews and self-identity (King, 2008). Life stories are individual works because they are told historically at a specific time and place. They are based on the rules, patterns, and other narratives of that period, which determine how story elements are linked into the logic of time. Life stories facilitate comprehension of not only the motivations of individuals but also the construction of the social organisation of life. This chapter utilises Miller's (2000) "real" behaviour approach to illustrate how shifting historical contexts give rise to divergent models of conformist innovative behaviour.

Conformist Innovative Behaviour in Soviet Times

Lithuanian social life in the Soviet era exhibited extensive standardisation, institutionalisation, and homogenisation (Brückner & Mayer, 2005; Hillmert, 2005; Kraniauskiene, 2016). The Lithuanian social order was predicated on a single-party regime, a centralised planned economy, state ownership, and the pervasive influence of a single ideology across all facets of life. According to Kraniauskiene (2016), the life course in Lithuania was subject to extensive standardisation and institutionalisation, primarily facilitated by the education system and further reinforced by Soviet employment practices. Individuals were compelled to align their existential behaviours with the prevailing norms and regulations established by these architects of social order.

Conduct of this nature is directed at those perceived as responsible for the "crisis," who may rightly be treated with hostility. One method of responding to such a "crisis" is by adopting conformist-innovative behaviour. In the context of Soviet life, individuals who have adopted this behaviour share a common characteristic: a sense of personal injustice coupled with a strong sense of moral rectitude. Conformist innovation is perceived as a form of retribution, a perception that is further reinforced when individuals act collectively rather than individually. This phenomenon is particularly pronounced among individuals who perceive that legitimate privileges are being misappropriated by others wielding positions of authority. Conformist innovation is a means of ensuring one's own or one's family's survival and the attainment of a better life. This phenomenon can be perceived as either a high-risk strategy in the absence of viable alternatives or a deliberate act of retribution against the architects and overseers of the Soviet system.

The empirical material collected enables the identification of the economic and political aspects of conformist-innovative behaviour during the Soviet period. The economic factors associated with this phenomenon include dissatisfaction with one's financial situation or the aspiration to live in a more advantageous position than one's social environment. However, despite these factors, individuals perceive their socio-economic situation as more unfavourable than they think. This perception is attributed to the actions of the architects of the Soviet system, leading to a sense of under-recognition and undervaluation among the populace. This sentiment often catalyses individuals to engage in innovative endeavours to enhance their well-being. One notable manifestation of this phenomenon is the involvement in illegal activities. The following example illustrates this behavioural motive:

> We used to go as tourists to Tallinn. On the way back, you bring a box of Vana Tallinn and chocolate, and all the petrol pays for itself...people ask <....> "bring me some fish...". If we buy a box and pay a symbolic amount of 10 roubles for that box of fish at the Riga market, I do not even touch the fish...I gave it to my neighbour, she gave it away, and I got 20 (roubles). <...> there was a shortage of goods...people were grateful... and people did it automatically<...> (M, 1955).

Conformist innovation behaviour is also evident when individuals engage in the illicit appropriation and sale of products obtained illegally for financial gain. The following examples illustrate this phenomenon:

> As my dad worked in the butter factory at that time, it was then called the cheese factory <....> It is, of course, no secret that in those (Soviet) times, at least for myself, there was certainly sour cream, milk, and cheese. (Man, 1959).
>
> Stealing and combinations were also widespread in the hosiery factory. A good part of the production consisted of women's underwear. I don't know by what means, from what resources, but all the workers, including my mother, would bring in one, and sometimes two, articles every day,

> which were often made from scraps, sometimes good ones. They were usually women's T-shirts - "overalls" <...> The women would go to work without a T-shirt and return with one. They used to sell these "overalls" <...> My mother did not go to the factory empty-handed either - she would bring products from the village to sell, and later on, chocolate products made in my father's sister's house, the composition and labels of which were no different from the ones sold in the shops at that time. Thus, only my mother's illegal trade could save her from starvation (M, 1955).

Conformistically innovative behaviour was regarded as permissible by these individuals, as they perceived collective property as belonging to all members of society, including themselves. This perception engendered a sense of moral rectitude, justifying the appropriation of a portion of the collective property for personal use. This "decisive" conduct was prevalent.

In rural areas, the situation was particularly dire. The process of collectivisation, a fundamental restructuring of rural society, profoundly impacted the lives of rural populations. Individuals were compelled to engage in labour on collective farms; these collective farms, rather than ensuring a life of dignity and security, became sites of profound hardship, where the mere survival of individuals was a struggle. A portion of wages was remitted in cash, while the remainder was exchanged for agricultural produce. However, most rural households' income is derived from personal auxiliary farms. Despite the severe penalties associated with misappropriating collective farm assets, the prevailing rational choice was to adopt conformist-innovative behaviours. This behaviour was rationalised not only as a survival strategy but also as a response to rural policies. Conformist innovation was manifested through collective action. The subsequent illustration exemplifies the implementation of the "act decisively" or conformist-innovative model in the countryside:

> Something else that sticks in my mind from my childhood, that terrible blackness, when my mother not only worked as a milkmaid, but also went to work in the fields, digging potatoes for the collective farm. Not for money, because they paid very little, but you could steal and take those potatoes home. So, first they dig the potatoes, then they put them in a

> basket and fill it with earth. In the evening, they would put the basket of potatoes near a bush and after dark, they would take the potatoes home from the bush. All in a row, like anything <...> The same was true with rye when it was threshed. It was just an accepted way of life; nobody was surprised. Otherwise, you couldn't make a living. Finally, maybe because people thought it was their land too, it was everybody's land, and they worked it. So they took it as their own, only secretly. Just like from the farm, my mother used to bring beetroot and flour on her shoulders. Some three or four kilometres were needed to get there. We used to go to meet them. And everybody was stealing, everybody was carrying. (M, 1954).

This phenomenon was also observed in interactions with subordinate officials. As one participant in the study notes:

> In 1950, a collective farm was forcibly organised in our district. People were forced to do agricultural work, and the pay was just for show. A few hundred grams of grain per working day. For a year, the collective farm workers earned a terbel of grain, which they could easily carry on their shoulders. In the first year of the collective farm, people were still living on reserves, but in the second and third years, hunger began to stare people in the face. There was a shortage of bread in the village. In July 1954, when I came home from Vilnius, I saw my father and his foreman carrying rye from the collective farm field to the barn. I jokingly asked: So, how come the government is helping to steal here now? My father replied: When you are hungry and you come to help <...>.In those first years of the collective farm, everything was stolen from the fields, barns, and warehouses, even though armed *Stribs*[1] would keep watch in the barns at night. But all kinds of *Stribs* even helped. Theft was severely punished. For a bag of rye, a man in a neighbouring village was sentenced to several years in prison... Theft was ingrained in people's consciousness. Because one did not feel guilty for such an act. Man was raped by the government by creating forced labour and not giving him a livelihood. And the consequences are obvious today. Pregnant women who, together with their husbands, would go trembling into the fields of the collective farm to dig potatoes, to fetch fodder for the animals from the meadows, would already give birth to babies who, when they were grown up, had

[1] *Stribs* (stribai) – Lithuanian term for local Soviet collaborators who helped enforce Soviet rule and suppress resistance, especially in rural areas after WWII.

> the urge to take everything from everywhere. I have such an example in my own family. (V, 1937).

An additional facet that facilitates the interpretation of the reaction as "acting decisively" and, consequently, punishing the custodians of Soviet ideology is the political nature of the conformist innovative behaviour. From the perspective of conformist-innovative behaviour, such actions can be characterised as a form of adaptation through protest. This phenomenon of bottom-up punishment is facilitated by various innovative practices within educational and professional contexts. The following illustration exemplifies the manifestation of conformist innovative practices during academic pursuits:

> It was a good time for us as young people. Since we were in session at Christmas, we would cover the door with a blanket. Thirteen of us lived in one room, from different regions. So one would make his region, and the other one would make his dishes. We used to celebrate Christmas with dishes from all regions of Lithuania. And at the university we had to pay tribute - all those atheisms, scientific communism. But we needed a result, we studied, we tried, and that was it. (M, 1950).

This innovative approach to the system was adopted not only by young people studying but also by those working in the education system, who were expected to serve as the "backbone" of Soviet youth. As one representative of the education system articulates:

> As soon as I came to work, I joined the Comsomol organisation. So I was told to go and see who was going to church. So we would go ourselves, we would go to confession, we would drive back and say that we didn't see anyone (in the church), we didn't know anything. (M, 1949).

A variety of innovative protest strategies were also implemented in the workplace. One participant in the study offers the following illustration:

> I was maybe 23-24 years old when I was working [in the paramilitary factory]. And my dad instilled that in me, and my dad didn't like the Russian system. And we didn't like it. It used to be February 16th, and I

> used to organise it at work. It's like a bottle of alcohol, sandwiches.... In my warehouse, we used to close up, lock the door, and we would celebrate <...> (M, 1948).

Conformistically, innovative behaviour is not regarded as problematic; rather, it is seen as a response to the architects of Soviet life who unfairly share the good produced by collective ownership. The concept of "acting decisively" is not merely a means to enhance one's circumstances or ensure survival; it is also regarded as a desirable instrument. As one participant in the study articulates:

> God forbid there should be more of these thieves. You buy yarn, you knit cheaper; you buy meat, you eat cheaper. (M, 1959)

The following example illustrates the essence of conformist-innovative behaviour:

> Work in the Soviet system, like society as a whole, is a realm of distorted mirrors. Some pretended to work, others pretended to pay. Thus, theft, combinations, impersonations, and deceptions were rife everywhere. The Soviet system went on and on and came to the end of the stick.

The Soviet system did not promote competitiveness and initiative; rather, it sought to produce an "average" citizen (Schwartz, 1965) who would be obedient and ideologically correct. Individual activism was tolerated only in the interest of one's own or family welfare. The scarcity of financial resources and constrained access to them contributed to pervasive sentiments of helplessness, insecurity, vulnerability, fear, and frustration. Conversely, these conditions have catalysed "decisive action," whereby individuals have expressed their position vis-à-vis the architects of the system through their actions. This behaviour exemplifies an ignorance and disregard for the punitive measures imposed by the Soviet system.

Conformist Innovative Behaviour After the 1990s

A series of radical social changes took place in Lithuania from 1990 onward, marking the conclusion of the nation's period of socialist modernity and the commencement of its transition to a market economy. The transformation process underwent several stages. The initial phase, spanning from 1991 to 1995, focused on the establishment of an institutional framework conducive to privatisation, accompanied by the formulation of pertinent legal regulations. A salient feature of this period was the rapid privatisation of formerly state-owned assets. This period was distinguished by spontaneous privatisation, which occurred concurrently with the accumulation of political capital. Consequently, this period is often referred to as "wild capitalism" or "post-Soviet egotism." During this period, privatisation was often enforced by recourse to illegal or semi-legal means, taking advantage of loopholes in the legislation. The second stage of the privatisation process, which lasted from 1996 until 2001, was characterised by a shift towards more structured and formalised privatisation processes.

This stage is regarded as a period of intensive institutional and economic reforms. In 2001, novel ownership regulations were instituted, establishing the foundational frameworks for institutional and legal oversight. This stage is also regarded as the conclusion of the economic transformation phase, thereby establishing the foundational elements of the structures that are characteristic of a market economy, labour relations, and social welfare institutions. The life course in Lithuania underwent a radical transformation characterised by de-standardisation, de-institutionalisation, individualisation, pluralisation, and differentiation (Kraniauskiene, 2011).

In the context of these radical changes, people have faced the challenges of readaptation. The nature of these readaptation experiences has exhibited significant variability. For some, this period has been characterised by the pursuit of novel opportunities, facilitating capital accumulation, and personal development. Conversely, others encountered difficulties in securing or maintaining employment, leading to the adoption of semi-legal or illegal work practices. The inability to adequately care for oneself was perceived as a sign of failure and a potential threat. Even those engaged in legal employment expressed discontent with wages. Saar and Helemae (2006) and Saar and Kazjulja (2016) proposed that the subjects could be divided into two categories, "winners" and "losers", based on their ability to adapt to the changing circumstances. This dichotomy was primarily influenced by educational attainment. This dynamic was further reinforced by the concept of "economic individualism", which posits a correlation between economic prosperity, individual effort, and personal responsibility (Kornhauser, 2015). This dynamic has given rise to considerable tensions and has spurred the exploration of diverse survival strategies. Concurrently, the nascent private business sector during the period of transformation offered limited appeal due to the disparity between the demands of the workforce and the financial stability. To evade tax obligations, a portion of the salary was remitted through legitimate channels, while another portion was discreetly disbursed in "envelopes". This period was characterised by a combination of conformist and innovative behaviours, exemplified by the tendency to "act decisively" and prioritise the interests of the individual.

According to one participant in the study (V, 1981), the individual in question completed ten grades. Following his disengagement from formal education, he engaged in illicit employment with farmers. However, he stopped working for the farmers due to financial constraints. He subsequently secured employment at a meat processing facility. This work was physically demanding, yet the compensation was commensurate with the effort exerted. The participant noted that he had no opportunity to save money. He resided with his parents, sharing their residence. The financial constraints he faced precluded the possibility of acquiring his own residence. Concurrently, his acquaintances secured employment in the construction sector in one of the Scandinavian countries. The subject's earnings were sufficient to enable a year-long work hiatus and procure 30,000 litas. He maintained his approach of acting decisively, and his strategy for achieving a better life was as follows: upon his return to Lithuania, he submitted an application to the Labour Exchange for unemployment benefits. Concurrently, he initiated a period of unauthorised employment in the field of apartment repair. After terminating the unemployment benefits, he secured a position that lasted for one month, subsequently resigning from the job a month later. Thereafter, he reapplied for benefits from the Job Centre. This pattern of financial "activity," punctuated by episodic construction work abroad and short-term unemployment benefits, has been further exacerbated by illicit activities in Lithuania, such as repairing flats and houses. This behavioural pattern is driven by a sense of frustration at the perceived disregard and neglect of the needs and interests of "ordinary" people by the system.

The conformist-innovative or "act decisively" model of behaviour is also applicable in the public sector when confronted with financial difficulties. A participant (M, 1965) employed in the cultural sector proffered the following illustration of survival: she orchestrated exhibitions, convened with poets and writers, and extended invitations to the urban community for these meetings. Given the paucity of events in the town, such initiatives were highly sought after by the local populace. However, to optimise the budget, the municipal authorities reduced the hours and salary, which were already modest in the cultural sector. Despite these challenges, the participant expressed a strong dedication to her profession, evidenced by her willingness to take three months of unpaid leave each year to care for the elderly in foreign countries. This practice was maintained for a considerable duration. The financial resources she procured through these efforts not only enabled her to meet her own needs but also to assist her son in settling the debts he owed her for the construction of his residence and the challenges he encountered in his business ventures.

According to Sommers and Woolfson (2014), the year 2014 marked a return to normalcy, with a significant portion of the population experiencing an improvement in their living conditions. The transition to liberal policies during the period of transformation resulted in a critical attitude towards the architects of the transformation. In response, conformist innovative behaviour, accompanied by manifestations of collectivist behaviour, was observed. During the system's transformation, the practice of "acting decisively" manifested in various forms. Private businesses tended to allocate a portion of their salaries through what has been termed "envelope payments," while employees sought to address their existential challenges by engaging in semi-legal or illegal activities, thereby evading tax obligations. This phenomenon has been termed deliberate punishment from below, signifying the awareness of the consequences of such actions, including criminal prosecution.

Concluding Remarks

Punishment constitutes an integral component of maintaining order within the system. The political, economic, and social context exerts a significant influence on the formulation of punishment policy from a top-down perspective. The process of adapting to this "order" varies in different historical contexts. From a macro-level perspective, this variation is determined by the opportunities, expectations, and controls provided by the system. From a micro-level, the individual's adaptation is determined by social class, education, opportunities, and the ability to fulfil those expectations. In instances where these mechanisms are deficient or constrained, individuals and their families encounter substantial impediments in shaping their lives, compelling them to seek alternative solutions, even if these diverge from the prevailing order and are subject to sanctions. This phenomenon, characterised by the pursuit of alternative solutions that defy established norms, is referred to as "punishment from below." This phenomenon is typified by a combination of conformist and innovative behaviours. In periods of system failure, this behaviour can gain considerable momentum, driven by the search for ever more innovative and "creative" solutions. These solutions are not merely intended to enhance personal circumstances; they also aim to condemn those perceived to have inflicted harm, thus seeking retribution and redress.

The empirical material demonstrates that the Soviet project, which existed in Lithuania for fifty years, exerted a multifaceted impact on the phenomenon of "punishment from below." Conformist-innovative behaviour, propelled by economic imperatives, emerged as the predominant behavioural strategy for personal gain. This phenomenon is also characterised by collective action. Conformist-innovative behaviour became the prevailing "norm" during the Soviet period. This phenomenon is further entrenched by the adoption of this behavioural pattern by subsequent generations, whose economic well-being surpassed that of the Soviet standard. Another aspect that encourages "punishment from below" or "decisive action" is political. This phenomenon is not primarily driven by economic well-being at the individual or family level, but rather by reactions and responses to the ideology promoted during the Soviet period.

Concurrently, during the period of Lithuania's post-1990 transformation, the ideological underpinnings of punishment became obsolete, while the economic dimension retained its pertinence. The phenomenon of "punishment from below" is associated with economic factors due to a deficiency in adaptation and resources within the context of system transformation. This dynamic perpetuates a self-perpetuating cycle, whereby society punishes punishers from above through various means, including tax evasion. A comprehensive investigation is imperative to elucidate the distinctive characteristics of this phenomenon across diverse social contexts. Each generation bears the "baggage" of the past and is contingent on future trends.

References

Atkinson, W. (2020). Fields and individuals: From Bourdieu to Lahire and back again. *European Journal of Social Theory, 24*(2), 195–210. https://doi.org/10.1177/1368431020923281(Accessed:9May2025)

Bauman, Z. (2000). Social issues of law and order. *British Journal of Criminology, 40*(2), 205–221.

Bertaux, D. (1981). From the life-history approach to the transformation of sociological practice. In D. Bertaux (Ed.), *Biography and society: The life history approach in the social sciences* (pp. 29–45). Sage.

Bertaux, D., & Thompson, P. (1993/2005). *Between generations: Family models, myths and memories.* Transaction Books.

Bourdieu, P. (2004). Structures and the habitus. *Material culture: Critical concepts in the social sciences, 1*(part 1), 116–77.

Brückner, H., & Mayer, K. U. (2005). De-standartization of the life course: What it might mean? And if it means anything, does it actually take place? *Advances in Life Course Research, 9*, 27–53.

Carvalho, H., & Chamberlen, A. (2018). Why punishment pleases: Punitive feelings in a world of hostile solidarity. *Punishment & Society, 20*(2), 217–234.

Carvalho, H. (2017). *The preventive turn in criminal law.* Oxford University Press. https://doi.org/10.1093/acprof:oso/9780198737858.001.0001(Accessed:9May2025)

Christie, N. (1977). Conflicts as property. *The British Journal of Criminology, 17*(1), 1–15.

Costelloe, M. T., Chiricos, T., & Gertz, M. (2009). Punitive attitudes toward criminals. *Punishment & Society, 11*(1), 25–49.

Fassin, D. (2018). *The will to punish.* Oxford University Press.

Garland, D. (2002). *The culture of control: Crime and social order in contemporary society.* The University of Chicago Press.

Hallsworth, S. (2004). Make my day: Images of masculinity and the psychodynamics of mass incarceration. In R. R. Lippens (Ed.), *Imaginary boundaries of justice* (pp. 141–160). Hart.

Hillmert, S. (2005). From old to new structures: A long-term comparison of the transition to adulthood in West and East Germany. *Advances in Life Course Research, 9*, 151–173.

King, A. (2008). Keeping a safe distance: Individualism and the less punitive public. *British Journal of Criminology, 48*, 190–208.

Kornhauser, R. (2015). Economic individualism and punitive attitudes: A cross-national analysis. *Punishment & Society, 17*(1), 27–53.

Kraniauskienė, S. (2011). *Tapsmas suaugusiuoju: Jaunimo socialinė branda Lietuvoje.* Lietuvos socialinių tyrimų centras.

Kraniauskienė, S. (2016). Pirmosios sovietinės kartos gyvenimo eigos ypatybės tapimo suaugusiuoju tarpsnyje. In L. Žilinskienė, S. Kraniauskienė, & I. Šutinienė (Eds.), *Gimę socializme: Pirmoji sovietmečio karta* (pp. 35–80). Vilniaus universiteto leidykla.

Kury, H., Kania, H., & Obergfell-Fuchs, J. (2004). Worüber sprechen wir, wenn wir über Punitivität sprechen? Versuch einer konzeptionellen und empirischen Begriffsbestimmung. *Kriminologisches Journal, 36*, 51–88.

Mathiesen, T. (1990). *Prison on trial: A critical assessment.* Sage.

Merton, R. K. (1938). Social structure and anomie. *American Sociological Review, 3*(5), 672–682.

Millburn, M. A., Niwa, M., & Patterson, M. D. (2013). Authoritarianism, anger, and hostile attribution bias: A test of affect displacement. *Political Psychology, 35*(2), 225–243.
Miller, R. (2000). *Researching life stories and family histories.* SAGE Publications.
Saar, E., & Helemae, J. (2006). Employment careers of men in Estonia. In M. Mills, F. Bernardi, & H. P. Blossfeld (Eds.), *Globalization, uncertainty and men's careers: An international comparison* (pp. 239–268). Edward Elgar Publishing.
Saar, E., & Kazjulja, M. (2016). Winners and losers in the generation of winners. In R. Nugin, N. Kanneke, & M. Raupsepp (Eds.), *Generations in Estonia: Contemporary perspectives on turbulent times* (pp. 256–279). University of Tartu Press.
Schwartz, H. (1965). *The Soviet economy since Stalin.* Lippincott.
Sommers, J., & Woolfson, C. (2014). Introduction: The Baltic and the political economy of austerity. In: Sommers, J., & Woolfson, C. (Eds.), *The contradictions of austerity: The socio-economic costs of the neoliberal Baltic model.* Routledge.
Sparks, R. (2012). States of insecurity: Punishment, populism, and contemporary political culture. In S. McConville (Ed.), *The use of punishment* (pp. 149–174). Routledge.
Srubar, I. (2016). Lifeworld and trauma: Selectivity of social memories. In G. Sebald & J. Wagle (Eds.), *Theorizing social memories* (pp. 17–31). Routledge.
Thompson, P., & Bornat, J. (2000). *The voice of the past: Oral history* (4th ed.). Oxford University Press.

6

Punitive Attitudes Towards Difference: Bullying Perception in the 1980–2000 Generation

Goda Damaševičiūtė and Jovita Žėkaitė-Maconko

Introduction

Following the restoration of independence in 1990, Lithuania experienced a systemic transformation that affected all spheres of life. The country confronted economic crises, inflation, high unemployment, income inequality, declining industrial output and privatisation of state-owned enterprises, as the previously used planned economic system changed to capitalism. Economic reforms have resulted in an escalation

The original version of the chapter has been revised. A correction to this chapter can be found at
https://doi.org/10.1007/978-3-032-05538-5_14

G. Damaševičiūtė (✉) · J. Žėkaitė-Maconko
Faculty of Philosophy, Institute of Sociology and Social Work, Department of Criminology, Vilnius University, Vilnius, Lithuania
e-mail: goda.damaseviciute@fsf.stud.vu.lt

J. Žėkaitė-Maconko
e-mail: jovita.zekaite-maconko@fsf.vu.lt

A. Dobryninas and S. Nikartas (eds.), *Understanding Crime Control and Punishment in Lithuania*, Crime Prevention and Security Management,
https://doi.org/10.1007/978-3-032-05538-5_6

of social stratification, characterised by a pronounced divergence between different income groups. Social tensions manifested themselves in various forms, including alcohol abuse, suicides, and an increase in crime in the first decade after independence. In particular, the number of offenders among young people aged 14–29 increased. According to official data, between 1990 and 1995, half of all offenders with a criminal record were juveniles (Juska et al., 2004).

Lithuania's accession to the European Union and NATO in 2004 marked a turning point in the country's development. Still, it also contributed to significant emigration, as many Lithuanians left for better economic opportunities abroad. Many children whose parents became work migrants were raised or looked after by grandparents or other adults. There was concern that such children would grow up with a propensity to violence, delinquent behaviour, unwanted interpersonal relationships, loneliness, and a self-image marked by a lack of love (Juozeliūnienė & Budginaitė-Mačkinė, 2023, p. 51). The results of the 2002–2004 International Youth Violence Experiences Survey showed that children in Lithuania and other post-Soviet countries were relatively more likely to be exposed to parental violence and to be more likely to be violent themselves (Dünkel et al., 2007; Sakalauskas et. Al., 2022). The use of corporal punishment against children in Lithuania was banned in the latest of all EU countries—only in 2017 (Sakalauskas et al., 2022, p. 104).

Transformational changes have also impacted the education system and the social environment of schools. Teachers had to retrain to adapt to the new education system, while education lost its value in the face of new rules of an uncontrolled market. Between 1993 and 1994, it was observed that some pupils dropped out of school and started working or setting up their own businesses. (National Education Agency, 2013) The difference in the socio-economic situation among young people was perhaps the most striking feature.

The context of the period underlines that young people had to experience change and insecurity in both private and public spheres. In this chapter, we will focus on the school environment, where young people spend a great deal of time and are in close contact with both adult teachers and a large community of peers. This will allow us to delve into the fundamental aspects of children's perception of the social world, moral values, and behavioural strategies at that time. In order to reconstruct the culture of punishment and bullying that existed in Lithuania at the beginning of independence, the memories of adults born between 1980 and 2000 will be analysed.

This chapter analyses bullying in the school environment from structural/institutional and individual perspectives. The analysis draws upon Ahmed and Braithwaite's (2011) Shame Management Theory and concepts from Braithwaite's (1989) restorative justice regulation process. Shame management theory explores how individuals respond to shame and its management in social and institutional contexts, emphasising the role of reintegrative and stigmatising shaming in shaping behaviour.

According to Gilligan (1996), there is a moralistic approach to analysing bullying, and this common method offers little in terms of understanding the root causes of bullying as a form of violence. Condemning and moralising bullying without considering the possibility of integration into a social group shuts down avenues for exploring the underlying motives behind bullying (De Haan et al., 2011, p. 38).

Furthermore, bullying has increasingly been recognised as a form of emotional violence against children in various official documents, including guidelines issued by the World Health Organisation (Vileikienė et al., 2011, pp. 16–17). Building on this scholarly foundation, this study analyses bullying experiences and their long-term impact on individuals' life courses, highlighting how these experiences contribute to forming personal and generational identities.

It is frequently the case in research on bullying in school settings that teachers and, in some cases, parents are regarded as key elements of control (Shariff, 2014, p. 24). Although teachers have attributed the role of controllers, some, even now, are convinced that children have to cope with teasing or bullying on their own (Glover et al., 1998, p. 55; Shariff, 2014, p. 6; Žėkaitė & Buzaitytė et al., 2021). It is assumed that this "struggle" is not theirs but the children's. A similar view is shared by some parents, who express the position that the child has to learn to "stand up for himself" because, at one time, they themselves were faced with similar problems, which no one helped them to solve (Žėkaitė & Buzaitytė et al., 2021).

In Lithuania, research on bullying as a phenomenon gained momentum only after 2000, primarily focusing on psychological (Grigutytė et al., 2018, 2019, 2020; Pilkauskaitė-Valickienė et al., 2009; Povilaitis & Valiukevičiūtė, 2005; Skerytė-Kazlauskienė et al., 2012) and educational perspectives (Klanienė & Skališienė, 2021). While some interdisciplinary efforts have emerged, incorporating insights from sociology, criminology, and psychology (Buzaitytė-Kašalynienė & Žėkaitė et al., 2021; Žėkaitė & Buzaitytė et al., 2021), criminological approaches to bullying remain underdeveloped (Kruopštaitė & Šupa, 2020; Šupa, 2021). This study expands on existing research by applying a historical-criminological perspective, contributing new insights into the phenomenon of bullying and its development in Lithuania and the broader Central and Eastern European region.

This chapter is based on data collected between 2021 and 2024 as part of the funded research project "Growing Up in Independent Lithuania: Life Course, Behavioural Strategies, and Their Contexts of People Born in 1980–2000." It draws on material from 67 life history interviews. The quota sample was based on age, gender, place of residence, and nationality. The participation rate was 53.7% for women and 46.3% for men. 82.1% of respondents have higher education (both non-university and university), 7.5% are still studying for a bachelor's degree, 4.5% have vocational school training, and 4.5% have secondary education. The research follows a generational approach, defining the cohorts born between 1980 and 2000 based on Corsten's (1999) framework and the concept of discursive models. In this perspective, *"generations are created, labelled, and reproduced in discursive fields […], and the core of generational identity consists of an understanding of past events and the future"* (Nugin & Kalmus, 2018, p. 301). Thus, the study conceptualises a generation as a birth cohort whose members share a conscious generational identity (Thomson, 2016). To explore generational identity and life experiences, the study employs a life course approach combined with biographical methodology. This qualitative research relies on life history interviews, integrating narrative and thematic interview methods. Participants first recount their life stories in a free-flowing narrative, then the focus shifts to key themes that emerge during the interview. One of the central themes identified in this study is childhood bullying within the school environment. Since interviewees reflect on their entire life course up to the moment of the interview, the prominence of bullying in their narratives suggests that it was a significant and formative experience in their lives.

Reintegrative Shaming: Conditions for Bullying Emergence, The Bullying Process, and its Participants

According to Braithwaite (1989), the idea of restorative justice focuses on building relationships between the victim, the perpetrator, and the community. The community's immediate reaction significantly influences an individual's behaviour. A community responds to those who breach its agreed-upon norms of coexistence either by imposing punitive measures that cause discomfort or pain, or by opting for reintegration and acceptance, all while striving to correct the undesirable behaviour. A caring and engaged community plays a crucial role in fostering individual responsibility, encouraging repentance, facilitating apology, and nurturing feelings of forgiveness (Braithwaite, 1989, p. 11).

Conversely, a community that resorts to punitive measures and engages in destructive shaming not only condemns the individual's actions but also the individual, resulting in marginalisation and exclusion. As a result, the stigmatised person may be driven to persist in their criminal behaviour, seeking acceptance within criminal subcultures and attempting to construct a deviant identity.

Braithwaite (1989) argues that stronger social ties result in less deviance within a community, partly because these ties enhance the effectiveness of informal social control. Conversely, behaviour that goes unashamed is more likely to be repeated, as it may be interpreted as tacitly approved by society or certain subgroups within it (Braithwaite, 1989, p. 1).

One of the main ideas in restorative justice theory (Braithwaite, 1989) is that if a society fosters relationships based on respect and social ties, crime and deviance are less likely to occur because of a desire not to disappoint others. Even if crimes are committed, society forgives through reintegrative shaming techniques that allow the offender to continue to feel part of the community. Braithwaite (1989), in introducing the concept of reintegrative shaming, described it as the intolerance of a person in a position of power (parent, teacher, employer) to the behaviour in question, in this case, bullying (Braithwaite, 1989, p. 78).

Recognising and effectively addressing bullying within a community or institution is far from straightforward. Bullying often occupies a grey area, subject to various interpretations and complicated by the desire to avoid victim-blaming. Although its harmful effects are widely acknowledged, perpetrators — those who should be held accountable and publicly shamed — are not always identified promptly or effectively.

In Ahmed and Braithwaite's (2011, pp. 56–59) Shame management theory, bullying is conceptualised as a synthesis of power and pride — a deliberate strategy for asserting dominance within a social group. This is achieved through the humiliation of rivals or by signalling consequences to potential challengers who might disrupt existing power dynamics.

In Shame management theory, forms of personal shame and pride play a crucial role. These emotions can be either constructive or destructive (see Table 6.1). Within this theoretical framework, shame is regarded as one of the core emotions which, if not properly recognised or acknowledged, can contribute to the erosion of an individual's social bonds (Ahmed & Braithwaite, 2011, p. 55). According to Shame Management Theory, a community's passive reaction to bullying does not necessarily imply approval by those witnessing it. Rather, such passivity may stem from fear — a concern that expressing disapproval or resisting the behaviour could result in becoming a target themselves (Shariff, 2014, p. 31).

Shame emerges when individuals perceive that they have violated the norms associated with their identity and integrity within the social group (Ahmed & Braithwaite, 2011, p. 69). Consequently, the individual is subjected to shame, and the intensity of this experience is closely tied to the strength of their attachment to the group (Karstedt, 2011, p. 12).

Table 6.1 Synthesis of shame and pride

	Shame	Pride
A constructive expression of social solidarity	Recognition of shame	Humble pride
Destructive expression of social alienation	Transfer of shame	Narcissistic pride

Within this theoretical framework, the pursuit of pride is considered a central emotion that reinforces existing social bonds (Karstedt, 2011, p. 1). However, these bonds are only strengthened when pride is pursued in constructive ways. A constructive synthesis of shame acceptance and humble pride (see Table 6.1) can promote positive relationships by emphasising respect, dignity, and social inclusion. According to the theory's authors, fostering pride in one's achievements, without comparing oneself to others or trying to prove superiority, should help create conditions that reduce bullying.

In contrast, a narcissistic pursuit of pride—marked by disrespect, dominance, and arrogance—poses a threat to interpersonal relationships (Ahmed & Braithwaite, 2011, p. 57). For instance, individuals prone to bullying may become trapped in a recurring cycle of shame and anger, where each outburst of anger deepens the underlying sense of shame. This shame is then repressed or neutralised, further perpetuating the cycle (Haan et al., 2011, p. 41). Ultimately, bullying, as viewed through this theoretical lens, is tied to individuals' desire to reinforce their social standing through destructive communication and deliberate humiliation of selected victims (Ahmed & Braithwaite, 2011, p. 60).

The Social School Environment: Social Ties, Authority Shifts, and Their Impact on Bullying

This chapter will examine the first decades of Lithuania's independence in the school environment through the childhood recollections of individuals born between 1980 and 2000. It will investigate the strength of social ties or their disruption and their potential impact on the prevalence of bullying. Additionally, it will assess the extent to which the authority figures identified in the theoretical framework, such as teachers, parents, and other adults, were genuinely influential in addressing bullying within their communities during that era.

In participants' life stories, the role of adults in relation to childhood bullying at school was described as passive. The adults manifested indifference, inaction, distancing from the problem, or urged children to defend themselves. There was a perception among adults that the issue was not within their remit, resulting in a somewhat dismissive approach. However, informants tended to be ambivalent about teachers' indifference, inability or lack of knowledge to respond to bullying. Reflecting on the bullying process from the current perspective, they argue that the ability of teachers or school administrators to stop bullying during breaks or after school was indeed limited due to its vast and varied scope.

In some cases, teachers or social workers implemented structural and formal measures to address bullying. It is challenging to determine whether the reintegrative shaming approach was ineffective or if more punitive forms of shaming were employed. The following quote is provided as an illustration of an initiative to resolve conflicts and its poor effect due to the methods that were primarily demonstrative and oriented to intimidate rather than practices that fundamentally changed attitudes or situations:

> Well, of course, then they think about how to solve it, they call the students to the social pedagogue, they try to solve it there, but there have been so many times when they went to the social pedagogue that they just, well, you cannot do anything about it, they just do not care, they just sit there and sleep, because they have been there so many times that they do not care any more. So you could not really teach them anything with words, [...] they used to scare the children there or say we are going to call someone here, or the police, or something, but, well, the children, you know, if they were not still afraid of the police, che-che-che, it did not change much. M/1997

Furthermore, it was not uncommon for teachers to become victims of bullying. Adolescents often lacked respect for teachers' authority, so they dismissed their role entirely and even mocked them. Teachers could be bullied for various reasons, including personal characteristics, teaching style, or appearance. It should be noted that aggression towards teachers was not necessarily direct. It could also take the form of actively ignoring them. Only class teachers or principals, who had a closer relationship with the young people and could thus at least partially mobilise or control them, could exert more authority. Some teachers engaged in bullying themselves. In informants' accounts, memories of teachers who displayed a proclivity for aggression towards pupils were particularly vivid. These teachers employed harsh disciplinary methods during lessons and also singled out and ridiculed children due to their socioeconomic status, learning abilities, or social skills. While not a common occurrence, these incidents were remembered not only by the victims but also by their relatives, and the impact was felt significantly after the events. Even in adulthood, individuals continued to experience difficulties coping with the stigmas that had been instilled. The following quote illustrates such bullying practices and their effects:

> She had a very bad teacher in primary school who publicly ridiculed her poverty in front of the class. [....] They used to make fun of her; the teacher used to say that she could not read. Not that she did not know how to read, but that she stuttered when she read aloud. And my sister still cannot read aloud in front of others. She even had a check-up, thinking maybe it was dyslexia, but actually, the doctor said that there was no dyslexia, and there was no disorder. It is probably post-traumatic something. It is because there were situations: someone had lost something, and someone had stolen something. And, in a word, my sister's rucksack was shaken out in front of the whole class, in front of everybody, well, because they suspected it was her. Well, it was not her... W/1991

The informants' accounts indicate a pervasive sense of mistrust and disbelief in the capacity of parents and older family members to meaningfully intervene in instances of bullying. Moreover, a high level of concern was expressed about the potential for the situation to deteriorate further following the involvement of relatives. Relatives themselves often felt powerless in the matter, with the majority of assistance expected from older siblings attending the same school, who were more familiar with the context of bullying. During the period under study, bullying was perceived as an issue that should be addressed only between the individuals involved. The following quote illustrates the passive reactions of parents and the help of a sibling to fight against bullying:

> Father, he used to get very nervous, and he used to go and talk to these children and, well, scare them because, well, father is father. I mean, they used to leave me alone when my father talked to them, but he has done it very few times. How can I put it here... not because they did not want to help, but because they just did not really know how to deal with it. My mother was just very overwhelmed by it, so I did not even bother her. I used to tell my brother straight away, because my brother was the best weapon against all those children. M/1997

While Braithwaite's (1989) theory emphasises the role of authoritative communities in effecting change in established power relations, the influence of teachers or parents as social authorities in the period under study was limited. It is evident that a paradigm shift has occurred in the role of teachers, who have transitioned from positions of authority to becoming victims of bullying. Some teachers have been observed to engage in bullying behaviour towards pupils. Parents have expressed uncertainty regarding how to respond or support their children. It is essential to emphasise that during the first decades of independence, amidst significant social and economic transformations within the state and the family unit of each citizen, the established communication norms were subjected to rigorous examination and redefinition. Social cohesion was low, with communities experiencing fragmentation and parents/teachers lacking significant social influence. During this period, there was a strong focus on overt displays of power through financial resources, physical strength, or connections. Education has lost its value, given how quickly influence could be gained through the display of physical strength and the rapid acquisition of financial resources. It was not the parents or teachers who held the position of authority, but rather the adolescents and the street culture prevalent at the time. Therefore, attempting to shame the bullies was not an integrative strategy. It was, in fact, divisive, and any criticism was usually met with open conflict.

Bullying as a Punitive Strategy Among Peers

This section will examine the community attitudes, involvement, and impact of peer bullying. It will investigate strategies of adaptation and resistance, reactions, effects, and contemporary reflections. As Braithwaite (1989) notes, the response to bullying can be significantly influenced by the wider community. Peers occupy a unique position of influence, and their approval or disapproval of bullying is reflected as an essential part of the social interaction that determines the aggressor's behaviour. However, the opposite trend can be observed in the period under study. The prevailing view was that one or more individuals could exert control over an entire social group, whether by intimidating it or influencing it to adopt a particular stance. Based on interviewees' accounts, individuals or peers regarded as both authorities and aggressors were physically strong, came from affluent backgrounds, and had influential social connections.

The majority of informants indicated a neutral stance on bullying. However, this neutrality was often employed as a proactive measure to prevent their involvement in bullying situations. It was believed that remaining passive would prevent unpleasant attention. Interviewees presented risks and constant tension in choosing the correct behaviour that would not provoke bullying. It could be wrongly chosen subjects of conversation, the company of peers with whom to spend time, or what is being laughed at. In some cases, even a minimal connection with the individual being bullied was perceived as a direct threat to becoming a potential target and risked the integrity of the dominant social group. It eventually prompted young people to take sides. In most cases, informants chose the side they perceived to be stronger for their safety, despite initially feeling that their actions were inappropriate. These quotes reflect the tension of choice and feelings of wrongdoing:

> I had to be involved in bullying myself to survive [....] if you are silent, others will come to you....[....] because there was a lot of bullying, and it seemed to be for the smallest things, and you had to be very careful about what you talked about and who you talked to about it.[....] M/1998

> There was a boy in my class, I do not know why, but everyone did not like him very much. [...] Well, he had no friends. And I started to notice that when he spends time with me, the others do not spend time with me. And then there was this first crisis that I do not want to be rejected by others, but at the same time, there is a betrayal of that person. And the boy always came up to me because I was the only one who did not say "eww, you stink" or something. [...] When somebody saw that I was very uncomfortable or upset, he came up to me already, then classmates attacked him and said: 'Get away from her, stop it. You see, she does not want to. W/1994

Complying with bullying and passive reactions towards it could also be explained by the frustration and hopelessness of experiencing situations where resistance to bullying has led to increased aggression against the one who resisted. Conversely, a more assertive and physical response from the victims of bullying averted further incidents. It was often found that a distinct physical superiority and aggression helped resolve the issue of bullying altogether. Without strong support from others or being able to prove one's physical superiority, alternative coping strategies were required. One such strategy was laughter. The initial step was to adopt a light-hearted approach to oneself, which then enabled the criticism of others to be more readily accepted. Another strategy was to avoid reacting to bullying altogether, which required patience and depended on the perpetrators' social environment and emotional maturity.

> But if you show that you are not willing to back down, then in a way, those who initiate the main aggression decide that maybe it is too much to deal with here, that they need to choose a weaker victim. M/1990

Those who were bullied reported that they eventually exhibited a range of negative behaviours, including stress, insecurity, fatigue, withdrawal, harshness, unsociability, apathy, and distrust of others. Even after the bullying stopped, they continued to experience social anxiety and felt compelled to adopt a defensive stance in social situations. This condition had a significant and long-lasting impact on personality traits and emotional states. The informants reported that they began to constantly assess the safety of their environment, to look for ways to hide, to avoid being bullied, or to adopt strategies to reduce the likelihood of being bullied. The victims of bullying were unable to see the environment in a positive light due to the constant tension and stress they experienced. This led to a lack of motivation to seek change, as they believed that no matter what they did, the situation would remain the same. As a result, they often chose to stay in their current educational setting, believing that integrating into a new environment would be more challenging.

> All the time, it was a war with all the boys in the class, and you had to guard your backpack and your pencil case, so that they would not take it. So that they would not break your backpack, because then all the ink would spill out on all the books, and you had to sit somehow in a place where they would not stab you in the back with a pen [...] during a technology class it was the worst, because, there were all sorts of sharp things, [...] they used to try to hit you with an object, try to hurt you with something... M/1997
> All the time, of course, the feeling of insecurity. [...] At one period it seemed that if someone was laughing, it was at me. [...] M/1990

Furthermore, those who were bullied sought social support and protection but were marginalised and excluded from their social groups. The prevailing logic in the children's community was "attack or be attacked". The informants confirmed a widespread feeling of having no one to turn to, being left alone, not knowing what to do, and having to deal with the problems themselves. It might reflect the lack of authoritative figures during that time or a contemporary stance on bullying, prevention, and condemnation. Research participants could not identify their social role and kept their recollections abstract even when considering past events.

> I do not know, now that I think about it, we should have called the police. But I did not know as a child. Nobody told us how to behave. Well, you have to take action, stand up, and defend. We did not know that. And it seemed that it was our world, where we had to manage ourselves then. W/1994

The transition from childhood to adolescence during the period under review was characterised by a fierce struggle for survival, frequently manifesting as bullying. In the adolescent phase, peers assumed more significant social influence as the authority of parents and teachers was diminished. Therefore, the position of peers, who were recognised as social leaders, determined whether bullying occurred. The social environment was defined by a distinct evaluation of physical power, with bullying being the norm rather than the exception. Those who exhibited behaviours that set them apart from the social group or were identified as weaker were subjected to direct aggression and its forms. It is evident from the defined situation that there was no neutral stance towards bullying. A lack of engagement was perceived as an indication of weakness or approval. This decision to conform and avoid confrontation was associated with a reluctance to differentiate oneself from the social group. However, those who were bold enough to challenge the status quo often faced consequences as a result.

Deconstructing the Bullying Process: Memories of its Motives and Forms

This section will examine the motives and forms of bullying characteristic of a specific period. Bullying researchers agree that aspects such as appearance, special needs, race, gender, and sexual orientation are often used as a pretext for bullying (Cesaroni et. al., 2012, p. 209; Shariff, 2014, p. 29; Markanski & Melander, 2018, p. 1075). Bullying, in the specific time period under study, is characterised by its causality related to style of dress, non-standard behaviour, personal traits based on socio-economic status and stereotypical gender roles. These aspects have become more pronounced during Lithuania's systemic transformation and the emergence of more opportunities to define lifestyles or attitudes. Society could not change at the same rate as it was experiencing innovation. The new opportunities were also unavailable to everyone, leading to more social tensions. Individuals who did not align with the changing mainstream culture or significantly stood out were frequently subjected to bullying.

Exceptionalism was expressed as being "above the norm", having more significant financial resources, affording more than the majority, and creating a distinctive identity, which could result in resentment or envy from others. The following quote illustrates the distinctiveness of different personal traits, which have been met with curiosity on the one hand, and negatively and as something to be bullied by on the other:

> And that's when I think I had my first encounter with bullying. Because she was very different from everyone else. She was very creative, she liked to dress very brightly, she liked to dress in a very interesting way. Well, not like on a magazine cover, but like you could see that she was some kind of artistic soul. I don't know. And I was very curious about that. Plus, she was very fond of drawing, so her drawing and her imagination in general were very different from all the other people around. W/1994

Another form of exclusivity was "failure to meet the required standard" due to a lack of financial resources, inability to purchase desired clothing, and failure to conform to behavioural norms, which collectively prevented integration. Bullying over dressing style and the value of clothes related to the socio-economic status of children was prevalent. The following quote illustrates the tension of answering appearance requirements and lying while trying to disguise the truth and meet expectations:

> I had been bullied because of my clothes. [...] They kept asking where did I buy this, where did I buy that and so on. It's like they're letting you know that it's important where it's bought from. [...] Well, I thought it was kind of strange. And then I was puzzled. And I remember I lied about buying something from a specific shop. Well, yeah, because I've been cornered. And it's really so embarrassing, I don't know, I didn't get too much into that talk there. But anyway, they asked, they kept asking. W/1996

Other markers were employed to differentiate between children from affluent backgrounds and those from less privileged ones. One such indicator was travel. Before independence, opportunities for international travel were limited. However, after opening national borders in 1990, individuals with the financial means to travel extensively began doing so. The emergence of private schools, which brought together children from very different backgrounds, had further accentuated these differences. A quote illustrates differences in travel opportunities and their manifestation among peers:

> Maybe because it was a private school. At least 60-70% of the children were from very wealthy families. And that was very noticeable, the difference between the very different children and the Russian-speaking children, who just lived nearby. [...] It was very noticeable during the holidays. We always had the possibility after the holidays, if somebody had travelled somewhere, he would say so and would bring a little souvenir. He had about twenty minutes to tell everybody where he had been. The difference was very much felt when they told me, already in the first or second grade, how they had been to Dubai, how they had been to Tenerife, how they had travelled through America. And you were at your grandmother's in Pabrade (laughs). W/1994

The socio-economic dissonance that existed was manifested in the relationships between students. If efforts were made at the state level to help less well-off families, their children could be perceived as inferior and second-class at school. Children who did not have the financial means to fit in tried to make up for their shortcomings elsewhere. Hiding their socioeconomic status, they tried to achieve the best results at school and offered their expertise to their peers in exchange for approval:

> I did not even say that my parents were divorced, because it was a huge shame. And I used to cover it up and hide it. [...] Of course, we did not dress terribly luxuriously there, and you could see there was deprivation. However, somehow, I built that school identity very strongly on the fact that I was the best student in the class. I used to give up my homework to other classmates. It did not pay to be angry with me because, well (laughs), but maybe it was a kind of adaptation strategy, a kind of discovery of my place. W/1991

The period was characterised by frequent references to sexual harassment, which could be regarded as an exceptional feature. The prevailing narrative was that if a boy exhibited behaviours such as annoyance or physical abuse towards a girl, it was interpreted as a manifestation of affection. There was a pronounced contrast in the treatment and justification of gender roles in relation to this issue. Masculinity was stereotyped and inextricably linked to aggression and active pursuit of sexual desires, while femininity was related to passivity, sensitivity, and advocacy for victims of bullying. However, receiving girls' sympathy could only lead to more aggression towards the victim. A significant number of matters about sexual maturity were typically left to the discretion of the adolescents themselves. Furthermore, recollections indicated that efforts were made to mitigate the impact of harassment. A notable absence of sex education in both the family and the school environment was evident.

> The thing that makes me most reluctant to go back to school is sexual harassment. Because I don't know if it was like this everywhere, but at our school, they liked to come up, lift up your skirt, feel you up, corner you in threes, put your hands up your skirt, while one of them is holding you. And the teachers never did anything about it, and they said, "Boys will always be boys." W/1994

Interviewees also noted the presence of stereotypical gender role-based bullying, with boys exhibiting the most aggressive behaviour. This may have been influenced by the prevailing standards for what constituted a "real man" at the time and the lack of alignment with those standards. The distinctiveness of appearance, like long hair or peculiar clothing, was unacceptable. For boys who visually did not appear to be out of place in the social group, but who were already aware of their sexual orientation, the social dissonance was particularly acute.

Informants share that wanting to fit in, they mocked others and called them gay (in Lithuania at that time, this epithet had a negative connotation), even though they felt that this kind of insult was intended to define their identity.

> There used to be a lot of bullying against boys... and, yes, there were a lot of insults that, you know, a person is called gay…[...] I had been

pointing my finger at someone and shouting it as an insult, when I'd already realised it myself. Because I realised it at about thirteen, fourteen, something like... about my orientation. M/1998

In fact, the period under study is characterised by extreme cruelty and a lack of empathy. Bullying was most often expressed in physical aggression rather than verbal abuse. This is evidenced by the examples of bullying given by the informants and the unsafe general atmosphere described. The interviewees describe the school environment as a place where students must learn to adapt and survive, regardless of their personal opinions or emotions. It should be noted that this observation does not single out public or private schools, which were not yet numerous at the time. The competitive environment was a standard feature of all schools. In schools where academic achievement was strongly promoted, the same rules of survival applied, with each individual competing for success on their own merits.

We were in the tenth grade, and he came in and started beating our classmate [...], and then we saw that he had a knuckle duster in his hand, and he was hitting a boy, and the boy was bleeding. [...] But that's the first thing when you see that, well, you realise that they can fight, that they can bring a knife to school, that they can do all that kind of thing [...] W/1988

The most violent episode was probably when... There was a joke about a student's mother dying - she committed suicide, and it was laughed at, and it was so... very unpleasant event, because it's just... and I didn't say anything because I knew I couldn't say anything. It was just a pure survival game in a way. M/1998

The complexity of bullying motives in a socio-historical context shows how broader societal changes affected individual experiences. The interplay of economic status, gender expectations, and socio-cultural shifts created an environment in which bullying became pervasive, normalised, and often violent. The lack of adequate gender and sexuality education contributed to a hostile environment for girls, where sexual harassment was part of everyday school life. On the other hand, boys also had to adapt or hide their sexual orientation if it did not meet aggressive masculinity standards. Personal characteristics such as unique fashion choices, lifestyle, or creative skills were met with mixed reactions, and children often felt pressured to conform to their peers' standards. Financial constraints affecting differences in dress style and international travel led to social status disadvantages. The environment was marked by extreme cruelty and distrust.

Concluding Remarks: A Bullying Society?

Individuals who have experienced bullying in the past are now adults actively shaping society — they are employed, financially independent, involved in decision-making processes, and serve as role models for the younger generation. As parents, they have developed a revised understanding of bullying, one that differs significantly from the earlier societal perceptions. Many research participants reflect on this shift through their own observations of bullying in the current context, particularly as it now affects their children. Although individual experiences with bullying may vary considerably, a shared sensitivity to the issue has emerged. This tendency is echoed in various statistical reports, which show that bullying is often recognised as one of the most pressing issues in Lithuanian society (WHO, 2024, p. 5).

Those who shared their experiences often associated bullying with anger, which stemmed from difficult social, psychological, or financial circumstances at the time. Young people who engaged in bullying behaviour were described as lacking motivation to align with the culture and goals of the educational institution. For the same reasons, they were also seen as potential victims of bullying. The school environment at the time was described as markedly different, often perceived as unsafe, and defined by constant struggles for survival. This heightened sensitivity to bullying coexists with a broader punitive attitude in society, suggesting that personal experiences from the past may be shaping strong public support for punishment-based responses to deviant behaviour. Notably, what was labelled as "deviant behaviour" could simply reflect differences in appearance, clothing style, or ways of communication.

During the period under review, punitive attitudes and behaviours were notable. There was a pervasive atmosphere of mistrust between children, teachers, and their parents. In the context of the constant struggle for survival, bullying became a means of separating those who were weak from those who were strong, both emotionally and physically. It was not possible to adopt a neutral approach to bullying. The standards of behaviour and social interaction deemed acceptable in the past are starkly different from those currently considered appropriate. This is reflected in the participants' responses to the study, which indicate a shift in attitude towards the situation at the time.

In the initial decades of independence, the significant shifts occurring across all societal spheres resulted in a notable absence of social authority. Accordingly, the concepts outlined in Braithwaite's (1989) and Ahmed and Braithwaite's (2011) Shame management theory on authority and its impact on individual conduct are not entirely reflected in this context. The traditional authority figures, namely parents and teachers, are subject to displacement and rethinking during adolescence. In some cases, these authority figures themselves become the victims of bullying or lack the ability to exert influence. The focus was on specific symbols of power, namely money and physical strength. Any discrepancy between these symbols risks exclusion from the group and a position as a target for bullying. As a result, the majority attempted to conform and lacked the motivation and the capacity to resist the prevailing aggressive culture. The bullying and its manifestations served to underscore the established norms and expectations of that era. These included a clear delineation of gender roles, with men occupying the dominant position and women assuming a more passive and submissive role.

The synthesis of shame and pride is evident in the way former social roles are conducted. The prevailing uncertainty in society resulted in a lack of trust between individuals, which in turn hindered the development of social empathy. The absence of emotional intelligence in society has resulted in the formation of destructive perceptions of both shame and pride. Any display of empathy or consideration for others could be perceived as a sign of vulnerability. In the context of bullying, women were the only individuals who could demonstrate greater emotional expressiveness, but their opinions and positions were often dismissed as insignificant.

In a society where any deviation from the prevailing norms was met with anger and aggression, it was not socially acceptable to shame those who engaged in bullying behaviour. Frequently, the blame for the bullying itself was attributed to the victim, based on the assumption that their own behaviour, appearance, or other characteristics had provoked the anger.

References

Ahmed, E., & Braithwaite, J. (2011). Shame, pride and workplace bullying. In S. Karstedt, I. Loader, & H. Strang (Eds.), *Emotions, Crime and Justice* (pp. 55–79). Hart Publishing.

Braithwaite, J. (1989). *Crime, shame and reintegration.* Cambridge University Press. https://doi.org/10.1017/CBO9780511804618(Accessed:9May2025)

Buzaitytė-Kašalynienė, J., Žėkaitė, J., Jusienė, R. & Stonkuvienė, I. (2021). Elektroninių patyčių paplitimas pradinėse ir pagrindinėse klasėse pirmojo karantino dėl COVID-19 pandemijos metu. *Pedagogika*, 144(4), 202–220. https://doi.org/10.15823/p.2021.144.11 (Accessed: 9 May 2025)

Cesaroni, C., Downing, S., & Alvi, S. (2012). Bullying enters the 21st century? Turning a critical eye to cyber-bullying research. *Youth Justice, 12*(3), 199–211. https://doi.org/10.1177/1473225412459837(Accessed:9May2025)

Corsten, M. (1999). The time of generations. *Time & Society, 8*(2–3), 249–272.

Dünkel, F., Gebauer, D., Geng, B., & Kestermann, C. (2007). *Mare-Balticum-Youth-Survey – Gewalterfahrungen von Jugendlichen im Ostseeraum.* Forum Verlag.

Gilligan, J. (1996). *Violence: Our deadly epidemic and its causes.* National Criminal Justice Reference Service. https://www.ojp.gov/ncjrs/virtual-library/abstracts/violence-our-deadly-epidemic-and-its-causes (Accessed: 9 May 2025)

Grigutytė, N., Pakalniškienė, V., Raižienė, S., & Povilaitis, R. (2018). Lietuvos vaikų naudojimosi internetu 2010 ir 2018 metais ypatumų palyginimas. *Psichologija, 58*, 57–71.

Grigutytė, N., Raižienė, S., & Pakalniškienė, V. (2019). Vaikų (ne)dalyvavimas elektroninėse patyčiose ir emociniai bei elgesio sunkumai. *Psichologija, 60,* 72–85.

Grigutytė, N., Raižienė, S. & Pakalniškienė, V. (2020). The role of school teachers, parents and friends in supporting children online. *ICERI2020 Proceedings*, 658–667. https://doi.org/10.21125/iceri.2020.0210 (Accessed: 9 May 2025)

Haan, W. D., Strang, H., Karstedt, S., & Loader, I. (2011). Making sense of 'senseless violence.' In S. Karstedt, I. Loader, & H. Strang (Eds.), *Emotions, Crime and Justice* (pp. 37–55). Hart Publishing.

Juozeliūnienė, I. & Budginaitė-Mačkinė, I. (2023). Gyvenantys mobiliame pasaulyje: 1980–2000 m. gimusiųjų migraciniai ketinimai ir šeiminio gyvenimo įsivaizdavimas. *Filosofija. Sociologija*, 34(4), 49–60.

Juska, A., Johnstone, P., & Pozzuto, R. (2004). The changing character of criminality and policing in post-socialist Lithuania: From fighting organised crime to policing marginal populations? *Crime, Law and Social Change, 41,* 161–177. https://doi.org/10.1023/B:CRIS.0000016224.65627.68(Accessed:9May2025)

Karstedt, S. (2011). Handle with care: Emotions, crime and justice. In S. Karstedt, I. Loader, & H. Strang (Eds.), *Emotions, Crime and Justice* (pp. 1–23). Hart Publishing.

Klanienė, I., & Skališienė, R. (2021). Encouraging responsibility of teenage girls in online social networks. *Pedagogika, 143*(3), 157–175.

Kruopštaitė, I., & Šupa, M. (2020). Etinės prieštaros internetinių bendruomenių kriminologiniuose tyrimuose. *Kriminologijos studijos, 8*, 8–37. https://doi.org/10.15388/CrimLithuan.2020.8.1 (Accessed: 9 of May 2025)

Markanski, A., & Melander, L. (2018). Intimate partner violence victimisation in the cyber and real world: Examining the extent of cyber aggression experiences and its association with in-person dating violence. *Journal of Interpersonal Violence, 33*(7), 1071–1095.

Nacionalinė švietimo agentūra. (2013). *Nepriklausomos valstybės švietimo kūrimo pamokos: 1988–2012*. https://www.nsa.smm.lt/wp-content/uploads/2016/01/bs_Nepriklausomos-valstybes-svietimo-kurimo-pamokos-1988-2012-2013-12.pdf (Accessed: 9 May 2025)

Nugin, R., & Kalmus, V. (2018). Social generations and societal changes. In P. Vihalemm, A. Masso, & S. Opermann (Eds.), *The Routledge International Handbook of European Social Transformations* (pp. 298–311). Routledge.

Pilkauskaitė-Valickienė, R., Raižienė, S. & Žukauskienė, R. (2009). Elektroninių patyčių paplitimas tarp Klaipėdos apskrities vyresniųjų klasių moksleivių, 114–121.

Povilaitis, R. & Valiukevičiūtė, J. (2005). Patyčių problema ir jos prevencijos bendrojo lavinimo mokykloje analizė, 16–17.

Sakalauskas, G., Kalpokas, V., Buzaitytė-Kašalynienė, J. & Švedaitė-Sakalauskė, B. (2022). Latentinės nepilnamečių delinkvencijos apraiškų ir tendencijų Lietuvoje tarptautinis palyginimas. *Socialinė teorija, empirija, politika ir praktika (STEPP)*, 24, 101–117.

Shariff, S. (2014). *Sexting and cyberbullying: Defining the line for digitally empowered kids*. Cambridge University Press. https://doi.org/10.1017/CBO9781139095891(Accessed:9May2025)

Skerytė-Kazlauskienė, M., Barkauskienė, R., & Povilaitis, R. (2012). Paauglių, turinčių mokymosi sutrikimų, savęs vertinimas: Ar svarbi patyčių patirtis? *Tiltai, 3*, 99–110.

Šupa, M. (2021). Socialiniai tyrimai apie elektroninius nusikaltimus: globalus temų diapazonas ir Lietuvoje atliktų tyrimų sisteminė analizė. *Kriminologijos studijos*, 9, 8–46. https://doi.org/10.15388/CrimLithuan.2021.9.1 (Accessed: 9 May 2025)

Thomson, A. (2016). Australian generations? Memory, oral history and generational identity in postwar Australia. *Australian Historical Studies, 47*(1), 41–57.

Vileikienė, E., Šidlauskienė, A., Vaicekauskaitė, L., Narkauskaitė, L., Smirnova, K., Povilaitis, R. (2011). *Smurto paplitimas ir jo prevencija Lietuvoje* p. 77. Higienos institutas.

World Health Organisation. (2024). *A Focus on Adolescent peer violence and bullying in Europe, Central Asia and Canada. Health behaviour in school-aged children international report from the 2021/2022 survey, 2*, 32. https://iris.who.int/bitstream/handle/10665/376323/9789289060929-eng.pdf?sequence=2 (Accessed: 9 May 2025)

Žėkaitė, J., Buzaitytė-Kašalynienė, J., Jusienė, R., Speičytė-Ruschhoff, E., Schoroškienė, V., & Stonkuvienė, I. (2021). Vaikų ugdymo nuotoliniu būdu technologinės perspektyvos: kilę esminiai iššūkiai ir atsiradusios galimybės. In *Nuotolinis vaikų ugdymas pandemijos dėl COVID-19 metu* (10–15). Vilniaus universitetas. https://www.fsf.vu.lt/dokumentai/Nuotolinis_vaiku_ugdymas_pandemijos_del_COVID-19_metu.pdf (Accessed: 9 May 2025)

Part II

Suitable Punishable Subjects

7

Disciplining the Poor: The Politics of Responsibilising the Underclass in Lithuania

Arūnas Poviliūnas and Arunas Juska

Introduction

In 1998, Dr. Irena Zaleskienė, a researcher at the Lithuanian University of Educational Sciences, published an article titled *Person, Society and State: Social Exclusion* (Zaleskienė, 1998). In this study, she presented the first systematic outline of the underclass phenomenon in Lithuania. Zaleskienė defined the underclass as *socialiai atskirti asmenys* (in Lith.) or

We sincerely thank Dr. Romas Lazutka for his insightful comments and valuable suggestions on the initial draft of this chapter.

A. Poviliūnas (✉)
Faculty of Philosophy, Institute of Sociology and Social Work, Vilnius University, Vilnius, Lithuania
e-mail: arunas.poviliunas@fsf.vu.lt

A. Juska
East Carolina University, Greenville, USA
e-mail: juskaa@ecu.edu

A. Dobryninas and S. Nikartas (eds.), *Understanding Crime Control and Punishment in Lithuania*, Crime Prevention and Security Management,
https://doi.org/10.1007/978-3-032-05538-5_7

"socially excluded persons," identifying them as belonging to "the lowest class" of society. She wrote:

> Currently, there are no statistical data or empirical studies on marginalised groups, often referred to as the "lowest class" of society. This includes individuals living on the fringes of society, such as chronic alcoholics, drug addicts, people with physical disabilities, ex-convicts struggling to reintegrate, and the homeless. However, indirect data—primarily derived from municipal reports and assessments by social assistance units—indicate that the number of such individuals has nearly doubled over the past 5–7 years. These individuals face significant barriers in accessing social security, charitable aid, and even basic healthcare services like ambulances. While municipalities do provide limited support, a comprehensive social protection policy for this vulnerable group of individuals is still lacking (Zaleskienė, 1998, pp. 21–22).

In addition to raising concerns about the rapid increase in socially excluded persons, Zaleskienė sought to describe their composition (Table 7.1). Using data from municipalities, she categorised and ranked the subgroups that, according to her, constituted the underclass in Lithuania. This typology highlighted the inconsistent and ad hoc metrics employed by different municipalities to identify and count members of the so-called "lowest class of society." The list included a mix of groups, individuals, and locations associated with social exclusion. Many of the categories were poorly defined and overlapping, such as those distinguishing between individuals forced into or voluntarily engaging in begging, or among "slums," "abandoned flats," and "gathering places of asocial families." Despite these ambiguities, the data indicated that nearly 3,000 so-called "asocial families" formed the core of the underclass dominating the overall count.

Zaleskienė's study was one of the first in Lithuania to propose consolidating previously distinct and heterogeneous categories of marginalised individuals—those who experienced rapid downward mobility from various social subgroups in post-Soviet Lithuanian society—into a single classification: the underclass. Consider that among the impoverished segments of the post-socialist population were individuals pauperised by deindustrialisation and privatisation of state-owned assets that was

Table 7.1 Socially excluded persons in selected cities in Lithuania (1997), Zaleskienė (1998, p. 21)

Groups of socially excluded	Cities and towns			
	Kaunas	Šiauliai	Vilnius	Visaginas
Asocial families	2 000	350	568	49
Persons without a permanent place of residence	500	60	150	–
Homeless children and adolescents	294	570	563	–
People forced into begging	10	130	116	–
People voluntarily engaging in begging	90	120	116	–
Drug addicts		129	958	94
Others	108	160	9 100	47
Slums and abandoned flats	23	20	76	30
Gathering places of asocial families	10		150	10

riddled with corruption, insider dealings and influence of organised criminal groups; the rural déclassé, who emerged due to the dismantling of the collective farming system and the conflict-ridden land restitution reforms aimed at returning property to pre-WWII owners and their descendants, many of whom resided in urban areas. Additionally, there were old age individuals, single parent families with children, and those with fixed incomes who were pauperised by high unemployment, elimination of public subsidies, currency devaluations and high inflation at the same time as the universal social protection system inherited from the Soviet era was being rapidly dismantled.

The newly introduced category of the underclass obscured the heterogeneity of the post-socialist "residuum" population. Instead of analysing the multiple downward trajectories triggered by large-scale structural transformations in post-socialist Lithuanian society, it shifted the focus towards a newly constructed subject of analysis and a new target for social policy and governance: the "asocial family."

This symbiotic relationship between the categories of underclass and asocial families is not unique to Lithuania. Although the term underclass was coined in the United States by sociologist Gunnar Myrdal (1965) to describe those permanently marginalised and trapped in poverty, it became a highly politically charged concept upon publication of Senator Daniel Patrick Moynihan's report, *The Negro Family:*

The Case for National Action (Moynihan, 1965). The report argued that the decline of the Black nuclear family was a key factor contributing to entrenched poverty and welfare dependence in the Black community. In other words, the discovery of the underclass in American society served to deflect attention from structural processes that generated new forms of inequality, poverty, and exclusion. Instead, it narrowed the focus to the generational reproduction of poverty within families, reframing systemic issues as familial or cultural deficiencies (Wacquant, 2022).

The cultural shift in poverty analysis also shaped Zaleskienė's conceptualisation of the genesis of the underclass in Lithuania. She attributed this phenomenon to the inability or unwillingness of marginalised individuals to adapt to the changing relationship between citizens and the state brought about by the democratisation of Lithuanian society. If, under the Soviet regime, the state maintained dominance and provided paternalistic care for individuals, the democratic reforms of post-Soviet Lithuania necessitated a new social contract with the poor. In its post-socialist reiteration, the primacy of the state was to be replaced by the primacy of individual responsibility. Citizens were now expected "to take responsibility for their well-being instead of asking the state to solve their personal problems" (Zaleskienė, 1998, p. 17).

Reining in the Poor: Imposing the New Punitive Social Contract on the Post-Socialist Underclass

In this chapter, we expand on the themes of punitiveness introduced earlier in this volume by examining the socio-political and socio-cultural processes involved in constructing and enforcing a new social contract on the post-socialist poor. At its core, this punitive contract represented a distinct class conflict settlement particular to post-socialist Lithuania. On one side were the increasingly affluent, predominantly urban classes who successfully adapted to the new service- and knowledge-based economy, with lifestyles and consumption patterns closely mirroring those of the Western European middle class. On the other side were the ones left behind, who failed to adapt to the post-socialist socio-economic realities, experiencing rapid downward social mobility and a dramatic decline in their living standards.

It reminds the central argument in Wacquant's book "Punishing the Poor" that the neoliberal state has shifted from a welfare state model to a "centaur state"—one that is "liberal at the top and paternalistic at the bottom." It involves the simultaneous retraction of social assistance for the poor and the expansion of punitive measures to control and discipline them (Wacquant, 2009, p. 312). The "underclass" has become a key target of this punitive approach, as the poor are increasingly stigmatised and seen as the source of "urban pathologies and antisocial behaviours." The language used to describe the "underclass"—as "mired in immorality and welfare dependency" (Wacquant, 2009, p. 62)—reflects this moralising and punitive perspective.

The new configurations of class delineation and conflict between the new haves and have-nots emerged prominently in the late 1990s, as the economy rebounded following a deep and protracted crisis across the region (Starkeviciute, 1998). Up until then, the dramatic rise in poverty and morbidity due to the collapse of centralised economies was widely regarded as a temporary issue that would subside once the transition to market economies advanced and economic growth resumed (Grinspun, 2001; UNDP, 1999; UNDP, 1998). Unexpectedly, rapid economic growth coincided with indicators of a "hardening of poverty," where prolonged unemployment and poverty began to result in unemployability, the proliferation of social pathologies, and the spatial segregation of the poor. Consequently, by the late 1990s, discussions within post-socialist studies began to shift towards examining the marginalisation of the poor. A substantial body of research emerged, arguing that an underclass—a marginalised stratum characterised by chronic unemployment and social isolation from mainstream society—was forming in post-socialist countries (Emigh & Szelényi, 2001; Genov, 1998; Hutton & Redmond, 2000; Tarkowska, 1999).

Conflicts between the emerging new winners and losers of post-socialist transformation were pervasive across former socialist countries, with different nations responding to their prominence in varying ways.

We propose to analyse these responses along two closely related dimensions: the *type of accommodation* and the *mode of accommodation* provided to the new post-socialist poor.

The *type of accommodation* can range from policies emphasising redistribution, social solidarity, and social protection for the new poor. According to Gøsta Esping-Andersen's (1996) typology, such policies align with social democratic welfare responses to poverty. At the opposite end of the spectrum are policies typical of the liberal welfare model, which emphasise individualism and self-reliance, rely on residual and means-tested eligibility criteria, limit the role of the state, and rely on the market as the primary provider of welfare.

Modes of accommodation can range from the "ideal type" of coalition and compromise-building through good-faith negotiations, which reflect the duties, responsibilities, and interests of both post-socialist haves and have-nots. At the opposite end of this spectrum lies an antagonistic approach, where conflicts over the new poverty are framed in zero-sum terms: a win for one side equates to a loss or punishment for the other, i.e., as taking from the "deserving" to give to the "undeserving" or casting taxation as a "burden" on capital, used to fund welfare dependency among the irresponsible new poor.

While Slovenia and the Czech Republic relied more on political accommodation, adopting policies that leaned towards social democratic rather than liberal welfare prescriptions, in Lithuania, liberal welfare policies were imposed in a zero-sum approach to class conflict resolution. This was largely due to the aggrieved have-nots of post-socialist transition suffering a decisive political loss in the electoral politics of the early 2000s, which delegitimised them as a political force.

In retrospect, the rise and fall of Rolandas Paksas, the sixth president of Lithuania (2003–2004), proved to be a pivotal development. Following the path dependency approach, we will characterise this episode of presidential political contention as a critical juncture, resolved through a distinctively punitive social contract with the post-socialist poor. In path dependency theory, a critical juncture refers to a period of disruption characterised by a high degree of uncertainty and openness, during which multiple paths in a political process become possible. However, once a "particular course of action <is> introduced, <it> can be virtually impossible to reverse" due to self-reinforcing mechanisms like vested interests, increasing returns, or social norms (Pierson, 2000, p. 251; see also Mahoney, 2000).

Similar to figures like Trump or Berlusconi, Paksas emerged as a charismatic proto-authoritarian populist of the kind popular today. He adeptly harnessed the grievances of large segments of the Lithuanian population who had failed to benefit from economic growth and experienced downward social mobility alongside a dramatic decline in their standards of living.

Part of Paksas's appeal stemmed from his status as a national aerobatics champion of the USSR in the 1980s, known for performing breathtaking piloting stunts—looping, rolling, and spinning in airshows and competitions. Like Trump or Berlusconi, Paksas was also wealthy and an oligarch of sorts. He launched his business career by leveraging his connections in ex-Soviet aviation and military industries in Russia (aerobatics was financed and operated by the Soviet air force) to fund his construction ventures in Vilnius.

By the time Paksas entered politics, academics in Lithuania were increasingly framing the underclass as emblematic of moral decay, while conflicts between the new haves and have-nots escalated on the streets. In March 2000, Lithuanian sugar beet growers organised a series of protests and marches, culminating in the blockade of major highways to demand increased state subsidies. Media coverage of these protests was overwhelmingly negative, popularising the derogatory term used to describe impoverished farmers as "the beets" (i.e., lazy, conservative, resistant to change, and primarily interested in lobbying for more welfare payments and subsidies). In response, farmers hurled an equally derisive label—"the elites"—at their critics, characterising them as snooty, distant, and arrogant urban classes who led pampered lives, ran the state and their businesses for their own interests, and remained disconnected from the lives and struggles of those they claimed to govern.

Sensing opportunities, a number of politicians were positioning themselves as "the voice of the people" victimised by post-socialist elites. Vytautas Šustauskas, a one-time mayor of Kaunas (Lithuania's second-largest city) and a single-term member of the Seimas, styled himself as "the king of the paupers." He staged "protest marches of the paupers" (mostly publicity stunts) and frequently spewed offensive rhetoric against "the elites," laced with antisemitism, homophobia, and anti-European Union and anti-NATO sentiments. In contrast, Rolandas Paksas avoided such crude rhetoric and proved far more effective in gaining prominence. Foreshadowing tactics later used by Donald Trump, Paksas mobilised his base by organising large rallies in economically depressed, dislocated, and depopulated provincial towns and rural areas. In 2003, he unexpectedly and decisively won the presidency. However, Paksas' background in aviation and his ties to Russian business interests became his undoing. When he was accused of corruption and accepting large bribes from a Russian businessman with connections to criminal groups, his supporters rallied to his defence, while his opponents framed the issue as a national security crisis (Juska & Johnstone, 2004).

Thus, the conflict between "the people" and "the elites" escalated into an antagonistic, zero-sum confrontation. To Paksas' opponents, no compromise was possible with a president under Russian criminal influence or his supporters supposedly harbouring pro-Russian and pro-Soviet sympathies.

The impeachment and removal of Paksas in April 2004 marked a decisive defeat for those disadvantaged by the post-socialist transformation in negotiating a new social contract. His downfall delegitimised their political protests, framing them as retrograde, subversive to the sovereignty of the Lithuanian state, and reflective of their supposedly Soviet mentality and pro-Russian sentiments. It also allowed to frame the protests, not as reactions to deliterious forms of exclusion and marginalisation produced by post-socialist transformation, but in moral terms as expressions of the lingering Soviet era dependency and a lack of personal responsibility among those dispossessed by the transition. In our view, the resolution of the 2003–04 crisis via decisive defeat of Paksas and his supporters had set Lithuanian policy towards poverty in much harder, more moralistic, and disciplinary terms than was the case in many other post-socialist countries.

While the political defeat of the populist threat facilitated the recasting of the new social contract into a harsher "tough love" rhetoric, it does not, on its own, explain the specific policies pursued and enacted in its aftermath. To analyse the deployment of the punitive responsibilisation approach towards the poor in Lithuania, we adopt the framework developed by the Birmingham School of Cultural Studies. The multidisciplinary research produced by scholars of this school is notable for its cultural turn in the study of politics and state power and their emphasis on the central role of popular culture in producing "common-sense" consensus and public support for changes in social policy (Connell & Hilton, 2016). Stuart Hall and his collaborators (Hall, 1998; Hall & O'Shea, 2013; Hall et al., 2013), along with other scholars working in this tradition (Hancock, 2004; Hills, 2015; Jensen, 2018), drew extensively on Gramsci's theory of cultural hegemony (Gramsci, 1973).

Specifically, we draw on Hall et al. (2013) and Jensen (2018) to develop a three-step iteration framework for tracing the consolidation of the punitive responsibilisation consensus that shaped post-socialist Lithuania's social welfare reforms. First, we examine how the dismantling of the universal welfare system and cuts to social expenditures were implemented through the creation and rationalisation of the social services market. These marketisation reforms were legitimised by technocratic discourses emphasising improved efficiency and effectiveness, aiming to reduce costs while ostensibly expanding services. Next, we will explore the socio-cultural process, unfolding simultaneously with the marketisation initiatives, of constructing a new "folk devil"—the underclass in general, and the "asocial family" in particular. The emergence of discourses surrounding the "asocial family" stigmatised the new poor and fuelled moral panic about the perceived threats they posed to societal norms and values. Finally, we examine how these moral fears surrounding "asocial families" were leveraged not only to legitimise reductions in social assistance but also to expand the punitive and disciplinary capacities of an increasingly intrusive and supervisory welfare apparatus.

Employing the Market to Reduce Social Expenditures on the New Poor in Lithuania

Since regaining independence in 1991, Lithuania zealously embraced neoliberal doctrines in building a new market economy, characterised by minimal controls on capital and open markets (Bohle & Greskovits, 2007; Hirschhausen, 1998; Kolodko, 2002). By the mid-1990s, neoliberal reforms extended to the social sphere, aiming to reduce the costs of social provisions. In 1996, the so-called system of "personal social services" was established in Lithuania, paving the way for funding of the non-state social service providers (Lietuvos Respublikos Seimas, 1996). By 2002, marketisation of social services proceeded further when the decree on the Framework of Social Services Reform was issued, aiming "to ensure the provision of individuals' most essential needs while incentivising active engagement in self-help" (Lietuvos Respublikos Vyriausybe, 2002). This was to be achieved by establishing the national social service market in which state, for-profit and nonprofit organisations will compete for contracts over the provision of social services. The 2006 Law on Social Services provided the legal base for the creation of a social services market (Lietuvos Respublikos Seimas, 2006).

More specifically, the law identified social service providers as well as their clients as participants in the social service market. For providers, it outlined the market incentives as well as benchmarking criteria designed to decrease costs and increase efficiency and service offerings. The law expanded the range of social service providers to include private entities, such as joint-stock companies, private firms, and individual enterprises, alongside public institutions like budgetary and public organisations. This represented a shift towards diversifying social service provision beyond the traditional public sector.

To operate, social service providers are required to obtain a licence, establishing a regulatory framework aimed at fostering a structured and competitive market for social services. Additionally, the law introduced the concept of "assistance money," allowing monetary allowances to replace standard social services and social care in certain cases. This provision incorporates elements of consumer choice and market-driven mechanisms into the social services system.

Social clients were now classified as participants in the social services market and divided into two overlapping categories: individuals and families. Individual clients were expected to comply with neoliberal requirements of being self-sufficient, autonomous, and enterprising. Families, similarly, were expected to be responsible, aspirational, and autonomous in raising children. Despite expressions of sympathy and solidarity, failure to meet these expectations relegated both categories of clients to a morally suspicious or deficient status, often with punitive and corrective implications of varying scope.

Finally, the 2012–2014 Social Assistance Reforms in Lithuania undertook to downsize social assistance, which had expanded during the 2008–09 economic crisis. The Law on Monetary Social Assistance for Low-Income Residents, which took effect on 1 January 2012, served as the legal foundation for providing social assistance. A key measure was to significantly increase the discretion of municipalities in administering funds allocated by the central government for social assistance.

Special commissions that included representatives of local communities were established to evaluate applicants' eligibility for assistance benefits. This introduced stricter criteria and additional hurdles, aligning with municipalities' objectives to reduce the number of benefit recipients. These reforms aimed to enhance the efficiency of social assistance by enabling municipalities to retain unspent funds for local development rather than returning them to the central government. These "savings" could be redirected to other expenditures, such as funding projects co-financed by the European Union and municipalities. Such projects, a priority for local business owners, who frequently dominate municipal councils in Lithuania, could benefit from the reallocation of these funds.

In the initial stage of the reform, five municipalities were selected to operate under increased budgetary discretion in social services provision. Figure 7.1 compares the performance of these pilot municipalities with that of a control group consisting of 11 municipalities operating under centralised allocation and spending directives.

The data demonstrate that the reforms were highly effective in reducing expenditures on social services. In the pilot municipalities, the ratios of recipients per 1,000 inhabitants and expenditures per inhabitant declined by more than one-fifth compared to the control group,

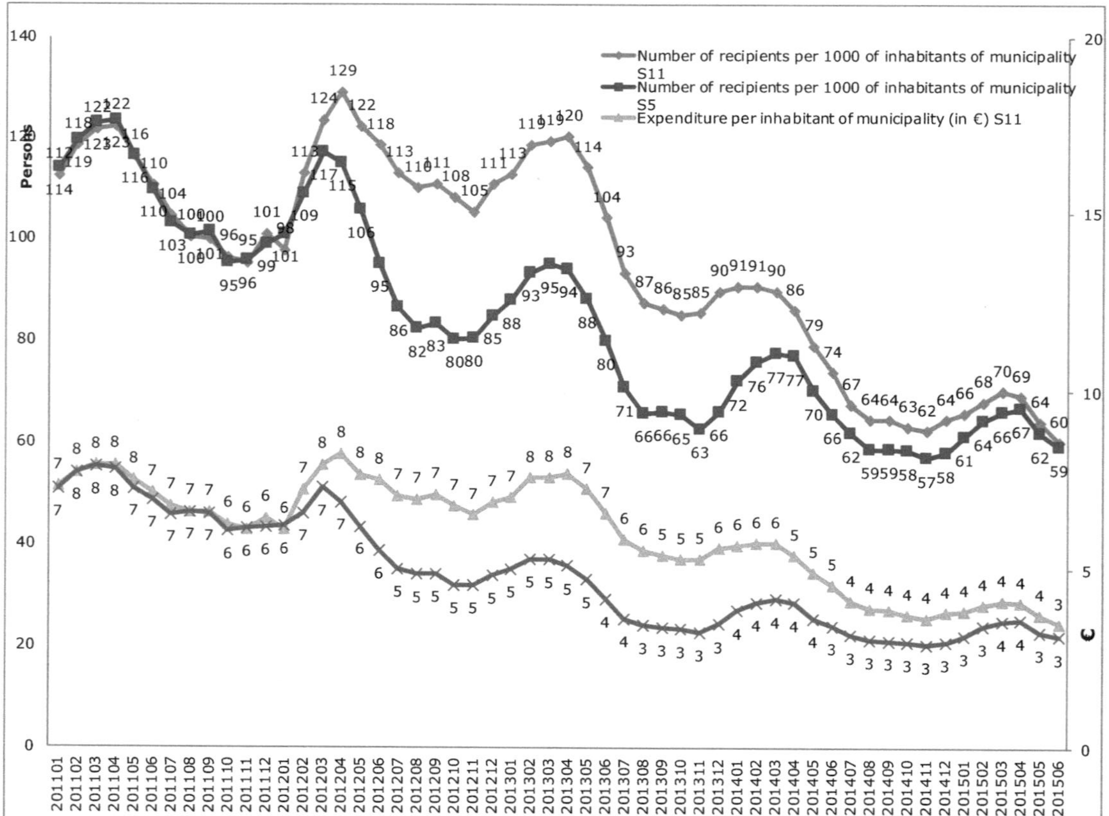

Fig. 7.1 Social services provision in five pilot municipalities (S5) operating under fiscal decentralisation compared to the control group of 11 municipalities (S11) operating under centralised allocation and spending directives, 2011–2015

by the late 2010s, administrative and bureaucratic pressure to reduce social assistance provision extended beyond the pilot municipalities to the control group, as new, lower benchmarks for the number of recipients and expenditures per recipient became the standard.

Similarly, the overall cuts to social assistance from 2012 to 2016 were also rapid and significant. Within just four years, the number of social assistance recipients was reduced by nearly 60%—from 222,000 in 2012 to 88,000 in 2016. Expenditure on social assistance also dropped sharply, decreasing by 66%, from €177.3 million to €60.7 million during the same period (Fig. 7.2).

However, with few notable exceptions among some academics and journalists, there was minimal public concern or opposition to the rapid dismantling of social protection for the country's poorest citizens. In comparison, local government representatives, tasked with managing municipal budgets, were more likely to support reform provisions that

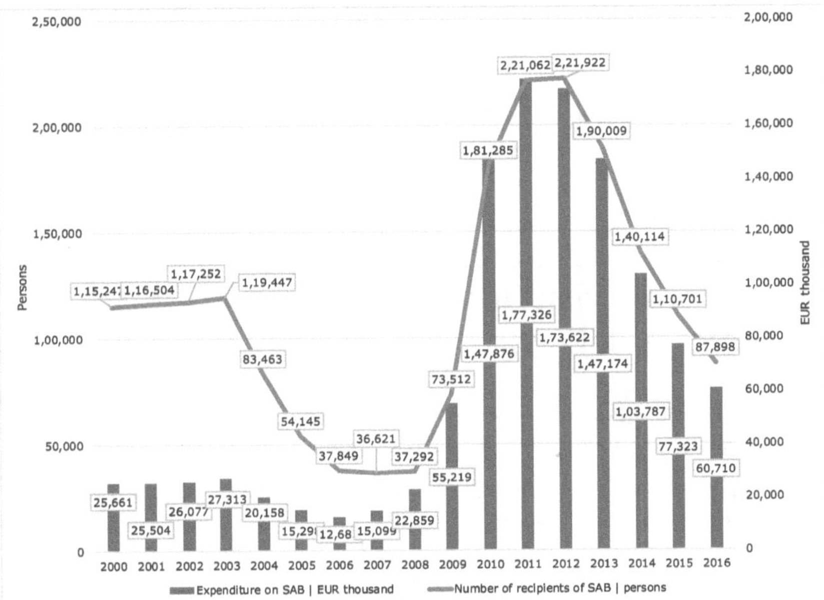

Fig. 7.2 Expenditures on social assistance benefits (SAB) and their recipients, 2000–2016

allowed savings from reduced social assistance to be redirected towards municipal needs. They also saw greater community involvement and stricter oversight of benefit recipients as steps to improve the effectiveness and targeting of assistance provision.

Social workers and social assistance specialists involved in administering and implementing the social assistance reform generally favoured stricter regulation of monetary benefits, considering it a way to promote social justice. However, they expressed greater scepticism regarding the benefits of community involvement and the efficacy of mandatory community service for benefit recipients.

Finally, community representatives, such as NGO members and neighbourhood elders, often had a closer connection to benefit recipients and their real-life circumstances. They were more likely to support community involvement in the social assistance decision-making process, viewing it as a way to enhance transparency and better target aid distribution. Additionally, they were less concerned about the increased administrative costs associated with home visits (Zalimiene et al., 2015).

In summary, although there were some differences in the positions of key stakeholders, the reforms reflected neoliberal policy preferences, with measures aimed at increasing control over benefit recipients and reducing their dependency on social assistance.

Turning the Post-Socialist Poverty into a Moral Crisis: Identifying and Counting the New "Folk Devils"

As the national economy has improved since the mid-1990s, the mass media coverage of the hardening post-socialist poverty has turned increasingly negative. Coverage of the rural poor became particularly skewed, inundated with sensational and grotesque portrayals of rural life. Lithuania's leading daily, Lietuvos Rytas, published headlines such as: "Villagers and their dogs in Biržai County got infested with lice" (August 15 1994); "In the morning [the villager] slaughtered a pig, in the evening [he] stabbed his wife" (January 3 1995); "Village teacher was stealing together with his teenage pupils" (April 24 1997); "Alcoholics are attempting to commit suicide by hanging and burning themselves" (September 10 1997); "A husband strangled his disabled wife" (October 18 1998); "After beating his wife, a drunken villager continued his debauchery" (February 24 1999); and "Everything that gets in the way [of the villagers] is stolen" (August 20 1999) (Juska, 2007, p. 245).

Parallel to increasing stigmatisation of rural poor, various labels for socially deficient families were becoming prominent, such as *families at social risk, social risk families,* or *asocial families.* By 2006, the new social services law had codified the criteria defining such families. More specifically, National Child Rights Protection and Adoption Service (NCRPAS) used seven indicators to define their charcateristics: alcohol and drug abuse by parents, lack of parenting skills, restriction of parental rights, placement of children under permanent guardianship, inapproprite use of social assistance, compulsive gambling by parents, and violence against children.

Figure 7.3 shows that two types of asocial parenting—alcohol/drug abuse and lack of parenting skills—accounted for 85% of the entries on the NCRPAS list. Other forms of deficient parenting were less significant: being restricted in parental rights and having children placed under permanent guardianship accounted for up to 5%, while violence against children was reported in about 2% of the families on the NCRPAS register.

This suggests that families labelled as "asocial" in Lithuania were predominantly those of alcoholic and hapless parents who endangered the safety and well-being of their children. These two categories of asocial parenting were deeply stigmatising, not because they identify alcoholic and abusive parents—many of whom undoubtedly exist—but because they are grounded in the assumption that irresponsible parenting is primarily a matter of "moral and personal conduct and choices about how to rise one's children <that> is postioned as *the most important factor* in determing child's life chances, more important than income, security, access to decent housing, healthcare, childcare, and so on. This *moral narrative* around good parenting distorts wider debates about widening social and economic polarisation and stagnant social mobility <because it

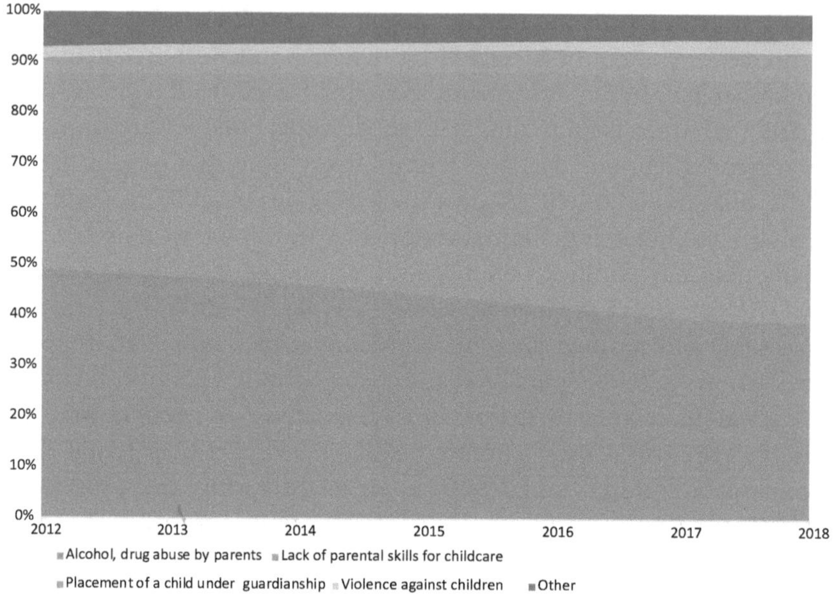

Fig. 7.3 Asocial families in Lithuania by type (%), 2012–2018. *Source* The Indicators Database of the State Data Agency

holds> that dispossession, disenfranchisement, poverty, and precarity are consequences of the failures of individual families" (Jensen, 2018, p. 16).

Therefore, the decrease and changes in the types of asocial families from 2012 to 2018 reflected not only the actual counts by NCRPAS officials of parents abusing alcohol and neglecting children but also shifts in moral concerns about such families, which can fluctuate relatively independently of the actual situation. For example, the significant decline of almost 20% in asocial families by 2018 likely reflects municipalities' incentives to reduce the overall number of social assistance beneficiaries to achieve "savings."

Similarly, there was a relative decline in the proportion of parents abusing alcohol or drugs, from 49% in 2012 to 39% in 2018, while the proportion of families categorised as lacking parental skills increased from 38 to 48% over the same period. While it is possible that alcohol abuse in families decreased alongside the moderate decline in alcohol consumption in Lithuania during the 2010s (Rehm et al., 2024), the relative increase in "lacking parental skills" counts is more likely attributable to a combination of two factors. First, by the late 2010s, categorisation of deficient parenting shifted towards the less stigmatising term "lack of skills," culminating in the discontinuation of data collection on asocial families in 2018. This change was driven by the diffusion and adoption of a more "neutral" nomenclature of poverty categories inspired by EU social policy initiatives and documents. Second, the growing emphasis on "teaching" parental skills was driven by the expansion of surveillance and intervention systems, as the popular pedagogy for addressing deficient families gained prominence since the late 2010s.

The Expansion of the Punitive and Disciplinary Capacities of an Increasingly Intrusive and Supervisory Apparatus

Defining asocial families through their moral failings, in turn, necessitated increased surveillance to assess the type and severity of these failings and to prescribe an appropriate combination of measures, including instruction, support, discipline, and, when deemed necessary, punishment. The 2012 Law on Cash Social Assistance for Low-Income Residents enhanced the disciplining measures targeting the poor.

Stricter eligibility and assessment criteria for social benefits were introduced. Municipalities established special commissions to evaluate applicants' eligibility for social assistance, implementing additional requirements and stricter rules with the aim of reducing the number of benefit recipients. The alleged goal of the commissions was to combat misuse of social assistance by dishonest recipients, whose increasing numbers on the welfare rolls, attributed to the fallout from the 2008–09 economic crisis, were seen as potential abuse of the system rather than a result of increased need.

Two new measures were introduced to incentivise employment among the poor. First, welfare benefit eligibility and amounts were reduced based on the duration of assistance. Specifically, social assistance was reduced by 20% after 36–48 months of eligibility, by 30% after 48–60 months, and by 40% after 60 months. For beneficiaries without children, no benefits were provided beyond this period. Second, a new partial benefit payment was introduced for former long-term unemployed individuals who gained employment. This benefit, amounting to 50% of the pre-employment total, continued to be paid if the recipient's earnings were between 100 and 200% of the minimum wage.

Finally, in order to continue receiving social assistance benefits, recipients were now required to participate in "socially beneficial activities" organised by municipal administrations. These activities were essentially mandatory work programmes, requiring up to 40 hours per month of work to remain eligible for continued benefits. Failure to participate in socially beneficial activities could result in the cancellation of social assistance payments.

The minimum income scheme reform in Lithuania appears to reflect a punitive logic towards the poor, as described in Wacquant's concept of "punishing the poor," through its emphasis on reducing dependency, increasing conditionality, and strengthening surveillance and control over the recipients of social assistance.

By 2018, the system for protecting children's rights also underwent a significant transformation. The term "family at social risk" was replaced with "family experiencing problems or crises," and the use of the "families at social risk" category was discontinued. The Child Rights Protection System was centralised in order to establish a unified, coherent framework for promptly and professionally addressing reports of child neglect and violence. This reorganisation aimed to work effectively with families facing problems or crises, fostering a supportive and child-friendly environment.

Mobile teams were established, comprising social workers and specialists from various fields under the State Child Rights Protection and Adoption Service, operating within the Ministry of Social Security and Labour. Led by case managers, these teams are tasked with providing intensive consultations and psychological and social assistance to families in crisis. The primary objective of case management was not only to deliver support to the families in crisis but also to empower them to achieve lasting changes, assuring the child's physical and mental well-being while safeguarding their interests.

To date, there is only limited and indirect data available to evaluate the effectiveness of the new team-based approach for addressing "families experiencing problems or crises." While the emphasis on more care-oriented and pedagogical interventions is undoubtedly commendable and worth supporting, a key concern emerges with this policy shift. Instead of aiming to reduce poverty, the approach seems to focus on increasingly specialised pedagogical strategies that emphasise the responsibilisation of the poor. Consider that despite numerous reforms, the at-risk-of-poverty rate over the last decade in Lithuania has not decreased, despite the real GDP per capita increasing from €12,400 in 2014 to €17,210 in 2024 (Eurostat, Real GDP per capita and At risk of poverty rate).

Concluding Remarks

In this chapter, we argued that Lithuania's distinctly punitive social policy towards the poor resulted from a peculiar settlement of class conflict between those who benefited from post-socialist reforms and those left behind, particularly in areas outside major cities that faced deindustrialisation, dislocation, and rapid depopulation. This struggle over the new social contract reflected diverging interpretations of post-socialist poverty, reflecting differing interests between the new "haves" and "have-nots."

Post-socialist poverty can be seen as a consequence of multifaceted structural processes—marketisation, privatisation, liberalisation, deindustrialisation, the rise of the service sector in the national economy, reintegration into regional and global markets, welfare retrenchment, widening inequality, and cultural individualisation. Such an understanding of poverty would favour social-democratic welfare responses rooted in social solidarity and redistribution.

However, in the conflict with those left behind, the rising classes decisively defeated populist opposition, discredited the president, compromised by his ties to Russian organised crime, and stigmatised his supporters, attributing their impoverishment to a supposed Soviet mentality, pro-Russian sentiments, and dependence on the state.

This decisive "cultural turn" in interpreting post-socialist poverty following Paksas' removal from office was further reinforced by the rise of a broadly popular consensus favouring punitive responsibilisation of the poor. This shift solidified the development of a distinctly punitive liberal welfare system in Lithuania.

The popular consensus around responsibilisation was shaped by a combination of (a) "value-neutral" technocratic discourses and initiatives that emphasised marketisation, rationalisation, and the increased effectiveness of social welfare provisions, and (b) the construction of new "folk devils"—the underclass in general, and the asocial family in particular—as threats to social values and norms. This framing, in turn, legitimised measures aimed at the moral reform of the poor, which became an ideologically hegemonic (in Gramscian terms) "common sense" in Lithuania.

This is not to suggest that statistics on the Lithuanian underclass fail to capture the deeply troubling social pathologies and self-destructive behaviours among the country's poorest. In this regard, a longer-term historical perspective on policies targeting abusive and alcoholic families in Lithuania might be valuable. The so-called "asocial families" are not a new social phenomenon in Lithuania, nor are the moral reforms aimed at addressing these issues. What has changed, however, at least since the mid-nineteenth century, is the moral framework underpinning these reforms.

In the 1850s, the Lithuanian temperance movement was spearheaded by the Catholic Church under the leadership of Bishop Motiejus Valančius. He believed that combating the problems of abusive alcoholic families required parents and communities to renew their Catholic faith and embrace a life of piety and strict religious observance. However, the nascent movement was soon banned by the General Governor of Vilnius, alarmed by its growing popularity, the rise of anti-Russian sentiments among temperance advocates, and opposition from local landlords who suffered economic losses due to the sudden drop in vodka demand.

During Soviet times, asocial families were to be "fixed" by re-educating parents to become model Soviet citizens, devout followers of the Communist Party and builders of socialism. These efforts faltered as Communist ideology crumbled under the rise of nationalism during *perestroika*. Similarly to Tsarist times, Gorbachev's poorly conceived anti-alcoholism campaign in the late 1980s resulted in significant budgetary shortfalls that the government could ill afford and caused sugar shortages due to the surge in illegal moonshining.

Today, the moral code has shifted once again, this time aligning with the neoliberal ideals of market-based morality. Instead of pious Catholics or devoted builders of socialism, the heroes of our era are business entrepreneurs and their vanguard, the *startuoliai* (startup founders in Lithuanian). Reflecting these new moral aspirations, asocial families are now expected to (a) curtail their abuse of alcohol and drugs and (b) develop their parenting skills to become self-regulating, entrepreneurial subjects. They are encouraged to invest their human capital in their children to maximise returns (self-discipline, better education outcomes, social mobility, jobs, etc.), ultimately making themselves and their children self-sufficient and less of a burden on society.

In a similar role to Bishop Valančius and the General Secretary of the Communist Party of the USSR, Prime Minister Saulius Skvernelis (2016–2020) initiated Lithuania's first post-socialist temperance campaign, which focused on limiting alcohol accessibility and increasing taxes on alcohol sales.

Regarding the development of parenting skills, the latest strategy emphasises the surveillance and guidance of asocial families by multi-disciplinary management teams. These teams are supposed to bring expertise in counselling, alcohol addiction, financial management, and professional training to support and reform these families.

The team-based approach can provide significant benefits to some social assistance clients and their families. However, the current social policy elevates the moral reform of the poor as the central strategy for poverty reduction. It prioritises addressing issues such as drunkenness, character flaws, disorganised daily lives, and child neglect in "asocial families," treating these as more critical factors than income security, access to decent housing, healthcare, childcare, or addressing widening social and economic polarisation and precarity.

Achieving substantive poverty reduction and a shift from punitive welfare provisions requires social policies grounded in solidarity and broader redistribution. For now, this remains a utopian proposition, as the prevailing "common sense" emphasises responsibilising the poor into self-regulating, entrepreneurial subjects. However, without addressing the broader structural conditions that perpetuate marginalisation, the team-based approach risks evolving into increasingly authoritarian forms of neoliberal governance.

Attempts to change individual motivation and behaviour inevitably generate widespread and diffuse resistance from the recalcitrant poor. Consequently, supervision by teams of experts can quickly evolve into a "cat-and-mouse game," as clients may find new ways to avoid, resist, or exploit welfare provisions. This, in turn, could lead to demands for new rounds of disciplinary reforms, potentially resulting in the evolution of what James Poulos (2014) referred to as "pink authoritarianism" in social assistance provision. This approach involves increasingly intrusive surveillance and intervention by regulatory state authorities into ever more intimate aspects of everyday life, ostensibly in the name of promoting self-reliance, health, and well-being for clients and their children, without resorting to oppressive and brutal police-state tactics.

There are indications that social policy in Lithuania is already moving in this direction. For instance, the most recent pension reforms, rather than mandating investments in private pension funds, employ a libertarian-paternalistic governance approach to "nudge" taxpayers into making such investments (Juska, 2021).

References

Bohle, D., & Greskovits, B. (2007). Neoliberalism, embedded neoliberalism and neocorporatism: Towards transnational capitalism in Central-Eastern Europe. *West European Politics, 30*(3), 443–466. https://doi.org/10.1080/01402380701276287

Connell, K., & Hilton, M. (2016). *Cultural studies 50 years on: History, practice and politics*. Rowman & Littlefield Publishers.

Emigh, R. J., & Szelényi, I. (2001). *Poverty, ethnicity, and gender in Eastern Europe during the market transition*. Praeger.

Esping-Andersen, G. (1996). *Welfare states in transition: National adaptations in global economies*. Sage Publications.

Genov, N. (1998). *Central and Eastern Europe: Continuing transformation*. UNESCO-MOST, Friedrich-Ebert Foundation.

Gramsci, A. (1973). *Letters from prison*. Harper and Row.

Grinspun, A. (2001). *Choices for the poor: Lessons from national poverty strategies*. United Nations Publications.

Hall, S., Critcher, C., Jefferson, T., Clarke, J., & Roberts, B. (2013). *Policing the crisis: Mugging, the state, and law and order*. Macmillan International.

Hall, S., & O'Shea, A. (2013). Common-sense neoliberalism. *Soundings: A Journal of Politics and Culture, 55* (Winter), 8–24.

Hancock, A. M. (2004). *The politics of disgust: The public identity of the welfare queen*. New York University Press.

Hills, J. (2015). *The welfare myth of them and us*. Policy Press.

Hutton, S., & Redmond, G. (2000). *Poverty in transition economies* (Routledge studies of societies in transition; Vol. 14). Routledge.

Jensen, T. (2018). *Parenting the crisis: The cultural politics of parent-blame*. Policy Press.

Juska, A. (2007). Discourses on rurality in post-socialist news media: The case of Lithuania's leading daily *Lietuvos Rytas*. *Journal of Rural Studies, 23*(2), 238–253. https://doi.org/10.1016/j.jrurstud.2006.02.003

Juska, A. (2021). A shift to libertarian paternalism in old-age income security: Discourses on pension privatization reforms in Lithuania 2016–2018. *International Social Security Review, 74*(2), 3–24. https://doi.org/10.1111/issr.12253

Juska, A., & Johnstone, P. (2004). The symbiosis of politics and crime in Lithuania. *Journal of Baltic Studies, 35*(4), 346–359.

Kolodko, G. (2002). *From shock to therapy: The political economy of postsocialist transformation*. Oxford University Press.

Mahoney, J. (2000). Path dependence in historical sociology. *Theory and Society, 29*(4), 507–548.

Moynihan, P. (1965). *The Negro family: The case for national action*. Department's Office of Policy Planning and Review. Retrieved May 15, 2025, from https://www.dol.gov/general/aboutdol/history/webid-moynihan

Myrdal, G. (1965). *Challenge to affluence*. Vintage Books.

Pierson, P. (2000). Increasing returns, path dependence, and the study of politics. *American Political Science Review, 94*(2), 251–267.

Poulos, J. (2014). Pink police state: An anatomy of the new American regime. *Society, 51*, 274–281.

Rehm, J., Rovira, P., Jiang, H., Lange, S., Shield, K. D., Tran, A., & Štelemėkas, M. (2024). Trends of alcohol-attributable deaths in Lithuania 2001–2021: Epidemiology and policy conclusions. *BMC Public Health, 24*(774), 1–9. Retrieved May 15, 2025, from https://doi.org/10.1186/s12889-024-18237-y

Seimas of the Republic of Lithuania. (1996). Law on Social Services of the Republic of Lithuania No. I-1579, 9 October. *Official Gazette*. Retrieved May 15, 2025, from http://www3.lrs.lt/pls/inter3/oldsearch.preps2?a=32093&b=

Seimas of the Republic of Lithuania. (2006). Law on Social Services of the Republic of Lithuania No. X-493, 19 January. *Official Gazette*. Retrieved May 15, 2025, from http://www3.lrs.lt/pls/inter2/dokpaieska.showdoc_l?p_id=270342&p_query=&p_tr2=

Starkeviciute, M. (1998). Ekonomika. In: Socialinės politikos grupė (ed.) *Pranešimas apie žmogaus socialinę raidą Lietuvoje* (pp. 25–38). UNDP.

Tarkowska, E. (1999). In search of an underclass in Poland. *Polish Sociological Review, 129*, 3–16.

UNDP, United Nations Development Programme. Regional Bureau for Europe and CIS. (1998). *Poverty in Transition?* United Nations Publications.

UNDP, United Nations Development Programme. Regional Bureau for Europe and CIS. (1999). *Transition 1999 – Human Development Report for Central and Eastern Europe and the CIS*. United Nations Publications.

von Hirschhausen, C. (1998). *New neighbours in Eastern Europe: Economic and industrial reform in Lithuania, Latvia and Estonia*. Presses des Mines.

Wacquant, L. (2009). *Punishing the poor: The neoliberal government of social insecurity*. Duke University Press.

Wacquant, L. (2022). *The invention of the 'Underclass': A study in the politics of knowledge*. Polity Press.

Zaleskienė, I. (1998). Asmuo, visuomenė ir valstybė. Socialinė atskirtis. In: Socialinės politikos grupė (ed.) *Pranešimas apie žmogaus socialinę raidą Lietuvoje* (pp. 17–23). UNDP.

Žalimienė, L., Poviliūnas, A., & Lazutka, R. (2015). Visuomenės grupių požiūris į socialinės pašalpos organizavimą kaip socialinės paramos politikos veiksnys. In: *Lietuvos socialinė raida. Užimtumo politikos ir socialinės pagalbos įtaka socialinei stratifikacijai* (pp. 104–127). Lietuvos socialinių tyrimų centras.

8

Technology and Future Trajectories of Punitivity: Lessons Learned from Selective Persecution of Online Offenders in Lithuania

Maryja Šupa, Vytautas Kaktinas, and Eglė Stankevičiūtė

Introduction

The notable decline in crime across the world in the 1990s (Tonry, 2014) was explained by some authors as the transformation of crime to online forms (Caneppele & Aebi, 2017; Lee, 2018) whose higher latency and liquidity may elude traditional forms of measuring crime levels. Reaction to online crime may not be properly integrated into the institutional processes in current criminal justice systems (Holt, 2018; Nouh et al., 2019), and law enforcement may lack the resources necessary to respond

M. Šupa (✉) · V. Kaktinas · E. Stankevičiūtė
Faculty of Philosophy, Institute of Sociology and Social Work, Department of Criminology, Vilnius University, Vilnius, Lithuania
e-mail: maryja.supa@fsf.vu.lt

V. Kaktinas
e-mail: vytautas.kaktinas@fsf.stud.vu.lt

E. Stankevičiūtė
e-mail: egle.stankeviciute@fsf.stud.vu.lt

A. Dobryninas and S. Nikartas (eds.), *Understanding Crime Control and Punishment in Lithuania*, Crime Prevention and Security Management,
https://doi.org/10.1007/978-3-032-05538-5_8

to online crime appropriately (Hadlington et al., 2021), resulting in specific forms of selectivity as to which online crime cases are registered, investigated, and brought to court (Cai et al., 2018; Smith et al., 2004), as well as extra-legal factors of selectivity, such as offender demographics, that determine potential differences in case outcomes (Dawei, 2021).

Online crime presents further problems for sentencing (Mason, 2006), which require answers to questions such as, how should the severity of online crime be determined, does the online nature of the crime change its seriousness in comparison to similar offline crimes, the role of experts in technical knowledge in explaining the essence of the crime and evaluating evidence. While these questions indicate there may be significant differences between outcomes in online and offline crime cases, sentencing differences have also been explained by judicial differences rather than the online nature of the crime(s) (Smith et al., 2004). To date, there is an ongoing discussion about factors appropriately describing the selectivity across criminal justice systems on online crime cases and its impact (Gřivna & Drápal, 2019; Dawei, 2021; Hartel et al., 2022).

Building upon the previous point, another significant debate is about the global or transnational nature of many (but not all) online crimes and how they are managed at the local level. Writing about online crime as far back as 2001, Snyder put forward that "a state-based perspective (…) is no longer appropriate or helpful in the context of globalisation" (Snyder, 2017, p. 254). However, as some authors point out, locally enacted online offences also exist, and there is a distinction between their types, offenders, targets, and modus operandi (e.g. Leukfeldt et al., 2017). Likewise, on the political and public meaning of online crime, some authors posit that political concern about online crime and criminal justice is diminished (Dockley, 2017). Others, in contrast, point out the heated (geo)political discussions about online security, and conflation of online crime with state security and foreign affairs (Brenner, 2006; Maskun et al., 2020). Therefore, the divide between transnational and local online crime is a useful point of analysis to understand the complex interrelation between (online) crime, politics, and globalisation.

The political and mediated reality of online crime, affecting the public imaginary, may stand in contrast to the institutional realities of online crime, in particular, the cases contained by the criminal justice system.

New technologies are also connected to innovations in social control and modes of governmentality which are inherent themes in the critique of the criminal justice system (Carvalho & Norrie, 2017). Thus, from a critical perspective, we feel the need to explore on a deeper level the disparities between criminal offences defined as ideal legal categories and how they are constructed in the criminal justice system, in order to establish the potential for novel means of social control to emerge.

The specific case of societies undergoing post-communist and post-socialist transformations is pertinent because the development and spread of computers and internet access occurred during a relatively short period of time after the dissolution of the Soviet Union in 1991. Having a clear starting point provides the possibility to observe the development of infrastructures, legal frameworks, and user experiences, and analyse the related development of new practices of social control. Within this broader perspective, we set out to contribute to the following debates: the selectivity and bias of criminal justice systems in online crime cases, the tension between online crimes carried out as local or transnational endeavours, and the implications of the institutional construction of online crime to innovations in social control.

Theoretical Perspectives on Online Offending in Somewhat Late Modern Flair

The theoretical underpinning of much online offending research in criminology is dominated by the positivist or neo-classical paradigm. It is based on the rational choice approach, routine (cyber) activity theory, and applications of situational crime prevention to "virtual" spaces (Maimon & Louderback, 2019). To a lesser extent, critical (Stratton et al., 2017), cultural (Yar, 2018) approaches are present, as well as voices from the (digital) Global South (Cross, 2018). This chapter focuses on aspects of punitivity and institutionalised justice which are more in line with theoretical frameworks focused explicitly on social control in late modern societies. We will specifically discuss Foucauldian and Deleuzian takes on social control that may be useful in explaining the empirical realities of the social control of online offending.

Foucault is an appropriate starting point in this theoretical debate because of his extensive work on those aspects of social control which permeate all forms of social interactions and societal structures. In the Foucauldian tradition, three entangled modalities of power—sovereign, disciplinary, and biopolitical—underlie patterns of social control that dominate in each society at a particular point in time. While sovereign power is reminiscent of its pre-modern origins and mostly relegated to the legal sphere (Foucault, 2007, p. 6), discipline and biopolitics explain trends in late modern societies at large. Discipline, enacted as control of individual bodies, is the microsocial counterpart of the macrosocial biopolitical control of populations. Metaphors are often used to describe biopolitics, such as controlling flows and promoting circulation (Foucault, 2007, pp. 6–42), norms as a form of risk management (Foucault, 2007, pp. 60–63), and planning and regulation (Foucault, 2007). The digital realm may be considered one of the several key biopolitical milieus (along with, for example, biotechnology itself, or physical spaces of globalised migration). In it, population is the vast information flow, abstracted from billions of individual bodies and circulated globally.

Biopolitical social control in the Foucauldian paradigm is enacted as *security*, contrasting with the other modalities, law and discipline. It illustrates many characteristics observed in contemporary security practices, such as integrating future developments into present-day designs, extracting maximum use and minimising harm, calculating probabilities to avert risk, and working in given conditions and with materials at hand (Foucault, 2007, pp. 18–20). The ultimate goal of biopolitical social control is *normalisation*, defined as a reduction of "deviant normalities" (Foucault, 2007, pp. 60–61). It is based on a vision of quantified representation of individuals integrated into a collective, risk identification leading to identification of danger, and natural or artificial mitigation of sudden crisis situations (Foucault, 2007, pp. 60–61). Both legal sovereignty and discipline, as modalities of social control, have a clearly expressed spatial dimension. In contrast, biopolitics, while also applicable to certain types of spaces and spatial control, is much better equipped to describe social control in terms of moving data. Indeed, the very nature of biopolitics implies that power structures feed on data and process it to ensure continuous cycles of normalisation.

In a similar manner, Deleuze has discussed *societies of control*, emphasising the role of *machines* as expressions of social control (Deleuze, 2017). In Deleuze's interpretation, late modern societies are characterised by social control as "short-term and of rapid rates of turnover", reflecting the needs of profit-oriented markets (Deleuze, 2017, p. 6). He also insists that social control must be studied as a socio-technological phenomenon (Deleuze, 2017, p. 7). While Deleuze only referred to Foucault's disciplinary societies in his essay, the traits he suggested for societies of control are closely reminiscent of Foucault's biopolitics. As in Foucault's case of quantified individuals, Deleuze suggests *dividuals*—individuals fragmented into multiple datasets.

This perspective, reflecting the development of communication technology in the early 1990s, already sets the stage for interpreting human agency in the context of continuous participation in information flows: as producers, consumers, data subjects, data objects, and nodal points in algorithmic determination of risk and utility (for rereadings of Deleuze in a more contemporary perspective see, e.g. Bruno & Rodríguez, 2022; Brusseau, 2020). However, Deleuze's *dividuals*, characterised as individuals participating in online interactions scattered across different online platforms and services, become consolidated back into a *quantified self*: an entity whose data is unified across multiple globally operating platforms and potentially also shared with state institutions in an ever-growing locus of data-driven power.

In contrast to optimistic promises conceptualised in such visions as McLuhan's global village (McLuhan, 1966) or Castells' networked society (Castells, 1997), the French perspective presents social control as inevitable and ingrained into the fabric of the relation between late modern states and individuals. The question of punitivity in such relations remains open, as it is often emphasised that biopolitical social control is manipulative and reliant on cancellation rather than obedience, working in an even more covert manner than discipline. However, one caveat of this perspective is that authors present technology as a given, as a practical means for the operation of power, rather than as a developing and changing field. Technological changes and innovations, therefore, are important aspects to consider when analysing developments of social control: not just as a tool, but a sign of mixing and remixing different modalities of power.

From the very practical point of view of theory explaining how new technology is adapted, Rogers' (2003) curve is a useful conceptual tool to illustrate how systems of social control adapt to changes in socio-technical milieus. While a technology spreads among innovators and early adopters, there are few set rules about its usage. Rather, the rules and limits are both developed and intensely discussed by the communities of practice focused on developing and testing the limits of the innovation. While some actions may be considered deviant (such as unauthorised access to telephone and computer networks in the 1970s and 1980s), they are seldom clearly regulated or legislated, and most often target the technology itself. Sanctions and punishments depend almost entirely on community reaction and informal norms. Only in rare cases do dedicated personalities from law enforcement take on novel technological cases (one of the best-known examples being T. Shimomura's personal hunt for renowned hacker K. Mitnick).

A new stage of development begins when a technology moves to mainstream usage, corresponding to Rogers' early and late majority, and becomes available to a larger part of society. It then becomes an attractive target for offenders using the technology as a tool for conducting regular offences such as theft, sexual deviance, or personal attacks, at a greater scale, speed, or convenience. At the same time, legislating bodies may come under pressure to regulate previously unregulated or under-regulated activities, and pass the baton on to the criminal justice system to adapt and carry out the new requirements. The birth of social control targeting a specific technological field is therefore shifted in relation to the development of the technology itself. The moment when a technology enters mainstream operation, it becomes the object of social control, and specific reactive patterns emerge in law enforcement, prosecution, and judiciary bodies.

How do social and institutional control systems adapt to the current development of emerging technologies? In a disciplinary and biopolitical world, in the society of control, what is the inflexion point where the criminal justice system adapts the existing ideological framework of social control to a seemingly novel and untamed field? This is precisely the question explored in the following sections using historical and contemporary evidence from the case of Lithuania.

Lithuanian Regulation, Policy, and Persecution in Online Offending from the Ground Up

Lithuania, during the period between the restoration of independence in 1990 and entry into the European Union in 2004, may be characterised as a society in transition. The period was characterised by rapid social, economic, political, and cultural change on one hand, and continuation of certain Soviet-era practices on the other hand, resulting in what Šaulauskas calls a development path combining continuation and imitation, rather than innovation (Šaulauskas, 1998). With the change in the system, it was inherently necessary to change the legal framework of the newly independent state. Although the legislative processes since 1990 have been rapid (Piesliakas, 2004), preparing the new Criminal Code took a decade. During the transitional period, until the new Criminal Code of the Republic of Lithuania came into effect in 2003, the Criminal Code of the Lithuanian Soviet Socialist Republic of 1961 was still in effect. However, it was subject to several changes and modifications.

According to Sakalauskas, it is challenging to find the criteria for the formation of an integrated criminal policy process in Lithuania (Sakalauskas et al., 2012). The restored independent Republic of Lithuania's criminal policy can be characterised by liberalisation tendencies and the maintenance of rather repressive punitivity. Although efforts have been made to adapt to international standards of the time and Western European trends towards lighter sentences, frequent imposition of custodial sentences, long periods of imprisonment and over-incarceration still prevailed. Despite recognising the importance of natural human rights and freedoms in criminal law, the abolition of the death penalty in Lithuania did not occur until 1998 (as a condition for Lithuania's accession to the European Union).

In the background of these processes, corporations, state institutions, and individuals gradually gained access to the internet. Figure 8.1 shows how the proportion of homes connected to the internet has increased from 2% in 2000 to 59% in 2010. This rapid expansion of the internet in the space of a mere 10 years directly corresponds to Rogers' innovation adoption curve. As such, it reflects the transformation from the internet as a niche resource used by innovators to a mass commodity available to both the early and late majority.

Therefore, the decade marked a seminal time, also from a legal perspective. The early days of the internet in Lithuania put a strain on law enforcement because few laws could be applied to online and computer-dependent offending. The first computer-dependent offence in Lithuania occurred in 1992, when an Ignalina atomic power plant employee modified the code of the power plant controller software "Titan". The modified program was supposed to manipulate data about the operation of the nuclear reactors. When the employee's case was brought to court, there were no appropriate articles in the Criminal Code

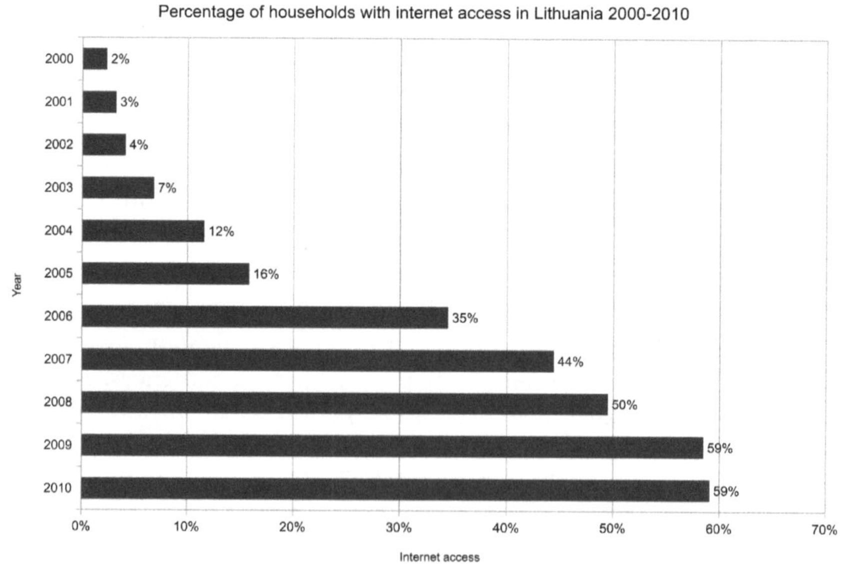

Fig. 8.1 Percentage of households with internet access in Lithuania, 2000–2010

to deal with the modification of computer programs. The article that was applied concerned damage to state property, but this particular article could only be applied due to the fact that the employer indeed *was* a critically significant state-owned facility (Leichteris, 1999).

This case illustrates both the fact that offending was only possible because the perpetrator had access to a rare and highly specialised technology. Additionally, its work as an early innovator and the absence of appropriate legislation to define the offence were key circumstances to success. According to oral history,[1] informal means of reacting to computer-dependent offending included system administrators from corporations inviting perpetrators to hold informal conversations, undercover law enforcement officials observing and sometimes participating in local online hacking forums, and, allegedly, fights (in specific cases of conflicts about internet traffic in student dormitories).

The next stage of development, marking the transformation from innovators to early majority, coincided with adopting the new Criminal Code in 2003. The new Criminal Code included Section 30, which described "Offences against informatics", later renamed to "Offences against security of electronic data and information systems" and included three articles pertaining to computer-dependent offending. Adopting this code marked a new era for law enforcement working with online offences.

In 2007, the focus of Section 30 shifted towards the security of information systems and their data instead of computer information and its programs. These changes also included a shift to virtues that the Criminal Code had to defend, and included the aspect of the security of national information systems and their data. Additionally, in 2007, the Criminal Code clearly separated the liability for illicit data disposal on a micro scale. These changes indicated separate focuses of the Criminal Code on the macro and micro levels of online offending. Finally, over 17 years until 2024, Section 30 of the Criminal Code has undergone a few minor changes, which increased the severity of incarceration by a couple of years for both computer-dependent and computer-assisted offences.

[1] From informal personal communication with members of the 1990s-2000s computer underground in Lithuania.

These changes to how online offending was defined in the Criminal Code show that, as the internet penetration moved from the early to the late majority stage, a refined understanding of computer-dependent offending has evolved and was integrated into the legal system. To a large extent, these changes were facilitated by the ratification of the Budapest Convention in 2004. At the same time, there was a movement away from informal means of social control in reaction to online offending. Instead, official law enforcement practices were expected to solve the growing problem of computer-dependent crime, and the need to develop official policy towards online offending became apparent.

For every year since 2012, the Public Prosecutor's Office has included computer-dependent crime on its list of priority areas. In its annual reports, the Public Prosecutor's Office emphasises investment in solutions for improving and successfully advancing online offending cases.

Since 2017, reports have highlighted a decrease in the effectiveness of investigations into these crimes and overall lengthy pre-trial investigations (usually lasting about 1 year). The main challenges identified in the reports: prolonged investigations of technological and electronic devices, high number of pre-trial investigations, problems of international cooperation between institutions (lengthy response times to requests for legal assistance), the growing gap between the theoretical knowledge and practical skills of law enforcement officers, and the sophisticated and transnational nature of these crimes. Law enforcement agencies address these problems by organising training for officers and developing methodological guidelines for investigating these crimes. A general pattern reflecting selectivity can be observed—the cases routinely presented in the reports do not correspond to the typical cases: various success stories (e.g. dismantling of criminal networks operating transnationally or uncovering large-scale data breaches) tend to appear in the reports rather than those prosecuted to a greater extent.

Despite being on the priority list of the Prosecutor's office, the reality of online offending cases brought to court and prosecuted paints a different portrait of dominant forms of offending and offenders. An analysis of actual cases brought to court with at least one of the articles from Sect. 30 of the Criminal Code in the years 2017–2021 shows clear trends of criminal justice selectivity in the prosecuted cases. A typical "online offence" in Lithuanian court case reality consists of illegal access to an IT system, in conjunction with fraud, illicit online payment, or illicit document possession (Šupa et al., 2023, p. 7).

A deeper dig into such cases reveals that rather than technologically advanced hacking to gain access, offenders typically use social engineering techniques to trick the victims out of their credentials, and then use them to log into online payment services or other online systems. Less than 10% of all prosecuted cases were related to offences involving computers and networks that did not co-occur with some form of financial fraud. Motives of financial gain accounted for 88% of all cases, with few instances of targeting individuals, IT systems, databases, or mixed targets (Šupa, 2023, p. 8). A typical online offender *prosecuted* in Lithuania operated single-handedly (82% of all cases), was male (77% of all cases), had completed secondary school education or less, including elementary school only (52% of all cases), and typically unemployed at the time of offending (47% of all cases) (Šupa et al., 2023, p. 8). A typical offence might be, for instance, gaining access to another person's payment card and PIN code, and taking out cash at the ATM, or using a former romantic partner's known social network password to post insulting messages.

The selectivity in Lithuanian online offending cases is characterised by both under-prosecution and over-prosecution. On one hand, technologically sophisticated and highly harmful offences most often remain uninvestigated. On the other hand, the overwhelming majority of cases brought to court and sentenced involve repeated scams (in most cases based on social engineering rather than technical skills) or other relatively minor cases. Selectivity is further apparent because 40% of prosecuted offenders have been previously convicted, and 66% had a lifetime history of offending, while 15% committed the offence while serving a prison sentence (Šupa, 2023, 9). This starkly contrasts with how the Public Prosecutor's Office presents online offending, which conveys images of highly skilled, international offenders working in organised groups (Public Prosecutor's Office, 2017, p. 23, 2019, pp. 20–21, 2022, pp. 17–18). While it is plausible that technologically savvy, computer-dependent online offending is conducted by offenders based in Lithuania or targeting victims based in Lithuania, there is little direct evidence of such cases reaching courts and getting prosecuted.

In "Chemical Illusions: Anthology of Cyberpunk Tales from Eastern Europe", the Bulgarian futurist and "Cyberpunk manifesto" author Christian As. Kirtchev's character mused about the fact that criminal justice is selective: "those who are outlaws are the poor" (Kirtchev, 2009, p. 68). Prison sentences are imposed in 73% of all cases labelled under online offending, with the most frequent sentence length ranging from 6 to 86 months (Šupa, 2023, 11). In conjunction with the proportion of supposed online offenders who have previous experience of the prison system, this statistic is an eloquent sign of harsh punitivity. It is directed at the usual suspects, who are ever cycling through the revolving door of the criminal justice system. These perpetrators, suitable for punishment, bear little resemblance to the technologically adept masters of machines alluded to in policy documents.

Innovations in Social Control: The Perspective of Emerging Technologies

Lithuania's case demonstrates that criminalising and penalising online offences has followed a clear-cut trajectory so far. The prosecution of online offending cases in Lithuania reveals three characteristics of social control in response to technological changes: (1) A specific form of selectivity, focusing on technically unskilled offences, often conducted by individuals already known to the criminal justice system. (2) A specific form of tension between the locality of the offences and the globality of the problem as presented in institutional public discourse. (3) A specific trajectory of adapting means of social control to new technologies with implications for future technological developments.

Criminal justice institutions in Lithuania frame the selectivity of online offences and persecution in official discourse as a result of a lack of resources. However, rather than failure to prosecute, this perceived lack of resources results in targeting and prosecuting a specific group of offenders. They operate alone rather than in groups, more often lack professional or tertiary education, are unemployed, and were previously convicted. This strategy shows the necessity to carry out and justify social control, even if it is carried out under limited conditions. The severity of offences is determined rather more often by their repeated nature, the suspect's previous criminal history, and peculiarities of local relationships (in case of offending targeting current or former romantic partners or family members). Expert knowledge, which in classical Foucauldian terms serves as a means of gatekeeping normality, has also been redefined. Rather than expertise in technology, the process and outcome of Lithuanian online offending cases depend on expertise in the usual perpetrators and access to the means of easily and effectively bringing them back into the criminal justice system.

This situation serves as an illustration of the indivisible *socio-cultural* nature of social control in one contemporary society. The suspects are labelled as online offenders because they are found guilty of breaching the precise articles from the Criminal Code that define online offending, when computers and networks are targets of offences. However, they become online offenders by virtue of their *social* status, not *technological* skills. The division between offline and online forms of offending becomes a grey area, where stereotypical offenders—internationally based and operating in organised groups, technically skilled, taking advantage of the scale and reach of global networks—may be replaced by single-handedly operating non-technical opportunists, many of them entering and exiting the revolving doors of criminal justice institutions.

As discussed in the previous section, there is a marked disparity between priorities declared by law enforcement institutions and actual contributions to the persecution of online offending. On the one hand, the prosecution office declares technically complex online offences a priority, requiring investment in appropriate tools and posing significant challenges. However, there is little trace of these investments and challenges in actual persecuted cases. In practice, they are simple, easily reachable, and often involve well-known offenders.

The public stance of law enforcement institutions reflects their willingness to participate in the discourse of online offending as a supra-national and complex set of risk-bearing events. High political concern about online offending is also apparent in its ties to national (cyber)security, with geopolitical implications referring to politically backed malicious actors from around the world, in Lithuania's case, most often attributed to Russia (NCSC, 2023). Moreover, the institutions demonstrate awareness of the technologically complex global nature of online offending (Public Prosecutor's Office, 2016, pp. 27–28, 2021, pp. 20–21, 2023, p. 15). Thus, they reproduce the dominant discourse in appropriate biopolitical terms.

However, the selectivity of institutional activities on the practical level shows that strategic global urgency is complemented and superseded by a local cycle of revolving-door tactics. They illustrated the interchangeability of the social and technical orientations of social control. The initial theoretical premise is that the mass adaptation of new technologies and innovations in offending automatically implies a novel means of social control.

The case of Lithuania and its comparison to several similar research results from other countries show that the trajectories of how social control develops may follow different patterns. As in Lithuania, old means of social control may be applied to new technologies, echoed by experience from other states with a post-Soviet or post-socialist legacy. Evidence to this effect is present in Estonia (Kikerpill, 2019) and Czechia (Drápal, 2018). Specific conditions are required to allow law enforcement to embrace new means of social control. Additionally, new circumstances are needed to apply them to new technological developments, as is apparent, for example, in the description of the types of online offences prosecuted in the Netherlands (Leukfeldt et al., 2017).

In a Deleuzian vein, the police need access to "the machine" to achieve better results in controlling deviance. However, they fall back on their existing access to the machinery of criminal justice when the former is unattainable. On the surface, there seems to be a contradiction in applying old social control to new technologies. It is a logical enactment of the socio-technical continuum in societies of control. They reflect the operational logics of law enforcement practice and emphasise the necessity of carrying out social control despite seeming resource limitations. The latter does not hinder institutions' participation in the discourse of complex global offending processes.

Concluding Remarks

In the Lithuanian case, the apparent priority given to online offending in policy documents starkly contrasts with the specific cases registered and heard in court. The latter shows a high level of selectivity typical of both the offences and the offenders prosecuted. Technologically sophisticated and highly harmful offences remain uninvestigated, while the usual suspects, such as repeated socially engineered scams or secondary school students involved in relatively minor cases, are over-prosecuted. This results in a specific pattern of technologically convenient persecution also found in other post-socialist states.

This finding has two further implications. Firstly, it will discuss adaptation to technological changes regarding old means of committing offences, and secondly, it will discuss the prospective adaptation to technological changes inherent in new technological paradigms. It is the case that if old means of social control are applied to new technologies, then the same will be applicable for offences facilitated by previous generations of technology (it may be noted that pure, non-technological offending is an exceptional state rather than the rule). Moreover, the (dis)ability to adapt to novel technologies in social control also implies the point on the law enforcement institutions' position on Rogers' technology adaptation curve. Thus, their skill in applying novel means of social control to old technologies of offending is also questionable.

The case of upcoming technological cycles and adaptation of social controls is pertinent since it is connected to questions of changing power relations (it is seen either as the modern state or the next iteration of a power entity). And changes of power within its subjects (again, either as modern individuals or more fluid networks of human and non-human actors). Developing machine learning algorithms, including adversary machine learning, signifies further disparities in the global reach, scale, and velocity of offending in the information technology cycle.

Further developments in the digitisation of objects and living organisms—the internet of things, internet of vehicles, machine-to-machine communication, internet of bodies, internet of nature—further exacerbate the challenges of the spreading reach of remote offending, and especially the physical impact of remotely enacting offences. In the socio-technological continuum, emphasis eventually shifts back from the technological to the social in terms of impact, visibility, and proximity, as mass-consumed technologies shift to invisible and lucid forms of networking. In this context, finding and prosecuting suitable perpetrators oriented at petty local offences will reinforce selectivity and application of existing well-known prosecution patterns.

The transfer of connectivity to the Internet of Bodies and Internet of Nature serves as a transition phase for the upcoming cycle of biotechnology. They include developments in wearable devices for digital health, synthetic biology, biological material science, genomics, proteomics, and other emerging forms of bioengineering. In terms of adoption of innovations, these are still in the innovator and early adopter stage. It is limited in access to lab developments and grass-roots biohacking communities. While recent developments in green criminology grapple with reversing the anthropocentric paradigm of both scientific research and institutional approaches to societal relations with nature, the future is already moving on to discussions of the possible "criminogenic potential" of emerging biotech (Elgabry et al., 2020).

The interchange of theory and methods between digital criminology and green criminology is still in its nascent stages. It indicates that the criminological discourse still has steps to take to understand—in the sense of criminological *Verstehen* (as per Ferrell, 1997) the cultural, societal, and punitive developments that are already germinating and will become apparent once the relevant technologies hit mass adoption. They will emerge with their own patterns of offending and social control. Providing direct access to both populations, the future digital and biotechnological milieus will serve as loci of legitimised means for (il)licit technology (ab)use. The shifting access from what is currently labelled socio-technical to the socio-bio-digital machinery may serve as a logical continuation of biopolitical risk management of flow—or as a breaking point for new forms of power to emerge.

References

Brenner, S. W. (2006). Cybercrime jurisdiction. *Crime, Law & Social Change, 46*(4–5), 189–206. https://doi.org/10.1007/s10611-007-9063-7(Accessed: 15May2025)

Bruno, F., & Rodríguez, P. M. (2022). The dividual: Digital practices and biotechnologies. *Theory, Culture & Society, 39*(3), 27–50. https://doi.org/10.1177/02632764211029356(Accessed:15May2025)

Brusseau, J. (2020). Deleuze's postscript on the societies of control: Updated for big data and predictive analytics. *Theoria, 67*(164), 1–25. https://doi.org/10.3167/th.2020.6716401(Accessed:15May2025)

Cai, T., Du, L., Xin, Y., & Chang, L. Y. (2018). Characteristics of cybercrimes: Evidence from Chinese judgment documents. *Police Practice & Research, 19*, 582–595. https://doi.org/10.1080/15614263.2018.1507895(Accessed:15May2025)

Caneppele, S., & Aebi, M. F. (2017). Crime drop or police recording flop? On the relationship between the decrease of offline crime and the increase of online and hybrid crimes. *Policing: A Journal of Policy & Practice, 13*(1), 66–79. Retrieved May 15, 2025, from https://doi.org/10.1093/police/pax055

Carvalho, H., & Norrie, A. (2017). In this interregnum: Dialectical themes in the critique of criminal justice. *Social & Legal Studies, 26*(6), 716–734. https://doi.org/10.1177/0964663917726839(Accessed:15May2025)

Castells, M. (1997). *The rise of the network society*. Blackwell.

Cross, C. (2018). Marginalized voices: The absence of Nigerian scholars in global examinations of online fraud. In K. Carrington, R. Hogg, J. Scott, & M. Sozzo (Eds.), *The Palgrave handbook of criminology and the global south* (pp. 261–280). Palgrave Macmillan.

Dawei, S. (2021). Sentencing disparity in China: A descriptive research on auxiliary cybercrime stipulated by Amendment IX of criminal law. *Iustum Aequum Salutare, 17*, 209–239.

Deleuze, G. (2017). Postscript on the societies of control. In C. Norris & D. Wilson (Eds.), *Surveillance, crime and social control* (pp. 35–39). Routledge. Retrieved May 15,2025, from https://doi.org/10.4324/9781315242002

Dockley, A. (2017). A chance to reimagine punishment and penality? *Social & Legal Studies, 28*(1), 118–123. https://doi.org/10.1177/0964663917746489(Accessed:15May2025)

Drápal, J. (2018). Sentencing disparities in the Czech Republic: Empirical evidence from post-communist Europe. *European Journal of Criminology, 17*(2), 151–174. https://doi.org/10.1177/1477370818773612(Accessed:15May2025)

Elgabry, M., Nesbeth, D., & Johnson, S. D. (2020). A systematic review of the criminogenic potential of synthetic biology and routes to future crime prevention. *Frontiers in Bioengineering & Biotechnology, 8*(571672), 1–18. https://doi.org/10.3389/fbioe.2020.571672(Accessed:15May2025)

Ferrell, J. (1997). Criminological Verstehen: Inside the immediacy of crime. *Justice Quarterly, 14*(1), 3–23. https://doi.org/10.1080/07418829700093201(Accessed:15May2025)

Foucault, M. (2007). *Security, territory, population: Lectures at the Collège de France 1977–1978*. M. Senellart & A. Fontana (Eds.). Picador. Retrieved May 15, 2025, from https://doi.org/10.1057/9780230245075(Accessed:15May2025)

Gřivna, T., & Drápal, J. (2019). Attacks on the confidentiality, integrity and availability of data and computer systems in the criminal case law of the Czech Republic. *Digital Investigation, 28*, 1–13. https://doi.org/10.1016/j.diin.2018.12.002(Accessed:15May2025)

Hadlington, L., Lumsden, K., Black, A., & Ferra, F. (2021). A qualitative exploration of police officers' experiences, challenges, and perceptions of cybercrime. *Policing, 15*(1), 34–43. https://doi.org/10.1093/police/pay090(Accessed:15May2025)

Hartel, P., van Wegberg, R., & van Staalduinen, M. (2022). Investigating sentence severity with judicial open data: A case study on sentencing high-tech crime in the Dutch criminal justice system. *European Journal on Criminal Policy & Research, 29*, 579–599. https://doi.org/10.1007/s10610-021-09503-5. (Accessed 15 May, 2025).

Holt, T. J. (2018). Regulating cybercrime through law enforcement and industry mechanisms. *Annals of the American Academy of Political & Social Science, 679*(1), 140–157. https://doi.org/10.1177/0002716218783679(Accessed:15May2025)

Kikerpill, K. (2019). Work, prey, love: A critical analysis of Estonian cybercrime case law 2014–2019. *Proceedings of the Estonian Academy of Security Sciences, 18*.

Kirtchev, C. A. (2009). *Chemical illusions: Anthology of cyberpunk tales from Eastern Europe*. CreateSpace Independent Publishing Platform.

Lee, M. (2018). Crime and the cyber periphery: Criminological theory beyond time and space. In K. Carrington, R. Hogg, J. Scott, & M. Sozzo, (Eds.),

The Palgrave handbook of criminology and the global south (pp. 223–244). Palgrave. Retrieved May 15, 2025, from https://doi.org/10.1007/978-3-319-65021-0

Leichteris, E. (1999). *Kompiuterinės technikos panaudojimas kaip nusikaltimų padarymo būdas. Thesis.* Vilniaus universitetas.

Leukfeldt, E. R., Kleemans, E. R., & Stol, W. P. (2017). A typology of cybercriminal networks: From low-tech all-rounders to high-tech specialists. *Crime, Law & Social Change, 67*(1), 21–37. https://doi.org/10.1007/s10611-016-9662-2(Accessed:15May2025)

Maimon, D., & Louderback, E. R. (2019). Cyber-dependent crimes: An interdisciplinary review. *Annual Review of Criminology, 2*(1), 191–216. https://doi.org/10.1146/annurev-criminol-032317-092057(Accessed:15May2025)

Maskun, A. N., Assidiq, H., Syafira, A., Napang, M., & Hendrapati, M. (2020). Qualifying cyber crime as crime of aggression in international law. *Journal of East Asia and International Law, 13*(2), 397–418. Retrieved May 15, 2025, from https://doi.org/10.14330/jeail.2020.13.2.08

Mason, D. R. (2006). Sentencing policy and procedure as applied to cyber crimes: A call for reconsideration and dialogue. *Mississippi Law Journal, 76*, 903–908.

McLuhan, M. (1966). *Understanding media: The extensions of man.* McGraw-Hill Book Co.

National Cybersecurity Center. (2023). *National Cybersecurity Report*. Retrieved May 15, 2025, from https://www.nksc.lt/doc/Nacionaline-kibernetinio-saugumo-ataskaita-2023.pdf

Nouh, M., Nurse, J. R. C., Webb, H., & Goldsmith, M. (2019). Cybercrime investigators are users too! Understanding the socio–technical challenges faced by law enforcement. In *Proceedings of the 2019 Workshop on Usable Security (USEC) at the Network and Distributed System Security Symposium (NDSS)* (pp. 1–11). Retrieved May 15, 2025, from https://doi.org/10.14722/usec.2019.23032

Piesliakas, V. (2004). Nusikalstamų veikų kvalifikavimo problemos, kylančios dėl baudžiamųjų įstatymų galiojimo laiko atžvilgiu. *Jurisprudencija, 60*(52), 12–30.

Public Prosecutor's Office of the Republic of Lithuania. (2012–2023). *Annual Reports.* Retrieved May 15, 2025, from https://prokuraturos.lt/lt/administracine-informacija/planavimo-dokumentai-ataskaitos/ataskaitos/138

Rogers, M. E. (2003). *Diffusion of innovations.* Free Press.

Sakalauskas, G., Bikelis, S., Kalpokas, V., & Pocienė, A. (2012). Baudžiamoji politika Lietuvoje: Tendencijos ir lyginamieji aspektai. *Teisės Instituto Mokslo Tyrimai, 8*, 1–168.

Šaulauskas, M. P. (1998). Postkomunistinės revoliucijos želmenys: Į postmodernią Lietuvą? *Sociologija. Mintis ir veiksmas, 2*(2), 77–94. Retrieved May 12, 2025, from SocMintVei.1998.2.6759

Smith, R., Grabosky, P., & Urbas, G. (2004). Cyber criminals on trial. *Criminal Justice Matters, 58*(1), 1–317. https://doi.org/10.1080/09627250408553240

Snyder, F. (2017). Sites of criminality and sites of governance. In D. S. Wall (Ed.), *Cyberspace crime*, 1st ed. (pp. 83–88). Routledge. Retrieved May 12, 2025, from https://doi.org/10.4324/9781315199627

Stratton, G., Powell, A., & Cameron, R. (2017). Crime and justice in digital society: Towards a 'digital criminology'? *International Journal for Crime, Justice and Social Democracy, 6*(2), 17–33. https://doi.org/10.5204/ijcjsd.v6i2.355(Accessed:12May2025)

Šupa, M., Kaktinas, V., & Rinkevičiūtė, A. (2023). Computer-dependent or computer-assisted? The social context of online crime in Lithuanian court judgements. *International Journal of Law, Crime and Justice, 73*(100577), 1–16. https://doi.org/10.1016/j.ijlcj.2023.100577(Accessed:12May2025)

Tonry, M. (2014). Why crime rates are falling throughout the Western world. *Crime and Justice, 43*(1), 1–63. Retrieved May 12, 2025, from 0192-3234/2014/0043-0007$10.00

Yar, M. (2018). Toward a cultural criminology of the internet. In K. F. Steinmetz & M. R. Nobles (Eds.), *Technocrime and criminological theory* (pp. 116–132). Routledge. Retrieved May 12, 2025, from https://doi.org/10.4324/9781315117249-8

9

Punishing Drug Users? A Sight at Lithuanian Drug Control Policy

Mindaugas Lankauskas

Introduction

"If it is true that a chain is only as strong as its weakest link, isn't it also true that a society is only as healthy as its sickest citizen and only as wealthy as its most deprived?" (Angelou, 1997). Although this quote addresses the grim reality faced by African Americans in the United States, it can also be applied to other marginalised social groups, such as drug users. When discussing how society views drug users and drug-related crime, "stigma" is a crucial concept that significantly influences societal attitudes and shapes drug control policies. More than 60 years ago, sociologist Goffman, in discussing different types of stigma, indicated that "...there are blemishes of individual character perceived as weak will, domineering or unnatural passions,

M. Lankauskas (✉)
Faculty of Philosophy, Institute of Sociology and Social Work, Department of Criminology, Vilnius University, Vilnius, Lithuania
e-mail: mindaugas.lankauskas@fsf.vu.lt

A. Dobryninas and S. Nikartas (eds.), *Understanding Crime Control and Punishment in Lithuania*, Crime Prevention and Security Management,
https://doi.org/10.1007/978-3-032-05538-5_9

treacherous and rigid beliefs, and dishonesty, these being inferred from a known record of, for example, mental disorder, imprisonment, addiction, alcoholism, homosexuality, unemployment, suicidal attempts, and radical political behaviour" (Goffman Erwing, 1963, p. 4). Stigma surrounding drug use and drug addiction appears to remain a significant issue in contemporary societies. For instance, according to Livingston et al. (2022), stigma produces a social context contributing to high rates of criminal justice involvement among people who use substances through inequitable social conditions, criminalisation of substances, and under-resourcing of substance use services. Substance use stigma is reinforced by harmful police practices, painful imprisonment experiences, and insufficient support offered to formerly incarcerated people living in the community (Livingston et al., 2022). Needless to say, there is a strong reliance on the criminal justice system's ability to curb drug use, despite evidence suggesting otherwise. Policies meant to prohibit or greatly suppress drugs present a paradox. Many policymakers portray and defend them vigorously as necessary to preserve public health and safety. Yet, the evidence suggests they have contributed directly and indirectly to lethal violence, communicable disease transmission, discrimination, forced displacement, unnecessary physical pain, and the undermining of people's right to health (Csete et al., 2016). In other words, the stigma attached to drug use significantly affects the lives of those who use drugs, and this should not be underestimated.

This chapter explores how punishment plays a central role in Lithuanian drug control policy, overshadowing rehabilitation efforts. To conduct this analysis, the author examined the provisions of Lithuanian criminal law concerning drug offences and relevant statistical data on drug use and drug-related crime. From the author's perspective, the emphasis on punitive measures in Lithuania could be a reflection of the stigmatisation of drug users. On the other hand, the precise reasons for the current legal *status quo* remain unclear and cannot be fully addressed within the scope of this brief chapter. However, plausible explanations can be found by considering research into the value system of Lithuanian society and its ongoing reckoning with its Soviet past. This chapter examines the current criminalisation of drug use in

Lithuania, the disproportionate impact of such criminalisation on individuals with addiction issues, and the over-reliance on incarceration as a response to drug offences. It highlights the urgent need for alternative sanctions and more compassionate, evidence-based approaches to addressing drug-related crime.

Illicit Drug Use: The Current State of Affairs

First, it is useful to glance at the data concerning illicit drug use in Lithuania. In the European context, Lithuania has always been a country with a comparatively low prevalence of illicit drug use. Conversely, it has consistently ranked among the top countries for alcohol consumption, ranking among the top countries globally in this regard. In 2013, the average consumption reached 15.6 litres of pure alcohol per person, representing a peak in this trend. In recent years, there has been a noticeable downward trend in alcohol consumption, although the figures remain relatively high. In 2020, the average consumption was 12.1 litres, with only three countries exceeding this figure: Latvia (12.9 litres), Georgia (14.4 litres), and Romania (16.8 litres) (World Health Organisation, 2024). If this downward trend in alcohol consumption continues in the future, other psychoactive substances may become more prevalent than they are now.

While the prevalence of illicit drug use among the general Lithuanian population remains relatively low, the number of young people engaging in drug use is gradually increasing. The issue of drug use among young people has become a prominent topic in the mass media. Recently, there have been numerous articles in the Lithuanian media portraying drug use among young people and in schools as an emerging and significant problem. For example, a recent article titled *Lithuania faces serious problem: drug addicts are getting younger and younger* emphasises that "drug use among minors is getting more and more popular, and the problem with their distribution and use in schools only continues to grow and worsen" (Zdanytė Gabija, 2023). Does such alarmist rhetoric reflect a genuinely growing social problem, or is it a case of moral panic escalated by mass media? If we want to search for the right answers, we should examine the most recently available data.

As shown in Fig. 9.1, the most recent data from a survey conducted in 2021 indicates that 14.1% of Lithuanian adults aged 15–64 have used illicit drugs at least once in their lifetime. Only seven European countries—Romania, Portugal, Greece, Bulgaria, Hungary, Türkiye, and Malta—reported lower lifetime prevalence rates of illicit drug use. This indicator was slightly or significantly higher in neighbouring countries, such as Latvia (16.8% in 2020), Poland (16.1% in 2018), and Estonia (25.4% in 2018). In contrast, Western European countries reported lifetime prevalence rates exceeding 30% (Netherlands, Italy, Germany, Denmark) and even surpassing 40% in some cases (Spain and France). In contrast, the prevalence of drug use among young adults (15–34 years old) in Lithuania increased from 17.8% in 2012 to 23.8% in 2021. Similarly, the use of drugs among the youngest adults (15–24 years old) increased from 14.5 to 22%. Therefore, the upward trend is noticeable and appears concerning. On the other hand, data from recent school pupil surveys appear more optimistic. According to the 2019 European School Survey Project on Alcohol and Other Drugs (ESPAD), 19% of Lithuanian students aged 15–16 had tried an illicit drug at least once in their lifetime, with 21% of boys and 18% of girls reporting such use. This was slightly above the European average, which stands at 17%. The majority of students who had used illicit drugs had used cannabis (representing 18% of the total student population). The proliferation of new psychoactive substances (NPS) is a concerning phenomenon. A relatively high proportion of pupils have tried them at least once in their lives. According to the data, 5.6% of all pupils reported having used NPS, including 4.8% of boys and 6.3% of girls (ESAPD group, 2020, 49–51; Rupšienė et al., 2020, p. 69). The most recent ESPAD survey, conducted in 2024, indicated a significant decrease in illicit drug use. In 2024, 13.3% of adolescents (11.3% of girls and 15.3% of boys) reported using illicit drugs (cannabis, ecstasy, amphetamine, methamphetamine, cocaine, crack, heroin, LSD, hallucinogenic mushrooms, GHB/GBL, or injecting drugs) at least once in their lifetime. This represents the lowest percentage recorded since 2003. Compared to 2019, the number of adolescents who have tried any drug at least once has decreased by 5.8 percentage points. Similarly, NPS also seem less popular, with only 3.7% of pupils reporting using such substances in 2024 (Rupšienė et al., 2024, pp. 60–63). As we can see, data from general population surveys and ESPAD surveys appear contradictory, with the former indicating an upward trend in illicit drug use among young people (15–24 years old) and the latter showing a downward trend among 15–16-year-old schoolchildren. Therefore, it is not possible to draw very strict conclusions about what to expect in the future.

Despite the comparatively low prevalence rates among the general population, drug users, particularly those suffering from severe addiction, constitute a significant proportion of the imprisoned population (Lankauskas, 2022). Maybe such a situation reflects a higher rate of "problem drug use"[2] compared to other countries? According to Goldstein's "tripartite framework", drugs and violence are seen as being related

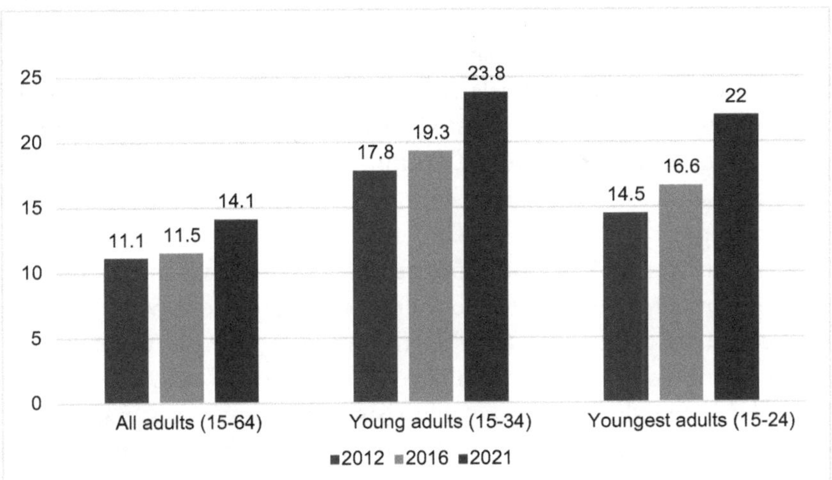

Fig. 9.1 Prevalence of illicit drug use in Lithuania (%)[1]

[1] According to the official data by the European Drug Agency (EMCDDA, 2023).

[2] "Problem drug use" is defined by the EMCDDA as "injecting drug use or long duration/regular use of opioids, cocaine and/or amphetamines". This definition specifically includes regular or long-term use of prescribed opioids such as methadone but does not include their rare or irregular use nor the use of other drugs, such as ecstasy or cannabis (European Union Drugs Agency, 2024).

in three possible ways: the psychopharmacological, the economically compulsive, and the systemic (Goldstein, 1985). It is widely acknowledged that the use of illicit substances, commonly referred to as "hard drugs" (i.e., opioids or strong stimulants), often leads to those mentioned above, "economically compulsive" engagement in criminal activities, primarily to finance the associated habit.

Data shows that, when it comes to opioid use, the situation in Lithuania is somewhat more concerning than the general prevalence of illicit drug use. For instance, the estimated number of opioid users is relatively high (3.92 per 1,000 residents in 2016), although not as high as in the United Kingdom (8.42 in 2014–2015), Finland, Italy, Ireland, and Austria (where recent surveys indicate rates higher than 6). In Latvia, the rate is also significant at 5.68 (2017). On the other hand, Poland has a very low rate of opioid use, with only 0.55 per 1,000 residents recorded in 2014. It is worth noting that it is impossible to determine precisely how many prisoners are incarcerated for crimes committed to finance their drug habit, as no such specific data exists. It can only be guessed that this number could be relatively high. In addition, Lithuania lacks programmes such as heroin-assisted treatment, leaving addicted users of opiates or opioids with limited options. For those without significant financial resources, criminal activity often becomes the only means to acquire drugs.

So far, Lithuania does not appear to be a country with a serious drug use problem; prevalence rates for illicit drug use are low compared to other countries in Europe and North America. On the other hand, it should be noted that the prevalence of illicit drug use among young people has been slowly but steadily rising in recent years, which could pose a significant challenge in the future. Whereas the relatively high rate of "problem drug use" could contribute to the disproportionate number of drug users in Lithuanian prisons, several other factors also play a role in this situation. This is not solely attributable to the drug of choice among so-called "junkies" but also depends on societal attitudes towards drugs and drug users, as well as the existing legal framework. Now, let's examine how drug offences are regulated under Lithuanian law.

Drug Offences: Legal Regulation and Statistical Data

Foremost, it is worth mentioning that the current regulations concerning drug offences have changed very little since 2003, when the Penal Code (Penal Code of the Republic of Lithuania, 2000) came into force. Lithuanian penal law regarding drug distribution and possession of drugs is strict, and a breach of this law results in lengthy custodial sentences. For instance, possession of a small amount of any illicit drug with the intent to distribute carries a custodial sentence of 2–8 years, while possession of a large amount results in imprisonment for 8–10 years. Possession of a very large amount (with or without intent to distribute) carries a custodial sentence of 10–15 years (Article 260 of the Penal Code). Interestingly, the sanctions for possession of a very large amount of drugs are similar to those for murder (imprisonment of 7–15 years, Article 129). The supply of a small amount is treated more harshly than grave crimes such as robbery (up to 6 years of imprisonment, Article 180) and even rape (up to 7 years of imprisonment, Article 149). This comparison demonstrates the perception that drug supply, technically a victimless crime, is potentially very dangerous to society. On the other hand, possession of a small amount of drugs for personal use is considered a misdemeanour. It is punishable by community service, restriction of liberty, a fine, or arrest (Paragraph 2, Article 259). Such a difference in sanctions for drug distribution and possession could be seen as a mere reflection of the widespread perception that drug users, while weak-willed, are primarily victims of predatory drug dealers.

It is noteworthy that the penal law of Lithuania does not provide for any alternative to incarceration for the offence of drug supply, even in cases where the perpetrator is addicted. Imposing lengthy prison sentences has been shown to have a profoundly detrimental impact on individuals, while efforts to facilitate rehabilitation and resocialisation within the prison environment have often proven ineffective. Moreover, contrary to the trends prevailing in the West, in 2017, Lithuania abolished administrative liability for acquiring and possessing drugs and criminalised this conduct, thus tightening legislative regulation (Lankauskas & Gutauskas, 2022). Interestingly, in Lithuania, there is a distinction between drug use and drug possession for personal use. While the latter was discussed above and incurs criminal sanctions under Paragraph 2, Article 259 of the Penal Code, the former is subject to administrative sanctions (small fines) under Article 71 of the Code of Administrative Misdemeanours (Code of Administrative Misdemeanours, 2015).

Despite recent efforts in Parliament to decriminalise drug possession for personal use, these initiatives have not been successful. Consequently, Lithuanian drug control policy remains heavily reliant on strict control measures. Therefore, in the face if an ongoing increase in drug use among the population, it is to be expected that the prison system will be subjected to an even greater influx of drug offenders (irrespective of whether they are addicted or not), with consequences for Lithuanian society that will be both long lasting and far-reaching. From a statistical perspective, such a dangerous trend can already be observed. Firstly, the total number of drug offences in Lithuania is consistently increasing, while overall crime rates are declining (Fig. 9.2).

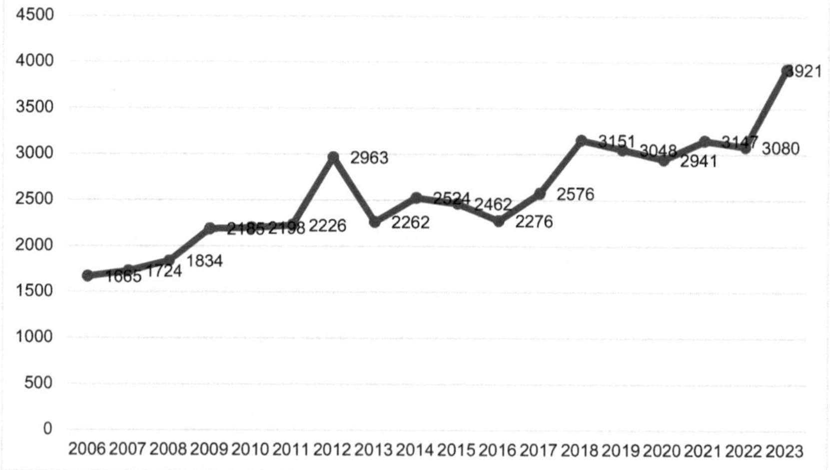

Fig. 9.2 Drug offences in Lithuania[3] (in total numbers)

[3] According to the official data (Information Technology and Communications Department under the Ministry of the Interior of the Republic of Lithuania, n.d.).

Secondly, the proportion of individuals incarcerated for drug offences in Lithuanian prisons is also increasing. According to the latest data from the Lithuanian Prison Service (Lithuanian Prison Service, n. d.), more than 20% of prisoners in 2023 were incarcerated for drug crimes, primarily for drug supply. It is important to stress that not all individuals incarcerated for drug offences are drug users themselves. Ironically, they can become such users within the Lithuanian prison system, which is infamous for weak drug-use control behind bars. In addition, it is worth mentioning that the number of drug offences among other crimes is not very significant, but the proportion of incarcerated individuals for drug crimes is alarming. One of the main reasons for this situation is the very nature of Lithuanian penal law concerning drug offences, which can be seen as a combination of strict sanctions and a lack of alternatives to imprisonment (Fig. 9.3).

Who is the typical offender sentenced for drug crimes? Perhaps they are some sort of "big fish" who are better off kept locked up for the safety of society? Unfortunately, according to official data, it seems that the main target of the criminal justice system in combating illegal drug use in Lithuania appears to be primarily cannabis users and small-scale dealers. In 2023, there were 635 cases of drug possession with intent to distribute

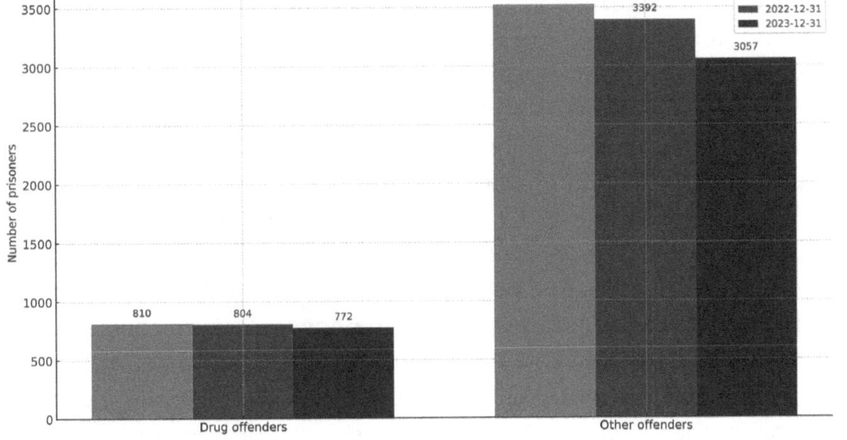

Fig. 9.3 People incarcerated for drug offences in Lithuania (in total numbers)

(up from 579 in 2022), while cases of possession for personal use rose significantly, with 3006 cases reported in 2023 compared to 2431 in 2022. 145 cases were recorded in 2023, compared to 103 in the previous year, regarding possessing very large amounts. Cannabis was involved in nearly half of drug possession cases and slightly less than one-third of drug distribution cases (Information Technology and Communications Department under the Ministry of the Interior of the Republic of Lithuania, n.d.). This emphasis on cannabis-related offences reflects a strong focus within the criminal justice system on this particular drug, despite its comparatively low harm profile relative to other substances. This could be explained by the fact that cannabis is the most popular illicit drug in Lithuania, making it the largest market for illegal drugs, with the highest number of users and dealers. Consequently, this prevalence likely drives the focus of the criminal justice system, as addressing cannabis-related activities affects a larger segment of the illicit drug landscape. In the author's opinion, this could also signal that police priorities are primarily directed towards statistical performance (i.e., more registered crimes or misdemeanours as an indicator of "good work"). One reason for such a policy is that in Lithuania, there is no differentiation between different illicit drugs based on their perceived harm to individuals and society.

In addition, many prisoners were convicted of other drug-related crimes (e.g., theft, robbery) committed to sustain their costly drug addiction. While it is not possible to indicate the exact number of such prisoners, there are statistical data concerning substance use disorders, which can provide insight into the prevalence of drug-related issues within the prison system, highlighting the significant portion of the incarcerated population affected by addiction.

As we can see from Fig. 9.4, in recent years, the percentage of prisoners officially diagnosed with substance (including alcohol) use disorders has ranged from 12.5% (the lowest point in 2016) to 21.7% (the highest point in 2019). One could even imagine how many prisoners also have such disorders but are not officially diagnosed. Research conducted in Lithuanian prisons revealed that drug use is a significant social and medical problem, closely linked to prison conditions and the atmosphere within prison facilities. Forbidden substances play a substantial role in the prison economy and contribute to the power dynamics within the informal prison hierarchy. The resulting drug debts often lead to crime and violence, undermining the stability and safety of prisons (Lankauskas, 2022, p. 121).

It is important to note that treatment and rehabilitation options for addicted offenders are limited. Addiction is not considered a mitigating circumstance according to Article 59 of the Penal Code; however, according to Paragraph 2, *courts may* theoretically recognise other circumstances (i.e., drug addiction) as mitigating, even if they are not explicitly stated in the article. There is no possible diversion mechanism, meaning that an addicted drug offender is not diverted to treatment but instead is subjected to criminal sanctions. In the prison system, treatment is mainly limited to 12-step groups, with only a small number of prisoners willing to participate. It is worth noting that opioid substitution treatment with methadone, which has been available outside of prisons since the 1990s, was only introduced into the prison system in 2018, following a court decision. Lithuania was among the last countries in

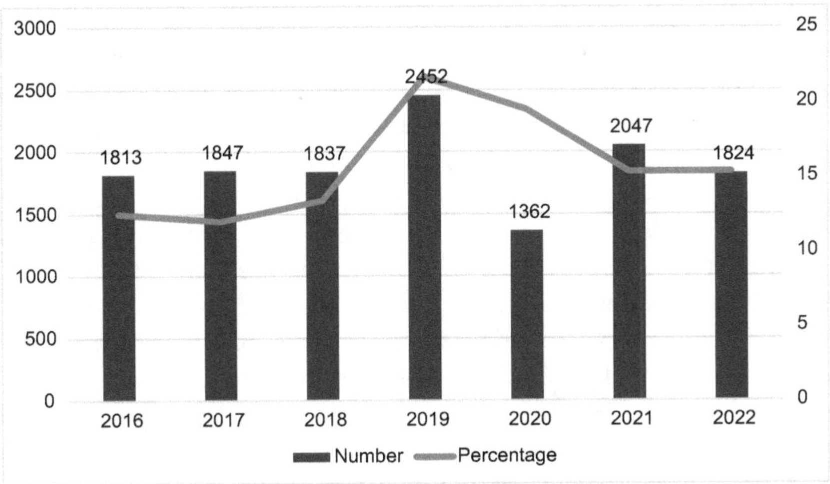

Fig. 9.4 Number of prisoners with substance use disorders[4] (in total numbers)

[4] Made by the author, using data provided in the report by Drug, Tobacco and Alcohol Control Department (Narkotikų, tabako ir alkoholio kontrolės departamentas, 2023, 86).

Europe to implement this measure. There are still no harm reduction measures, such as needle and syringe exchange programmes, in prison settings.

The existing legal framework, focused on criminal prosecution and lengthy sanctions, has the dangerous potential to criminalise a larger segment of society in the future, further ostracising them from the "normal" members of society. Accordingly, the growing prison population of "junkies" could become a significant burden on society as a whole, especially considering the "revolving door" phenomenon, where addicted drug users frequently migrate between prison and freedom. To address these issues effectively, it is essential to reconsider the punitive approach towards drug-using offenders and transition towards a more health-oriented strategy.

Despite the harsh penal provisions regarding drug offences in Lithuania, strategic political documents indicate a political will to shift towards a more humane and health-oriented drug control policy. According to the National Agenda (National Agenda for Drug, Tobacco and Alcohol Control, Use Prevention and Harm Reduction until 2035, 2023, Paragraph 114.3), the state should reconsider the existing penal policy directed at drug users, decriminalise less serious behaviour, and review current penal sanctions to achieve a more balanced approach to criminal liability for drug offences, as well as expand the possibility of applying alternative sanctions (to incarceration) where appropriate. These goals are supported by recent research in Lithuania. For instance, diverting offenders with problem drug use away from incarceration may have several positive effects, such as preventing the high risks of involvement in the criminal subculture, health risks (including the progress of drug use), risk of deterioration of social skills, receiving social stigma and also it may help reducing prison system costs(e.g., infrastructure, staff, etc.) (Bikelis & Lankauskas, 2024, p. 168). Also, there is a solid criminological background to distinguish the concept of less serious drug distribution, which refers to non-commercial or minimally commercially motivated activities of small scale and involving relatively low-risk substances. In many such cases, incarceration (especially long term) would appear to be a disproportionately severe penalty, bringing an unjustified burden for both a person and society (Bikelis & Lankauskas, 2024, p. 176).

However, before we can address these concerns, we must first answer the question of why our existing penal law and law enforcement practices are so harsh towards drug crime, which, by its nature, is often considered a "victimless" crime. Who drives us to treat drug offenders more as criminals than as individuals suffering from illness or making different life choices?

Why Are Drug Users Punished so Harshly in Lithuania?

It is not possible to answer this question in a very detailed fashion, as there are far too many reasons and variables that can influence penal culture in general and the punishment for drug crimes or drug-related crimes in particular. At the same time, certain assumptions can be made based on an analysis of the existing legal framework, historical circumstances, and the supposed value systems of Lithuanian society.

To begin with, the "harsh treatment" of drug users in Lithuania appears so when compared with the drug laws and attitudes of European countries. However, if we compare Lithuanian legal regulation with that of countries in the East, the picture may look a bit different. Different strategies towards drug use can lead to dramatically varying situations across countries. For instance, Cohen perfectly explained how "junky misery" ("junky elend") in different countries are not the same and that the level in the Netherlands seemed to be lower than in countries nearby (e.g., Germany or Switzerland) (Cohen Peter, 1992). This means that similar drug use patterns (prevalence, most popular illicit drugs, etc.) do not necessarily indicate that the situation of people who use drugs should be the same. Quite the opposite, because drug laws and police practices towards drug users vary significantly between countries and can lead to different outcomes. In this context, it is important to note that drug use in the Western world is more or less normalised. In contrast, it remains a largely marginalised and stigmatised activity in Lithuania. As

Dertadian points out, "the theory of the normalisation of drug use, especially among young people in advanced capitalist societies, has become a mainstay of contemporary drug scholarship".

In the contemporary drugs field, the theory of the normalisation of drug use has been used both to describe and evidence social change—how drug use has become normalised in society—and in a more instrumental way in drug policy: to set a standard for good public policy that seeks to reduce harm from the now-normal practice of drug use (Dertadian, 2023). The last statement clearly illustrates that normalisation and modern drug policy often go hand in hand. If we view drug use as a moral sin, we tend to favour strict drug control measures. On the contrary, perceiving it as an individual pathology makes us more inclined to support medical control (or "medicalisation"). Foucault was cautious about the potential expansion of disciplinary practices into all aspects of life, warning that "all the movements of extension that characterise modern penality problematisation of the criminal behind his crime, the concern with a punishment that is a correction, a therapy, a normalisation, the division of the act of judgement between various authorities that are supposed to measure, assess, diagnose, cure, transform individuals - all this betrays the penetra tion of the disciplinary examination into the judicial inquisition" (Foucault, 1995, 227). Therefore, while at first glance relocating the drug problem from the criminal justice system's shadow to the realm of medicine might seem beneficial, it could also carry specific dangers.

As a social glue of society, the Dominant religion often plays an important role in shaping the legal framework, particularly concerning the nature of penal law. Lithuania is a predominantly Catholic country, and Catholicism traditionally holds conservative views on issues like drug use, often equating substance use with moral failing. This religious perspective contributes to the stigmatisation of drug users and supports the criminalisation approach, as illicit drug use is seen as a violation of moral and ethical standards. According to Inglehart and Welzel's World Cultural Map, there are two major dimensions of cross-cultural values: traditional values versus self-expression values and survival values versus self-expression values. On this cultural map, Lithuania belongs to the cluster of "Catholic Europe" countries, displaying a relatively higher emphasis on secular-rational values than traditional ones. At the same time, Lithuania strongly prioritises survival values over self-expression. In this context, Lithuanian society is very far from "Protestant Europe" and is instead closely aligned with "Orthodox Europe" countries such as Bulgaria, Ukraine, Russia, and Belarus, as well as "Confucian" countries like China (Ronald Inglehart, 2023). Accordingly, when discussing drug policy or attitudes towards illicit drug use, Lithuania may share more similarities with these countries than with those of Western Europe. Research findings also support that assumption. For example, Cao and Zhao hypothesised that tolerance of illegal drugs is linked to human development and the strength of a nation's cultural axis: survivalism versus self-expressionism. Their research showed that "residents from nations with higher levels of human development and with higher self-expressionist scores are more tolerant of soft drug use than residents in nations with lower human development levels and lower self-expressionist scores" (Cao & Zhao, 2012). Accordingly, while Lithuania's less tolerant approach to drugs can be explained by its current value system, which is still heavily based on survivalism, this could change in the future if Lithuania shifts towards the values of Western Europe and experiences further economic growth.

As previously demonstrated, the Lithuanian legal approach to the drug problem can be defined as punitive rather than health-oriented. The possible root of this approach lies in the idea that drug use is a moral issue; therefore, drug users are solely responsible for their acts and should be punished harshly (Lankauskas & Gutauskas, 2022, p. 322). Negative societal attitudes towards drug users, especially those who are addicted, are evident in a recent survey conducted in 2019. According to the survey results, ex-drug addicts are the least popular potential collaborators, with only 3% of respondents willing to work with them. Only 8% of the population would agree to work with individuals who have returned from prison. In comparison, 20 and 23% would be willing to work alongside former alcoholics and homeless individuals, respectively (15min.lt, 2019). The results show that ex-drug addicts are perceived even more negatively than former prisoners or alcoholics, reflecting the pervasive belief that "once an addict, always an addict". Such a hostile societal climate fuels punitive attitudes not only towards drug traffickers, viewed as "evil drug pushers", but also towards drug users, who are often seen as sinful or weak-willed individuals who, to some extent, deserve punishment for their behaviour, regardless of whether they are addicted or not. Hence, it is possible to return to the issue from which we started, namely, the *stigma* attached to drug users. It could be argued that this stigma, which is itself a consequence of underlying social processes, continues to exert an influence on Lithuanian drug policy to the present day. In this context, the role of the police cannot be underestimated either. It is naive to expect that police officers would be more compassionate towards drug users than society in general, especially when they are daily exposed to the darker side of the drug underworld. Consequently, it is evident that a harsh criminal justice response to drug use could exacerbate the situation for hard drug users in particular. According to Becker, "the deviant is one to whom that label has successfully been applied; deviant behaviour is behaviour that people so label" (Becker, 1963, 9). Let's agree with this postulate of labelling theory. It becomes clear why it is so difficult for drug users to escape the "junkie" label, especially when it is reinforced through multiple incarcerations for drug-related offences. In the end, the life of an individual struggling with substance abuse often becomes a cyclical phenomenon, characterised by recurrent incarceration and subsequent release, which collectively diminishes the prospect of a positive outcome. Hard drug users are more likely to receive such a label compared to occasional drug users, who make up a sizeable hidden population (this becomes evident when comparing drug use statistics with the statistics of registered drug offences). On the other hand, recreational users, if caught, may experience a "self-fulfilling prophecy" and drift towards more problematic drug use behaviours and practices. This is particularly true if such users are incarcerated (e.g., for drug supply).

An analysis of Lithuanian drug control policy shows that it diverges significantly from contemporary Western standards, which are more health-oriented, instead embodying a more punitive, Eastern approach. Drug addiction remains one of the most challenging social and public health issues in modern Lithuania, where drug scares, fears, and the association of drug use with criminal activity often fuel punitive approaches in drug control policy. Despite advances in understanding addiction as a chronically relapsing disorder (Koob & Volkow, 2016), societal attitudes continue to stigmatise addicted individuals, reinforcing harsh legal measures against them. More work needs to be done to reduce drug use stigma and its negative implications for drug policy. According to Cohen, "the most promising strategies of lowering levels of junky elend among which junky dying, is to interfere in the process of social ostracism by creating neutralising institutions. These institutions have to work on the level of the daily problems of heavy drug users and not on the level of monolithic pharmacological or psychological constructions of their problems" (Cohen Peter, 1992).

Concluding Remarks

First, it is difficult to pinpoint the exact reasons behind Lithuania's drug control policy. Probably, strict and rigid penal laws concerning drug offences in Lithuania have a foundation in Lithuanian society, its history, religion, and social and cultural values. Likely, it stems from the generally conservative values of Lithuanian society, relatively recent exposure to illicit drugs, and an inherited post-Soviet attitude towards people. Lithuania's history, particularly its experience under Soviet rule, has contributed to the development of a strict legal and societal attitude towards many forms of deviance, including drug use. During the Soviet era, there was an emphasis on maintaining social order and conformity, which included harsh measures for criminal behaviour, including drug offences. The legacy of this past continues to influence current legal and societal responses to drugs.

Lithuanian drug control policy heavily relies on the criminal justice system, with limited emphasis on harm reduction and treatment options. This is a consequence of the prevailing value system in Lithuanian society, shaped by its Soviet past and relatively recent exposure to illicit drugs, which have been present in some other societies for centuries. As we can imagine, a drug user, regardless of their drug of choice or life story, is often perceived as a somewhat dangerous individual, most likely deeply connected to the criminal underworld.

Illicit drug use instils fear in Lithuanian society, and drug users are often perceived as convenient scapegoats to blame ("it is their fault"). This perception contributes to the further marginalisation and stigmatisation of people who use drugs, particularly those who are most vulnerable, such as users of "hard drugs". Such a hardline approach has severe implications for drug policy in Lithuania, placing a strong emphasis on so-called hard measures and prioritising the role of law enforcement in addressing the "drug problem".

Penal law can be seen as a mirror of a nation's value system, albeit distorted, often representing the values of elites and powerful interest groups more than society shares. Looking at this mirror, it becomes evident that drugs are perceived as a significant danger to Lithuanian society. Consequently, the penal law provisions concerning drug offences are extremely strict. Incarceration is the only available measure in almost all drug supply cases, regardless of whether it involves commercially motivated drug dealing or so-called social supply. While, on paper, penal law is aimed at addressing "drug crime", in reality, it often translates to punishing individuals who use prohibited substances. This has resulted in a substantial proportion of inmates being incarcerated for drug offences (about 20% in 2023). Additionally, some prisoners have committed other crimes (e.g., theft or burglary) to sustain their costly drug habits. To sum up, the prison population includes a significant number of individuals linked to drug use in one way or another. Treatment and rehabilitation options in prisons are limited, meaning drug use often continues behind bars or resumes after release.

Illicit drug use in Lithuanian society, while not currently widespread, is increasing among young people. If our approach to this issue remains unchanged, we may face an even larger prison population in the future, along with the accompanying financial and social costs. Decriminalising less serious drug offences, depenalising more serious ones, and expanding treatment opportunities for individuals with addiction could help avert such a crisis. Drug policy reform may also involve introducing a diversion system within the Lithuanian legal framework for drug-related crimes. Realistically, this cannot be achieved without a fundamental shift in deeply rooted societal attitudes towards people who use drugs.

References

Angelou, M. (1997). *Even the stars look lonesome*. Random House.

Becker, H. S. (1963). *Outsiders: Studies in the sociology of deviance*. Free Press.

Bikelis, S., & Lankauskas, M. (2024). Penal response to less serious drug distribution offences: The case of Lithuania in the regional context. *Baltic Journal of Law & Politics, 17*(1), 163–180. Retrieved May 12, 2025, from https://doi.org/10.2478/bjlp-2024-0008

Cao, L., & Zhao, R. (2012). The impact of culture on the acceptance of soft drugs across Europe. *Journal of Criminal Justice, 40*(4), 296–305. Retrieved May 12, 2025, from https://doi.org/10.1016/j.jcrimjus.2012.04.002

Code of Administrative Misdemeanours, Pub. L. No. 2015-11216. (2015). Retrieved May 12, 2025, from https://www.e-tar.lt/portal/lt/legalAct/4ebe66c0262311e5bf92d6af3f6a2e8b/asr

Cohen, P. (1992). Junky Elend: Some ways of explaining it and dealing with it. *Wiener Zeitschrift für Suchtforschung, 14*(3/4), 59–64.

Csete, J., et al. (2016). Public health & international drug policy. *The Lancet, 387*(10026), 1427–1480. Retrieved May 12, 2025, from https://doi.org/10.1016/S0140-6736(16)00619-X

Dertadian, G. C. (2023). Is non-medical use normal? Normalisation, medicalisation & pharmaceutical consumption. *International Journal of Drug Policy, 119*(104123), 2025. https://doi.org/10.1016/j.drugpo.2023.104123 (Accessed:12May

EMCDDA. (2023). *Statistical Bulletin 2023—Prevalence of Drug Use*. Retrieved May 12, 2025, from https://www.emcdda.europa.eu/data/stats2023/gps_en

ESAPD group. (2020). *ESPAD Report 2019: Results from the European School Survey Project on Alcohol and Other Drugs*. EMCDDA Joint Publications.

European Union Drugs Agency. (2024). *Statistical Bulletin 2024—Problem Drug Use*. Retrieved May 12, 2025, from https://www.euda.europa.eu/data/stats2024/pdu_en

Foucault, M. (1995). *Discipline and punish: The birth of the prison*. Random House, Inc.

Goffman, E. (1963). *Stigma: Notes on the management of spoiled identity*. Simon & Schuster, Inc.

Goldstein, P. J. (1985). The drugs/violence nexus: A tripartite conceptual framework. *Journal of Drug Issues, 15*(4), 493–506. Retrieved May 12, 2025, from https://doi.org/10.1177/002204268501500406

Information Technology & Communications Department. (n.d.). *Open Data.* Retrieved May 12, 2025, from https://ird.lt/lt/paslaugos/tvarkomu-valdomu-registru-ir-informaciniu-sistemu-paslaugos/nusikalstamu-veiku-zinybinio-registro-nvzr-atviri-duomenys-paslaugos/nusikalstamos-veikos-lietuvoje-2006-2023-metais/oid.1005

Inglehart, R. (2023). *The Inglehart-Welzel World Cultural Map—World Values Survey 7 (2023)* [Map]. Retrieved May 12, 2025, from https://www.worldvaluessurvey.org/images/Map2023NEW.png

Koob, G. F., & Volkow, N. D. (2016). Neurobiology of addiction: A neurocircuitry analysis. *The Lancet Psychiatry, 3*(8), 760–773.

Lankauskas, M., & Gutauskas, A. (2022). Chasing the high: Drug users as a vulnerable group in Lithuania. In A. Limantė & D. Pūraitė-Andrikienė (Eds.), *Legal protection of vulnerable groups in Lithuania, Latvia, Estonia and Poland* (Vol. 8, pp. 309–325). Springer. Retrieved May 12, 2025, from https://doi.org/10.1007/978-3-031-06998-7_14

Lankauskas, M. (2022). *Narkotikai ir įkalinimas: Kriminologiniai baudimo už disponavimą narkotinėmis ar psichotropinėmis medžiagomis aspektai ir jų vartojimo kalinimo įstaigose ypatumai.* Vilnius: Lietuvos socialinių mokslų centro Teisės institutas. Retrieved May 12, 2025, from https://teise.org/wp-content/uploads/2023/01/Narkotikai-ir-ikalinimas.pdf

Lithuanian Prison Service. (n.d.). *Open Data.* Retrieved May 12, 2025, from https://kalejimai.lrv.lt/lt/administracine-informacija/ataskaitos/metu/

Livingston, J., Bonn, M., Brown, P., Deveau, S., & Houston, A.-M. (2022). Experiences of stigma and criminal/justice among people who use substances. In G. Schomerus & P. W. Corrigan (Eds.), *The stigma of substance use disorders,* 1st ed. (pp. 46–67). Cambridge University Press. Retrieved May 12, 2025, from https://doi.org/10.1017/9781108936972.004

Narkotikų, tabako & alkoholio kontrolės departamentas. (2023). *Psichoaktyviosios medžiagos: Tendencijos ir pokyčiai.*

National Agenda for Drug, Tobacco and Alcohol Control, Use Prevention and Harm Reduction until 2035, Pub. L. No. 2023-09953. (2023). Retrieved May 12, 2025. from https://e-seimas.lrs.lt/portal/legalAct/lt/TAD/1bc8cc00faf111edbc0bd16e3a4d3b97?jfwid=dqracznun

Penal Code of the Republic of Lithuania, Pub. L. No. 89-2741. (2000).

Rupšienė, L., Šaltytė-Vaisiauskė, L., Bredelytė, A., & Laucevičius, E. (2024). *Alkoholio ir kitų psichoaktyviųjų medžiagų tyrimo ataskaita. ESPAD Lietuva—2024.*

Rupšienė, L., Šutinienė, I., & Saveljeva, R. (2020). *ESPAD-2019. Alkoholio ir kitų psichoaktyviųjų medžiagų vartojimas Lietuvoje.*

World Health Organization. (2024). *Alcohol Consumption. Total Alcohol per Capita (>= 15 Years of Age) Consumption (Litres of Pure Alcohol).* Retrieved May 12, 2025, from https://data.who.int/indicators/i/EF38E6A/EE6F72A?m49=440

Zdanytė, G. (2023). Lithuania faces serious problem: Drug addicts are getting younger & younger. *Delfi.lt*, 20 October. Retrieved May 12, 2025, from https://www.delfi.lt/en/my-impact/lithuania-faces-serious-problem-drug-addicts-are-getting-younger-and-younger-94859617

15min.lt. (2019). Apklausa: Didžiausią spaudimą darbe patiria buvę narkomanai & nuteistieji. *15min.lt*, 20 November. Retrieved May 12, 2025, from https://www.15min.lt/naujiena/aktualu/lietuva/apklausa-didziausia-spaudima-darbe-patiria-buve-narkomanai-ir-nuteistieji-56-1234930

10

Female Offender: Doubly Deviant and Hounded by the Media

Rimantė Gaičevskytė-Savickė

Introduction

Criminal news gained considerable popularity in the twentieth century as a relatively cheap genre of journalism. However, not all criminal stories find their way onto newspaper pages or news portals. Whether a specific news item has the potential to become sensational depends on several news selection factors (Jewkes, 2015). Crimes committed by women are among the most attractive subjects for the media due to their relatively rare occurrence, thus naturally arousing greater curiosity and interest (Heidensohn, 1996).

The image of the female offender in the media is typically constructed around patriarchal expectations, where criminal behaviour is portrayed

R. Gaičevskytė-Savickė (✉)
Faculty of Philosophy, Institute of Sociology and Social Work, Department of Criminology, Vilnius University, Vilnius, Lithuania
e-mail: rimante.gaicevskyte-savicke@fsf.vu.lt

A. Dobryninas and S. Nikartas (eds.), *Understanding Crime Control and Punishment in Lithuania*, Crime Prevention and Security Management,
https://doi.org/10.1007/978-3-032-05538-5_10

as opposing the idealised images assigned to women. The representations highlight stereotypical roles associated primarily with motherhood and partnership, juxtaposing them with criminal behaviour. A dedicated partner or caring mother is contrasted with a woman involved in crime, reinforcing negative social perceptions (Hartman, 1977). Furthermore, there is evidence that the representation and intensity of coverage of female and male offenders differ significantly (Ditton & Duffy, 1983; Jewkes, 2015; Kowalik, 2022; Marsh & Melville, 2009). Media coverage becomes more intense and prolonged when a woman commits a serious crime. Her image is portrayed more vividly and leaves a longer-lasting impression on the audience (Heidensohn, 1996; Jewkes, 2015). Additionally, the narrative surrounding the crime often serves as an excuse to dissect the details of her private life, transforming the crime story into a morality tale for other women (Hartman, 1977).

Despite the ostensibly noble goal of informing the public, media organisations also pursue commercial interests, aiming to attract as large an audience as possible (Birkbeck, 2014). This often results in sensationalist headlines, in-depth and dramatic narratives, and prolonged coverage of details about female offenders (Jewkes, 2015). Women involved in criminal cases are frequently depicted through certain recurring stereotypes (Jewkes, 2015; Lloyd, 1995; Morrissey, 2003; Naylor, 2001):

- *bad wife* (failure to comply with traditional domestic roles; notably, such narratives rarely apply to male offenders);
- *bad mother* (crimes involving harm to children breach not only the law but also profoundly held maternal ideals);
- *sexuality and sexual deviance* (sexual preferences, frigidity, or homosexuality are used to explain or amplify female criminality);
- *physical attractiveness* (women portrayed as dangerously seductive or emotionally manipulative);
- *mythical or archetypal figures* (witch, vampire, temptress, fallen woman, derived from pagan mythology, Christian theology, or classical literature and art);

- *manipulator* (when a woman commits a crime alongside her partner, the media portrays her neither as a victim nor as an independent criminal, but as manipulative);
- *non-woman or "unnatural" woman* (a female offender is depicted either as a childlike person, not entirely responsible for her actions, or as masculinised).

This chapter aims to reveal how images of female offenders are constructed in Lithuanian media through a detailed Delfi.lt news portal content analysis.[1] Delfi.lt was selected as one of Lithuania's most popular and longest-standing online news platforms.

Content analysis assessed how crime news involving female offenders is presented. The research focused on two main objectives: first, to identify the types of female crimes most frequently featured in the news; and second, to analyse and categorise the dominant media portrayals of female offenders.

Due to technical limitations (unsatisfactory results from automated searches), relevant publications were selected manually from the Delfi.lt news archive. Within 2000 to 2020, 128 relevant news articles were selected for qualitative content analysis within the chosen timeframe. The analysis focused primarily on identifying recurring representations and stereotypes in portraying female offenders.

[1] This research was conducted as part of the dissertation "Female Offender: The Criminological Perception and Media Portrayals."

"The Kingdom of Crooked Mirrors"[2]: Registered Crimes and Their Representation in the Media

The conducted quantitative analysis revealed that DELFI news portal publications reflect only a tiny portion of official crime statistics (see Fig. 10.1). However, it is precisely through this small, selective dose of crime news that audience knowledge and general perceptions of the criminogenic situation are shaped.

Upon reviewing the analysed publications, the DELFI news portal primarily focused on crimes and misdemeanours related to property, property rights, and financial interests (22.1%) and crimes against human health (17%). This thematic distribution of crime news directly

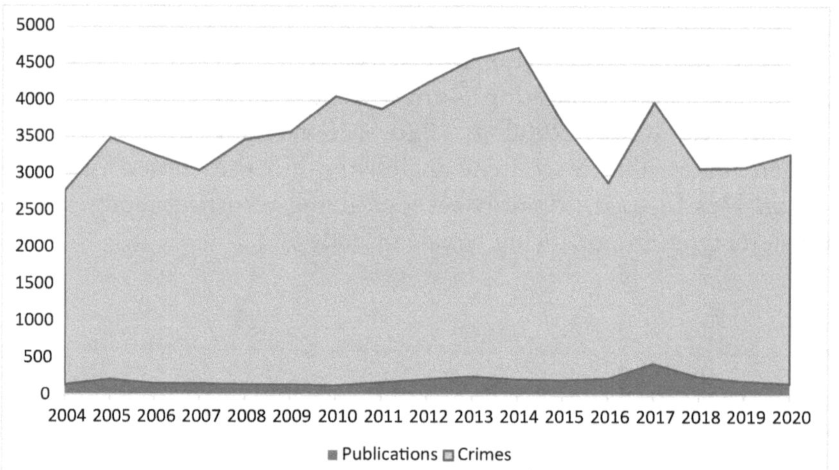

Fig. 10.1 Dynamics of publications on women's crimes and registered crimes and misdemeanours, 2004–2020 (total numbers)

[2] The title "*Kingdom of Crooked Mirrors*" is taken from a metaphor familiar in Eastern European culture (as well as from popular children's fairy tales during the Soviet era), referring to a world in which reality is systematically distorted through mirrors that reflect a warped image of the real world. In this context, the term is used to describe the discrepancy between actual crime statistics and their depiction in the media.

corresponds to actual crime statistics—these are indeed the offences for which women are most frequently suspected or accused. However, third in thematic popularity are news reports about murders (15.6%), even though these crimes occur relatively infrequently, ranging from 43 cases in 2004 to 11 in 2019 annually. Fourth in frequency are news about transportation safety crimes and misdemeanours (10.3%); fifth and sixth are crimes related to illegal possession of narcotic, psychotropic, toxic, or highly potent substances (8.1%), and crimes against children and families (7.3%). Meanwhile, 19.6% of news items belong to the "Other" category (crimes against personal freedom, sexual freedom and integrity, social rights, economy and financial systems, honour and dignity, privacy, etc.).

Crimes against human health and life account for nearly one-third of the relevant criminal news content. The prevailing themes in these publications align with scholarly insights about crime news presentation, highlighting that extreme cruelty characteristic of violent crimes and the risk of becoming a victim of property crime are among the most significant factors determining news selection.

Further, we will examine how the dynamics of registered crimes and the frequency of popular crime news changed during the analysed period. Evaluating the intensity of information coverage on different types of crimes reveals two key trends: (1) information dissemination about crimes against human life receives intensive attention, whereas (2) other types of crimes receive only episodic media coverage.

Media give exceptional attention to crimes against human life (Dobryninas et al., 2014; Lundman, 2003; Sorenson et al., 1998). As previously mentioned, media attention becomes disproportionately high, especially when women are involved in these crimes (Jewkes, 2015; Soothill et al., 2002). This tendency is reflected in Fig. 10.2: Since 2007, there has been periodic growth in news related to murders involving women, and from 2011 onwards, the number of such publications annually exceeds the number of registered crimes. The year 2017 was particularly notable for such news—several women in Lithuania were accused of murdering their young children. However, these tragedies were overshadowed by the story of Matukas, prompting politicians to initiate reforms in child welfare protection, known as the Matukas reform.[3] Another observed trend is that the number of publications remains relatively stable regardless of how many crimes are registered. This stability might reflect consistent news selection by journalists favouring the most intriguing, bizarre, or extraordinary stories. Thus, property crimes, drug-related offences, traffic safety violations, and crimes against human health are not extensively or frequently featured in the crime news category.

Property crimes and misdemeanours enter the news section typically when the committed crime is either exceptionally large scale or notably minor (e.g., "Gas station employee disappears with 18,000 €," "Woman did not pay for shampoos worth nearly 32 €"), or when the woman's professional role or status contradicts stereotypical notions of criminality (e.g., "University employee accused of money laundering," "Former child rights advocate avoids jail"), or when the offence is peculiar, unusual, or unexpected. Headlines highlighting these surprising female roles often

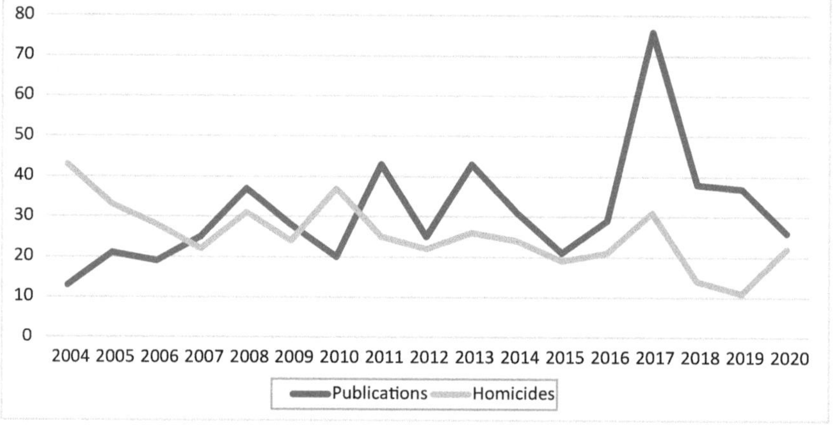

Fig. 10.2 Dynamics of women suspected of crimes against human life and a number of related publications (total numbers)

[3] Five-year-old Matukas died in January 2017 after being severely beaten by his mother and stepfather. The child was admitted to hospital with multiple bruises. Experts found that he had been hit with at least 135 blows. The crime was the subject of a major public outcry, with civic actions calling for more attention to be paid to combating violence against children. The Parliament very quickly banned all forms of violence against children and the use of corporal punishment.

use mockery and reinforce stereotypes portraying women either as seductive manipulators or naive and unintelligent individuals (e.g., "Liquor store clerk not only stole but also danced with customers," "Girl posing as a man scammed money," "Naive woman believed a stranger would gift her almost a million").

Additionally, heightened media attention to property crimes is observed when the suspect is a Roma woman. Their ethnicity is prominently featured in headlines, often employing the publicly unacceptable term "gypsy" (e.g., "Woman invited gypsies into her home and lost €15,000," "Elderly woman lost €20,000 after letting gypsies in," "Gypsy promising fortune-telling scammed company funds from a man," "Woman talking with gypsies on her way to the bank lost her savings").

Between 2012 and 2020, the proportion of women suspected of crimes against human health nearly doubled—from 6.2% to 11.2%. However, when offenses are committed intentionally, women are predominantly accused of minor bodily injuries and causing physical pain (Tereškinas et al., 2021, p. 28). Suppose a crime against health is neither severe nor unusually violent. In that case, audience attention is drawn by emphasising atypical assault weapons (e.g., "Jealous wife took revenge on husband with a scythe," "Son-in-law got hit in the forehead by a stone from his mother-in-law," "Woman struck sister's face with firewood," "Conflict in the municipality: woman stabbed another with a pen," "Girl knocked out boyfriend's teeth with a phone"), or exotic elements of harm (e.g., "The consequence of courtship—torn testicle," "Woman bit partner's ear and ended up in detention," "Woman stabbed partner in buttocks"). Publications frequently highlight violence towards minors or vulnerable relatives (e.g., "Woman got drunk, beat her children, and ended up in a psychiatric hospital," "Woman beat 9-year-old son with fire poker," "Violence against minors continues: woman allegedly beat son with belt and cable," "Granddaughter beat and stabbed grandmother with scissors, glass shard, then bit her"). Headlines often morally condemn women for failing in stereotypical roles as mothers, partners, sisters, or daughters.

For severe or potentially severe bodily injuries, headlines strive to encapsulate detailed descriptions of the crime (e.g., "Disabled father's liver ruptured after daughter's beating," "Little boy's drama: stepmother kicked him, hit his head with a backpack, dragged him around the room by the neck").

Women are often suspected of traffic safety violations. Official crime statistics separately categorise intoxication from narcotics, psychotropic, or other substances only since 2019. Although the number of traffic safety violations and driving under the influence cases is similar, the latter dominate crime news (e.g., "Drunk blonde sped out of a side street and hit hunters' car," "Doctor went to patient drunk, caught by police en route," "Massage parlour owner previously fined for prostitution wants to be queen of 'road roosters'," "Drunk woman, unable to park car, joyfully greeted police"). Headlines again mock and belittle female drivers, echoing persistent stereotypes about women's supposed inferiority in driving skills compared to men (Berger, 1986; Ercan & Ulug, 2015), further emphasising irresponsible behaviour associated with intoxicated driving.

Women are more commonly suspected of drug possession without intent to distribute. Yet, cases involving female drug distributors appear more frequently in crime news, accompanied by moralising headlines emphasising stereotypical roles (e.g., "Two-week-old infant's mother detained on drug trafficking charges," "An 80-year-old woman known as 'Grandma' arrested for drug dealing"). Intimate details are also intentionally highlighted ("Sister hid drugs for brother in her bra," "Drugs smuggled into prison hidden in yoghurt").

The state intervenes in parent–child relationships mainly when parental duties are neglected, endangering children's welfare. Such crimes gain media attention primarily when alcohol disrupts maternal duties.

In official crime statistics, the most frequently recorded crimes and misdemeanours against children and families are child maintenance evasion and abuse of parental or guardian rights and responsibilities. The state intervenes in parent–child relationships only when parental duties are inadequately performed, putting children's interests at risk. A sharp increase in officially registered offences observed over several years, starting from 2010, is not reflected in the abundance of media coverage.

The criminal news category predominantly includes cases of parental or guardian misconduct, significantly when alcohol impedes the fulfilment of maternal care responsibilities (e.g., "Another mother's drinking spree ends tragically: children temporarily placed in hospital care," "Alcohol became more important to a mother than her children," "Intoxicated 19-year-old mother abandoned baby by roadside," "Drunk parents sent their four children out overnight to seek shelter elsewhere").

Typology of Criminalised Female Images: Qualitative Analysis

The qualitative content analysis identified the most frequently recurring and prominently emphasised social images of women: the deceiver, bad mother, and bad wife (partner) (see Table 10.1).

The **woman-deceiver** seeks material benefit through illegal means: offering nonexistent social services to seniors or disabled people, promising help in obtaining high-paying jobs, then disappearing with an "intermediary fee":

Table 10.1 Most frequent images of criminalised women portrayed in the media

The Deceiver	Offers illegal or miraculous goods and a variety of services
	Borrows money at high interest rates that they never pay back
	Collects charity for the child and/or the sick
	In most cases, she does not have a legal job, and if she does, she cheats her employer in various ways
Bad Mother	Abuses or takes the life of a young child
	Lacking social skills
	Poor financial situation and household
	Lonely, without outside help
	Making irresponsible decisions, failing to ensure the safety of children
	Addicted to alcohol
Bad wife (Partner)	Victims or accomplices of long-term violence (especially when the victims are the children of the couple)
	Living in an anti-social or very poor way
	Alcohol is an integral part of everyday life

> The famous female swindler of Vilnius has slipped again, posing as Vita, an employee of the VIP Protection Department. She promised a man a well-paid job, but never fulfilled her promise. (Famous swindler slips again: promised the impossible, March 18, 2015)

In another publication, a Romani woman presents herself as a fortune-teller capable of healing various illnesses, removing curses, attracting good fortune, or warding off bad luck:

> A Roma woman was sentenced for fraudulently extracting property valued at 26,428 EUR in early 2012 by claiming to straighten the victim's hunchback and drive out the demon possessing her. <...> The fortune-teller explained that this required opening the 'Book of Life,' but, allegedly, that costs money. (How fortune-teller Veronika straightened a hunchback and chased out the demon living inside a woman, October 28, 2015)

She also borrows money at supposedly high interest or raises funds for charitable causes—children she does not have or diseases she does not suffer from—to resolve fabricated problematic situations:

> Two Facebook profiles published photos and the tragic story of a seriously ill little boy. The child's mother requested donations, claiming her son would not survive otherwise. (Invented a heartbreaking story about a sick child: could not escape consequences, January 22, 2015)

> A forty-year-old woman was found guilty of an unusual method of fraud. She demanded 500 euros from her lover to terminate a pregnancy, although she was not pregnant at the time. (Money demanded for a fake pregnancy brought a woman to court, November 6, 2020)

Alternatively, she engages in the illegal sale of supposed medications available only on the "black market" due to their powerful effects:

> The woman placed ads on various websites offering medications capable of terminating pregnancies. Although she had previously been convicted for this, she continued her activities, deceiving others. She advertised

> the unregistered drug 'Mifepristone,' supposedly capable of terminating pregnancies up to 9 weeks. <...> She claimed that she disagreed with women's choice to terminate pregnancies and therefore pretended to sell such drugs. 'I am against abortion; that is why I did it,' the woman told the court. (Woman, who invented unprecedented fraud, will now take care of elderly people, July 5, 2014)

> Medications enhancing sexual potency, such as 'Viagra' or 'Cialis,' were available without prescriptions. Two illegal pharmacies operated in Lithuania's capital, selling these medications even cheaper than in legal pharmacies. The business was so successful that even repeated confiscations by police did not stop the 'pharmacists'. (Queues for 'Viagra': How three Vilnius women helped men achieve miracles, October 10, 2016)

This type of woman is typically unemployed, lacking stable income, surviving on welfare or funds acquired through deceit, supporting young children or other dependent family members, and frequently suffering from addictions (drugs, gambling, alcohol).

In cases where the woman-deceiver holds a legitimate job, sometimes she finds it difficult to justify the trust placed in her:

> A woman working as a casino dealer in Vilnius managed to deceive her employers – she placed a magnetic card over stacks of chips during games, stealing chips valued at several thousand euros. Later, these chips were cashed at the casino's counter. (Two girls' trick: one stole chips in Vilnius casino, the other cashed them, March 24, 2014)

> I knew it was wrong; I realised I was committing a crime, but I needed the money," said a former liquor store saleswoman. The young cashier failed to get rich at the store's expense – management quickly noticed missing funds. Within just a few days, the store suffered almost 500 euros in losses. (...) Video footage captured the saleswoman consuming alcohol and even dancing with two men at her workplace around 2 AM, before closing. (The liquor store cashier did not just steal – she also danced with customers, January 26, 2015)

The prevailing belief that maternal and caregiving instincts in women are innate results in heightened attention to behaviours contradicting this expectation (Worrall, 1990). Analysed publications vividly portray the **violent or bad mother:**

> Social workers, called to the scene, were horrified upon examining the child: his entire body was covered in bruises from multiple beatings. <...> The 29-year-old mother admitted beating her son after he misbehaved at home. The woman, raising three children alone (the injured boy being the eldest), said she 'lost her temper' and beat him like a punching bag. (A mother beat her child, October 11, 2007)

> One and three-year-old children were found exhausted and with bruised faces. Their 26-year-old mother was intoxicated (2.76 % BAC). <...> The doctor stated that the children suffered not only from beatings but also from severe neglect. Both brothers were filthy, neglected, and possibly underfed. <...> Violence was not new to the woman's household—her eldest child, a 5-year-old son, had already been taken away due to abuse. (Exhausted and beaten children, aged 1 and 3, hospitalised, June 17, 2008)

Even mothers responsible for taking their childrens lives are depicted:

> Several weeks ago, in a drainage ditch, a newborn was found strangled with a rope. Authorities suspect the mother committed the crime due to poverty. <...> The multi-child family was registered among troubled families. <...> Although the woman did not abuse alcohol, the family, like many others, lived off welfare and farming. <...> Speculation arose that stress from familial burdens, lack of money, and psychological issues prompted the young mother's decision. <...> The young woman deeply loved and cared for her five children (Mother of five accused of infant murder, June 27, 2002).

This image of a dangerous, non-maternal mother is directly linked to the portrayal of a mother who drinks excessively, lives in poverty, is irresponsible, lacks social skills, and has limited family support. Such a mother fails to ensure her children's physical and emotional safety, leaves them unattended, neglects their nutritional needs, fails to provide a safe environment, reacts inadequately, or cannot care for her children due to her physical or mental health issues and the absence of support.

Two dominant portrayals emerge for the **bad wife or partner** (cohabitant, spouse, girlfriend)—violent and alcohol-abusing. In many reported cases, violence emerges because of drinking, sometimes with fatal outcomes:

> The woman argued with her husband over 3 euros, and she asked for vodka. The husband refused and started beating her. Having frequently endured beatings before, she inexplicably grabbed a kitchen knife and stabbed him. Afterwards, she cleaned up the blood and informed drinking companions outside that her husband had committed suicide. (An argument over 3 euros became a family tragedy, May 17, 2003)

> That day, the couple received a neighbour and his friend. They drank a litre of vodka and talked in a friendly way. When the neighbour left, the three of them drank intoxicating drinks and had a good time. Then the wife went out for a smoke and returned to find her husband naked and making love to the guest. She lost control and started screaming. The husband was not disturbed; on the contrary, he scolded her not to disturb them. Then the woman took an axe and hit him on the heel. (A woman who has hurt her unfaithful husband will atone for her guilt with a broom, April 28, 2012)

Many publications involving violent female partners share three common factors: the woman is a long-term victim of physical, psychological, or sexual violence, living in poverty or socially deprived conditions, with alcohol being a constant presence in the couple's daily life.

Concluding Remarks

The results of the study reveal that the image of women who commit crimes presented in the publications of the most prominent Lithuanian news portal, DELFI, is influenced by the patriarchal and cultural norms prevailing in society. Media narratives inform and moralise, reinforcing restrictions on women's behaviour, especially if they do not meet traditional expectations for stereotypical female roles, such as mothers, partners, daughters, well-moral, modest, gentle, etc. This analysis allows for several broader insights into the impact of criminal news on public perception and law enforcement practices.

In the discourse of criminal news, a woman who commits a crime is often presented as "doubly deviant"—she violates not only the criminal law but also the norms of "acceptable behaviour" imposed on her by society (Heidensohn, 1996). The study revealed that Lithuanian criminal news particularly reinforces this norm by emphasising the gender of offenders, their motherhood status, and their alleged "lack of femininity."

Moral condemnation dominates female offenders, which we will not find in analogous stories of male crimes. For example, an offender mother is usually treated in the media as the visible opposite of the image of a "good mother"; therefore, she is criminalised not only on a legal but also on a moral level. In this way, the media not only records crimes but also reproduces stereotypical social and moral norms dominant in society, which can affect the audience, law enforcement practices, and criminal policy.

Cases of female offenders presented by the media are often taken out of context, emphasising their "abnormality," but do not provide a more profound social analysis (Curran & Ranzetti, 2001). Crime news lacks a broader approach to the social causes of crimes, especially to the connection of female crime with economic factors, violence in the close environment or psychosocial problems, and the assessment of alternative situations that would allow us to understand the motives of crimes not only through individual moral "depravity," but also through structural factors.

Finally, mocking and demeaning headlines of a sexist nature indicate disrespect for the individual and a high level of bullying culture in the analysed media.

The influence of the media is very significant not only in shaping public opinion but also in criminal policy directions. Negative or stereotypical portrayals can arouse public fear and moral panic and form a false opinion about a person who has committed an offence, and politicians, in order to respond to public sentiment, may prioritise stricter criminal measures (Chesney-Lind, 2006; Frost et al., 2019; Jewkes, 2015; Simpson & Butler, 2015).

The growth in the number of women in prison is a trend observed worldwide (Covington, 2002). Have women started to commit many more crimes over the past few decades? To some extent, yes, but the changes in crime statistics are not so drastic, so the assumption is that women may be punished more severely (Chesney-Lind, 2006). What determines this? One possible factor is the portrayal of female offenders in the media, where gender becomes an essential ingredient of news (Dowler et al., 2006). Sensationalist media tend to raise public concern about supposedly growing crime trends and aggressive behaviour (Chesney-Lind, 2006). Such narratives are flawed for two reasons: first, they do not reflect the actual situation, and second, they create a self-fulfilling prophecy when believing in the supposed evil that is needed, many girls and women (especially from socially vulnerable groups) end up in the criminal justice system (Chesney-Lind & Irwin, 2004).

Criminologists sympathetic to feminism have expressed concern about these trends for more than a quarter of a century, emphasising the need to provide an answer and influence such narratives that are out of touch with reality (Barak, 2006). It is precisely to criminologists that this mission and duty is addressed—to familiarise the public with news and professional information worthy of status. In the author's opinion, one of the most important aspects of this mission is to remind that a person who has committed a crime remains a person. Moreover, a woman who has committed a crime is often a person who carries with her the burden of serious worries, problems, and various traumas.

Although intense media attention to the crime of girls and women has been observed for more than three decades (Chesney-Lind & Irwin,

2004; Faludi, 2006), the essential message sent to the audience has not changed—they are worse than they ever were (Chesney-Lind, 2006). Moreover, the concept of evil includes not only more assertive behaviour or manifestation of violent behaviour but also the failure to fulfil the roles imposed by patriarchy.

Exaggerated media attention towards women accused of crimes, their public con, and stereotypically portrayed images constitute highly appealing content that generates extensive audience attention. Even though only a tiny fraction of criminalised women's stories become news, the stereotypes associated with criminalised women affect them daily. This complicates their reintegration process, creates barriers to employment and daily activities, and has psychological effects.

In conclusion, this study reveals that criminal news not only reflects but actively constructs images of female offenders, which over time may influence criminal policy and societal attitudes towards female offenders. Criminalised women are often depicted as violators of moral norms rather than merely subjects of criminal law; this process illustrates how the media reinforces broader social power structures. To achieve more objective portrayals of criminalised women, it is essential to encourage broader discourse in the media, promote journalistic ethics, reduce bullying culture, and educate the public to foster a deeper societal understanding of the real-life circumstances, issues, and factors underlying women's criminal behaviour.

References

Barak, G. (2006). Newsmaking criminology: Reflections of the media, intellectuals, and crime. *Justice Quarterly, 5*(4), 565–587.

Berger, M. L. (1986). Women drivers! The emergence of folklore and stereotypic opinions concerning feminine automotive behavior. *Women's Studies International Forum, 9*(3), 257–263.

Birkbeck, R. (2014). Media representations of crime and criminal justice. In *Oxford Handbook Topics in Criminology and Criminal Justice* (pp. 1–13).

Chesney-Lind, M. (2006). Patriarchy, crime, and justice. Feminist criminology in an era of backlash. *Feminist Criminology, 1*(1), 6–26.

Chesney-Lind, M., & Irwin, K. (2004). From badness to meanness: Popular constructions of contemporary girlhood. *All about the girls: Culture, power, and identity* (pp. 44–56). Routledge.

Covington, S. (2002). Helping women recover: Creating gender-responsive treatment. In *The handbook of addiction treatment for women* (pp. 52–72).

Curran, D. J., & Renzetti, C. M. (2001). *Theories of crime*. Allyn & Bacon.

Ditton, J., & Duffy, J. (1983). Bias in the newspaper reporting of crime news. *British Journal of Criminology, 23*(2), 159–165.

Dobryninas, A., Kalpokas, V., & Mickevič, A. (2014). Murder in Lithuania: A sociological perspective. *Kriminologijos Studijos, 2*, 41–95.

Dowler, K., Fleming, T., & Muzzatti, S. L. (2006). Constructing crime: Media, crime, and popular culture. *Canadian Journal of Criminology and Criminal Justice, 48*(6), 837–850.

Ercan, N. & Ulug, O.M. (2015). *You see that driver? I bet that's a woman! A social psychological approach to understand sexism in traffic*. International Conference on Knowledge and Politics in Gender and Women's Studies.

Faludi, S. (2006). *Backlash: The undeclared war against American women*. Three Rivers Press.

Frost, N. A., Trapassi, J., & Heinz, S. (2019). Public opinion and correctional privatization. *Criminology and Public Policy, 18*(2), 457–476.

Hartman, M. (1977). *Victorian murderesses: A true history of thirteen respectable French and English women accused of unspeakable crimes*. Robson Books.

Heidensohn, F. M. (1996). *Women and crime*. Macmillan Press.

Jewkes, Y. (2015). *Media and crime*. Sage Publications.

Kowalik, K.J. (2022). *Media influenced perceptions of female offenders: Comparative analysis of gender and offense* (Doctoral dissertation). Fielding Graduate University.

Lloyd, A. (1995). *Doubly deviant, doubly damned: Society's treatment of violent women*. Penguin Books.

Lundman, R. J. (2003). The newsworthiness and selection bias in news about murder. *Sociological Forum, 18*(3), 357–386.

Marsh, I., & Melville, G. (2009). *Crime, justice and the media*. Routledge.

Morrissey, B. (2003). *When women kill. Questions of agency and subjectivity*. Routledge.

Naylor, B. (2001). Reporting violence in the British print media gendered stories. *The Howard Journal of Criminal Justice, 40*, 180–194.

Simpson, P. L., & Butler, T. (2015). Assessing the public's views on prison and prison alternatives: Findings from public deliberation research in three Australian cities. *Journal of Deliberative Democracy, 11*(2).

Soothill, K., Peelo, M., Francis, B., Pearson, J., & Ackerley, E. (2002). Homicide and the media: Identifying the top cases in The Times. *The Howard Journal, 41*(5), 401–421.

Sorenson, S., Peterson-Manz, J. G., & Berk, R. A. (1998). News media coverage and the epidemiology of homicide. *American Journal of Public Health, 88*(10), 1510–1514.

Tereškinas, A., Vaičiūnienė, R., Nikartas, S. and Jarutienė, L. (2021). *Moterys Lietuvos baudžiamojo teisingumo sistemoje: nuo baudimo praktikų iki bausmės patirčių: monografija*. Žara.

Worrall, A. (1990). *Offending women: Female lawbreakers and the criminal justice system* (pp. 8–42). Routledge.

Part III

Institutional Punitiveness

11

A Reform Again? Explaining Reorganisation Processes and Perspectives of Imprisonment in Lithuania

Jolanta Aleknevičienė

Introduction

Reforms of the penal enforcement system and reorganisation of prisons are widely debated in many countries worldwide, including Lithuania. The need for changes in the system arises from national strategic guidelines, international standards, and human rights protection requirements. In Lithuania, this issue remains remarkably relevant. Despite the standards outlined in the European Prison Rules (Council of Europe, 2020), inmate resocialisation and the protection of human rights continue to pose significant challenges in Lithuania.

The United Nations Standard Minimum Rules (United Nations, 2015) emphasise preserving prisoners' dignity and the importance of

J. Aleknevičienė (✉)
Faculty of Philosophy, Institute of Sociology and Social Work, Department of Criminology, Vilnius University, Vilnius, Lithuania
e-mail: jolanta.alekneviciene@fsf.vu.lt

A. Dobryninas and S. Nikartas (eds.), *Understanding Crime Control and Punishment in Lithuania*, Crime Prevention and Security Management,
https://doi.org/10.1007/978-3-032-05538-5_11

resocialisation. However, their integration into Lithuanian law and practice remains insufficient. The Lithuanian penitentiary system continues to face significant issues. The latest report by the National Audit Office (2024) highlights that inmates in six Lithuanian prisons in 2023 were provided with less than the recommended minimum of 4 square meters of living space. Furthermore, the goal of resocialisation remains unfulfilled, mainly because just over one-third of convicted persons participated in behaviour modification programs in 2023. Moreover, the Lithuanian penal enforcement system does not effectively encourage inmates to abandon criminal behaviours; it is declared that more than 60% of the incarcerated are repeat offenders. The penitentiary system also struggles with staff management issues, including an imbalanced salary system, insufficient staff competence to fulfil current and new duties, and a general lack of employees. The general staff shortage in Lithuanian prisons is 21%, while in the resocialisation units, it reaches 29% in 2023. Notably, in 2021, 87 million euros were allocated to maintain Lithuania's penal enforcement system. Additionally, extra funds were required to compensate inmates for poor detention conditions. In 2021, courts reviewed 592 cases concerning inmate compensation—an increase of 37% compared to 2020. As a result, courts awarded inmates 131,200 euros in compensation, representing a 29% increase from the previous year (National Audit Office, 2024).

Taking account of the problems, the 18th Government of Lithuania identified penal enforcement reform as one of its priority initiatives in its program (Government of the Republic of Lithuania,). The planned reform aimed to ensure detention conditions that comply with established standards, provide methodological support to officers and staff, enhance qualification improvement opportunities, foster internal motivation, and improve the reintegration process for inmates so that, upon release, they pursue their life goals through lawful means. A strategic objective was to develop a next-generation penal enforcement system. In 2021, the Lithuanian Government approved the implementation plan for this program, assigning the Minister of Justice a strategic task: establishing an efficient and modern penal enforcement system. These documents marked the strategic direction for overhauling Lithuania's penal enforcement system, which will be discussed there.

This chapter seeks to answer these research questions: What is the current incarceration situation in Lithuania, and what are its main challenges? How is the reorganisation of prisons progressing? Can this reform bring about significant changes in the penal enforcement system in Lithuania?

The chapter aims to analyse the situation of incarceration and its issues in Lithuania, examine the ongoing prison reorganisation process, and explore how the core objective of incarceration—prisoner resocialisation—is being shaped. Additionally, it discusses whether the current reforms can potentially drive more profound changes in penal enforcement. The research employs an analysis of international and national legal and strategic documents, a review of statistical data, an examination of qualitative research findings, and a study of academic literature.

It is also valuable to briefly introduce the research landscape concerning Lithuania's penitentiary system issues. Notably, criminologist G. Sakalauskas and colleagues contributed to the field by publishing the monograph "*Conditions of Imprisonment and Premises for Social Integration of Prisoners*" (Sakalauskas et al., 2020) and by addressing the concept and challenges of resocialisation in various articles (Sakalauskas, 2012, 2015). Likewise, R. Vaičiūnienė and V. Viršilas (2017, 2018) have examined the implementation practices of resocialisation and the application of resocialisation measures. The models of resocialisation, their application in Lithuania, and the implementation of social rehabilitation in prisons were analysed in the work of L. Žilinskienė and R. Tumilaitė (2011). The objectives of incarceration in Lithuania have been evaluated from the perspective of critical criminology by J. Aleknevičienė(2022). The topic of resocialisation has also been explored by J. Aleknevičienė and I. Kalinauskaitė (2023), R. Prakapas and R. Katinaitė (2008), and J. Piliponytė (Aleknevičienė) (2000). The reform of Lithuania's system of enforcement of sentences has been analysed by R. Uscila (2022).

The first part of this chapter discusses the current incarceration state in Lithuania, highlighting statistical data and criminological research findings while identifying key challenges in the penitentiary system, particularly concerning achieving its primary objective—resocialisation. The following part examines the goals and implementation process of penal enforcement reforms in Lithuania, focusing on restructuring correctional institutions. Furthermore, the study explores inmate resocialisation, including its definition, processes, and practical applications. Finally, drawing on the ideas of critical criminology, the impact and future perspectives of these reforms are discussed.

The Incarceration Situation and Issues in Lithuania

Incarceration statistics, criminological research, and penal enforcement policy reveal various challenges within Lithuania's penitentiary system, which will be discussed in this section. Despite efforts to modernise the system of enforcement of sentences, Lithuania has one of the highest incarceration rates in the European Union (EU). At the beginning of 2023, Lithuania had 174 inmates per 100,000 inhabitants, compared to 172 in Latvia and 151 in Estonia. Among EU countries, only Czechia (176), Slovakia (183), Poland (194), and Hungary (211) had higher incarceration rates than Lithuania, while the EU average was 116 (Aebi & Cocco, 2024).

The 2024 Human Rights Monitoring Report in Lithuania highlights that more than 25,000 individuals served various types of sentences, with about one-third serving custodial sentences. This proportion has remained essentially unchanged over the past seven years. As in many other countries, Lithuania's total number of prisoners has steadily declined, dropping by more than 50% over the past twelve years. Lithuanian researchers suggest that this decline may be attributed to amendments in the Lithuanian Criminal Code and the Penal Enforcement Code and an overall decrease in crime rates (Sakalauskas, 2024). However, despite this decline, Lithuania's incarceration rate remains significantly higher than that of other EU countries. In 2023, nearly 8500 individuals served custodial sentences, of whom approximately 6500 were serving fixed-term imprisonment, around 2000 were sentenced to arrest, and 99 were serving life sentences. The sentencing structure indicates that long-term imprisonment continues to dominate, with around 55% of convicted prisoners serving sentences of five years or longer. The frequent and prolonged use of imprisonment remains one of the main factors contributing to Lithuania's relatively high prisoner numbers.

A comprehensive qualitative study[1] identified key challenges in the Lithuanian penitentiary system at systemic, organisational, and individual levels based on expert and practitioner insights (Aleknevičienė & Kalinauskaitė, 2023).

Systemic-Level Issues: The study found that the officially stated aim of incarceration—resocialisation—is largely declarative and not prioritised in practice. Leadership roles within the penitentiary system are often assigned to individuals with a security or law enforcement background, primarily to maintain institutional control. At the same time, resocialisation is delegated to specific units and not treated as a systemic objective. Low political interest in prison reform drives a pronounced disparity between the declared goals and available financial resources. Prison conditions, including dormitory-style accommodations, lack of privacy, and inadequate facilities, undermine rehabilitation efforts. Employment opportunities for inmates are limited, with fewer than half engaged in work or creative activities in 2023. Post-release reintegration is hindered by the absence of a national support model and inconsistent service provision at the municipal level. Additionally, deficiencies in prison staff training and working conditions contribute to a punitive institutional culture and poor staff-inmate relations. Public stigma against former inmates remains a significant barrier to reintegration.

Organisational-Level Issues: The hostile social climate in prisons, driven by entrenched informal subcultures, obstructs participation in resocialisation programs and fosters mistrust. Behavioural correction programs are insufficient, and inmates have long waiting periods, reducing inmate motivation. Risk assessment methodologies lack precision, with inconsistent classification and subjectivity affecting access to resocialisation programs. Monitoring resocialisation efforts is limited to quantitative indicators, which do not capture program quality or effectiveness, hindering process evaluation and improvement.

[1] A comprehensive qualitative study was conducted between 2022 and 2023 by Ignė Kalinauskaitė. The research involved 20 semi-structured interviews with 22 participants, including experts from the Lithuanian prison system and prison staff. All participants were ensured confidentiality, and their data were anonymised following ethical research standards.

Individual-Level Issues: Many inmates are unable to participate meaningfully in resocialisation programs due to underdeveloped social skills, mental health conditions, addiction, or developmental disorders. These individuals require preliminary medical, psychological, and life skills interventions before resocialisation.

Thus, the Lithuanian penitentiary system faces significant challenges in implementing prisoner resocialisation as its primary declared objective of incarceration. Systemic deficiencies, such as insufficient funding, misalignment of priorities, and infrastructure problems, limit the potential for change. At the organisational level, there is an apparent lack of cooperation and communication between units, while the social climate in prisons remains unfavourable for behavioural change among inmates. At the individual level, prisoners often lack social skills and support mechanisms that would facilitate their successful reintegration into society after serving their sentence.

Systemic and structural issues have also been discussed in the works of Lithuanian criminologists (Sakalauskas et al., 2020; Slade & Vaičiūnienė, 2018; Uscila, 2022), as well as in the 2024 report by the National Audit Office, which highlights evident problems related to inadequate funding, staff shortages, and the absence of evaluation mechanisms for behavioural correction programs. Although incarceration statistics in Lithuania indicate a decline in the number of prisoners, experts generally agree that resocialisation is an appropriate goal of imprisonment, as outlined in strategic documents. The declared aim of resocialisation primarily serves to obscure the negative consequences of incarceration and the negative experience in prison. These research findings enrich the results of a previous quantitative study of prisoners (Sakalauskas et al., 2020), which revealed a significant gap between legal provisions and the actual conditions of incarceration. The problems identified by prisoners indicate that, under the current circumstances, imprisonment can only incidentally contribute to social integration or resocialisation. This is because prison resocialisation is not implemented systematically, individually tailored, planned, and step by step. There is no suitable infrastructure to support this process, while continuous confrontation with prison staff and prevailing distrust further reinforce criminal behaviour among inmates (Sakalauskas et al., 2020).

The information discussed highlights the persistent structural and systemic challenges facing Lithuania's penitentiary system, despite measurable reductions in the overall prison population and formal commitments to resocialisation as the core objective of incarceration. Lithuania continues to maintain one of the highest incarceration rates in the European Union, with a sentencing structure heavily reliant on long-term imprisonment. Criminological research and expert assessments reveal that resocialisation remains symbolic mainly in practice. The penitentiary system is characterised by underfunding, insufficient institutional coordination, inadequate infrastructure, and a lack of empirical evaluation mechanisms. Moreover, negative prison environments, limited inmate employment, and public stigma against former prisoners hinder reintegration efforts. At the individual level, many inmates lack the foundational support necessary for participation in resocialisation programs. The research data underscore a systemic misalignment between declared policy objectives and the actual conditions of imprisonment, raising critical concerns about the capacity of the Lithuanian penitentiary system to implement meaningful resocialisation outcomes.

It is evident that over the past thirty-five years of Lithuania's independence, the penitentiary system has been among those that have changed slowly and only a little. Therefore, it is important to examine the ongoing reform and its significance. The following section explores the reform process of the penal enforcement system and the aspects of prison reorganisation in Lithuania.

The Process of Reforming Lithuania's Penal Enforcement System and Peculiarities of Prisons Reorganisation

This section discusses the objectives, directions, and implementation of sentence enforcement system reform in Lithuania, focusing on reorganising correctional institutions to implement resocialisation.

Over the past decades, a few reforms have been implemented in Lithuania's sentence enforcement system, encompassing modernisation, renovation, and humanisation of correctional institutions. Although modernisation plans for places of detention were developed and initiated, their implementation was fragmented, lacking consistent funding and political support. Due to these shortcomings, the restructuring of the penitentiary system has been prolonged, and the ambition to establish a more effective penal enforcement system has been only minimally realised.

A new impetus for reforms was provided by the strategic goals outlined in the *Programme of the Eighteenth Government of the Republic of Lithuania*—to create a next-generation penal enforcement system. This objective was further supported by the *Justice System Development Programme for 2021–2030*, prepared by the Ministry of Justice, which emphasises that the current system is not sufficiently effective in altering offenders'criminal behaviour patterns. The main issues include inadequate infrastructure, insufficient resocialisation and social support for inmates, and a shortage of qualified personnel.

Considering these challenges, the reform aimed to enhance the efficiency of the penal enforcement system by ensuring effective resocialisation of inmates, incarceration conditions that meet the highest standards of human rights protection, and attractive, safe working conditions for system employees (Ministry of Justice of the Republic of Lithuania, 2021). The goal of increasing the efficiency of the penal enforcement system is also enshrined in the *National Progress Plan for 2021–2030* (Government of the Republic of Lithuania,), which highlights the necessity of systematically reforming the penitentiary system to achieve the objectives of justice, resocialisation, and public security.

External donors have played a significant role in the reform of Lithuania's penitentiary system. The Prison Department (now Lithuanian Prison Service) implemented the *Project Development of Quality-Based Lithuanian Correctional Service System* under the EEA and Norwegian Financial Mechanisms program, Justice and Home Affairs 2014–2021. Since September 2020, a joint project with Norway has been ongoing and is set to continue until 2024. The main objectives of this initiative are to reform the professional training, education, and competency development system for penal enforcement personnel, enhance the resocialisation process for inmates, strengthen inter-institutional cooperation, create modern infrastructure tailored for the vocational training of inmates, and develop electronic monitoring.

In order to fundamentally transform the resocialisation process of inmates, the Director of the Prison Department approved the *Concept of Resocialization Reform of Convicted Persons* on 7 January 2021 (Prison Department under the Ministry of Justice of the Republic of Lithuania, 2021a, 2021b). The primary goal of this document is to institutionalise systemic changes that position resocialisation as the central axis of penal enforcement. The concept defines resocialisation as a "complex process of social learning," wherein individualised and group-based interventions—including social work, psychological counselling, employment programs, treatment, and other measures that promote positive behaviour—build inmates' motivation to adopt a lawful lifestyle. The document emphasises applying the principles of "normalisation of life in correctional institutions and reducing the harmful effects of imprisonment" within the resocialisation process. Additionally, the concept highlights the importance of motivation enhancement as an essential condition for successful social reintegration. The long-term goal of the reform is to strengthen public security by reducing the risk of recidivism.

The *Concept of Resocialization Reform of Convicted Persons* outlines the main directions and activities of the reform, encompassing: (1) personnel: employee training and qualification improvement, structuring of positions and remuneration systems, and defining qualification requirements; (2) inmate management: differentiation of custodial sentences, individualised work with inmates, addiction treatment, employment organisation, application of short-term leave, and the implementation of incentive and disciplinary mechanisms; (3) institutional cooperation: inclusion of social partners, non-governmental organisations, and volunteers, management of the resocialisation process, and implementation of work reflection and supervision practices; (4) material resources: expansion of infrastructure, financing models, and coordination of the inmate release process; (5) synergy between science and practice: evaluation of the effectiveness of resocialisation measures based on criminological research.

The document analysis shows that this reform represents a paradigmatic shift in Lithuania's penal enforcement system, aiming to ensure that the sentence served adheres to international human rights standards and contributes to the successful reintegration of inmates into society.

Continuing the analysis of policy documents, it is important to note that following the approval of the *Concept of Resocialization Reform*, an action plan was developed, emphasising the necessity of conducting a comprehensive analysis of the resocialisation situation, preparing proposals, and establishing strategies for their implementation. The document highlights the importance of addressing the individual needs of inmates, reducing the risk of criminal behaviour, and ensuring their successful reintegration into society upon release (Prison Department under the Ministry of Justice of the Republic of Lithuania, 2021b).

Thus, the strategic documents examined identify the main directions for addressing the problems of imprisonment: infrastructure improvement, upgrading detention conditions by the highest human rights protection standards, and modernising the penal enforcement system; impact on inmates, creating conditions that encourage former inmates to pursue life goals through lawful means, developing an effective resocialisation system, applying advanced methods, and reducing the harmful effects of imprisonment; strengthening personnel, improving working conditions, enhancing qualifications, and balancing staff numbers with workload demands.

In 2021, the Ministry of Justice announced that, in pursuit of a more efficient penal enforcement system reform, it was planned to reorganise the Prison Department and its subordinate institutions by merging them into a single legal entity—the *Lithuanian Prison Service*. This institution aims to ensure more transparent and effective administration, greater security, prevention of recidivism, and uniform enforcement practices while simultaneously reducing corruption risks (Ministry of Justice of the Republic of Lithuania, 2021b). Thus, the reform of Lithuania's penal enforcement system was focused on enhancing overall operational efficiency and establishing uniform penal enforcement practices, improving staff qualifications and working conditions, modernising incarceration conditions, strengthening inmate resocialisation, and increasing public trust in the penal enforcement system. These changes indicate a fundamental shift in approach—from a traditional penal enforcement system to a model where resocialisation and recidivism prevention become priorities.

The *Strategic Operational Guidelines of the Lithuanian Penal System* for 2022–2030 were developed based on the discussed strategic documents. These guidelines were formalised in 2022 by order of the Director of the Prison Department, becoming the *Strategic Operational Guidelines of the Prison Department 2022–2030* (later—Lithuania Prison Service). The guidelines identify three main directions for improving the penal enforcement system: human resources management and development, management of operational areas, infrastructure development, and digitisation. These strategic objectives aim to ensure the effectiveness of the penal enforcement system, enhance the integration of employees and inmates into the reformed system, and improve the overall quality of system governance (Lithuanian Prison Service, 2022).

It is important to note that one of the key stages in the reform of the penal enforcement system was the separation of the Lithuanian Probation Service from the Prison Department on 1 July 2022. The Probation Service became an independent institution directly subordinate to the Ministry of Justice of the Republic of Lithuania. Further reform occurred on 1 January 2023, when the Prison Department was reorganised into the Lithuanian Prison Service. This new institution assumed all functions and responsibilities of correctional facilities, becoming the central governing body for penitentiary institutions. Now, eight prisons operate under the Lithuanian Prison Service, performing penal enforcement and resocialisation functions. According to former Justice Minister's Advisor R. Uscila, this reform established in Lithuania the dualistic model of the penal enforcement system, which is predominant in Europe, whereby two independent yet equivalent penitentiary institutions operate—the Lithuanian Probation Service, responsible for alternative sentences and the supervision of offenders in the community and the Lithuanian Prison Service, responsible for the enforcement of custodial sentences and the supervision of detainees (Uscila, 2022). R. Uscila, as one of the reform's implementers, emphasised that the main features of the reform of Lithuania's penal enforcement system are (1) centralisation—ensuring transparent institutional management and more efficient administration; (2) clarification of functions and areas of activity—distinctly separating the objectives of resocialisation, penal enforcement, and probation; (3) optimisation of staff work—emphasising direct work with offenders and their resocialisation; (4) enhancement of resocialisation effectiveness—strengthening inmates' preparation for integration into society after serving their sentence; (5) improve personnel competencies—increasing staff qualifications, organising training, and ensuring attractive working conditions; and (6) modernisation of infrastructure—digitising processes and improving detention conditions. Thus, the reform aimed to establish a penal enforcement system that is efficient, transparent, and oriented towards resocialisation, ensuring that correctional facilities provide not only conditions for serving a sentence but also opportunities for inmates' resocialisation and integration into society.

Next, we will examine offender resocialisation as a key priority in reforming the penal enforcement system.

At the international level, inmate resocialisation is emphasised in the *United Nations Standard Minimum Rules for the Treatment of Prisoners* (the Nelson Mandela Rules), which state that the primary objective of custodial sentences is public protection and recidivism reduction. To achieve these goals, the execution of a sentence must be oriented towards the gradual reintegration of offenders into society (United Nations, 2015).

In Lithuania's legal framework, resocialisation is enshrined in the *Penal Enforcement Code*. Article 1 of the Code emphasises that a sentence must be executed so that, upon completion, the offender pursues life goals through lawful means and methods. Article 52 of the Code specifies that inmate resocialisation is based on criminal behaviour risk management—the application of individualised measures aimed at reducing the likelihood of recidivism and implementing restorative justice, seeking not only to punish the offender but also to restore their social ties with the community. The resocialisation measures include social work, psychological and spiritual support, education and vocational training, inmate employment, and leisure activities. These measures should be essential for mitigating imprisonment's consequences and promoting offenders' reintegration into society (Seimas of the Republic of Lithuania, 2002).

In Lithuania, particular attention has been given to resocialisation in the penal enforcement reform and national strategic documents. The *Justification of the Development Programme for the Justice System for 2021–2030*, prepared by the Ministry of Justice of the Republic of Lithuania, aimed to "optimise the resocialisation and assistance system for convicted persons" (Government of the Republic of Lithuania, 2021). This demonstrates that resocialisation has become a priority not only within the penal enforcement system but also in the broader justice policy strategy.

The *Strategic Operational Guidelines of the Prison Service for 2022–2030* (Lithuanian Prison Service, 2022) state that "the sole objective of penal enforcement is the resocialisation of offenders." These guidelines outline three key strategic goals for resocialisation: enhancing the efficiency of resocialisation process management—establishing monitoring and analysis mechanisms to assess the impact of applied measures; expansion and optimisation of resocialisation measures—ensuring individualised resocialisation measures are applied to all offenders; monitoring the quality of resocialisation—creating a continuous monitoring system to evaluate the long-term effects of resocialisation measures.

The *National Progress Plan for 2021–2030* (Government of the Republic of Lithuania,) states that the conditions of incarceration and the implementation of advanced resocialisation measures must meet the requirements established in national and international standards. The *Programme of the Government of the Republic of Lithuania*, approved in 2020, emphasises the importance of reforming penal enforcement institutions, which should focus on inmate resocialisation and re-offending prevention. This document also formulates the main directions of the penal enforcement system reform: developing a clear vision for penal institutions, expanding resocialisation and behaviour correction programs, modernising the probation system, and ensuring appropriate conditions in penal enforcement institutions (Government of the Republic of Lithuania, 2020a, 2020b). These reform priorities are also reflected in the strategic documents of the Ministry of Justice of the Republic of Lithuania (Government of the Republic of Lithuania, 2021; Ministry of Justice of the Republic of Lithuania, 2021; Ministry of Justice of the Republic of Lithuania, 2022).

As mentioned above, *The Concept of Resocialization Reform for Convicted Persons in Lithuania,* approved in 2021, sets out the goal of establishing the foundations for the restructuring of the penal enforcement system, ensuring that resocialisation becomes the central objective of incarceration (Prison Department under the Ministry of Justice of the Republic of Lithuania, 2021a). Following the approval of the concept, an action plan was developed, emphasising the importance of analysing the resocialisation situation, drafting strategic proposals, and defining mechanisms for their implementation. This document also highlights the individual needs of inmates, the reduction of criminal behaviour risks, and the reintegration process into society (Prison Department under the Ministry of Justice of the Republic of Lithuania, 2021b).

In 2024, the Lithuanian Prison Service developed a *Regulation on Operation Resocialization Divisions in Lithuanian Prisons* (Lithuanian Prison Service, 2024a) to standardise penal enforcement processes across Lithuanian prisons. This document regulates the organisation and operation of the Resocialization Division staff, process management, and their interaction with other service units. The *Resocialization Standard for Convicted Persons* (Lithuanian Prison Service, 2024b) was also drafted and approved. This document establishes the fundamental principles, mandatory norms, rules of the resocialisation process, and the key requirements for the process and the professionals involved. It also includes a *Strategic Directions Matrix for Resocialization,* detailing the main aspects of the reform.

Thus, the analysed strategic documents highlight the positive impact on the individual as a fundamental approach to understanding and addressing incarceration-related issues. The content presented in these documents leads to the assumption that resocialisation should be implemented effectively. However, the various authors' criminological research presented in the first part of this chapter has revealed numerous critical issues within the penitentiary system.

When examining the implementation of inmate resocialisation, it is noteworthy that the resocialisation measures applied in Lithuanian correctional institutions include approved behavioural correction programs, among which are *The Motivational Program,* which assesses participants' suitability for further programs, and positive engagement activities upon completion, *Rehabilitation Program for Individuals Dependent on Psychoactive Substances*, a group program *EQUIP* targeted at individuals aged 14–25, an individual cognitive-behavioural correction program "*Just You and Me*" covering modules on violence prevention, psychoactive substance use prevention, and criminal behaviour modification, and a group program *SeNAT* designed for offenders who have committed sexual offenses against children. In 2024, additional resocialisation programs were approved, such as an *Anger Management Program, a Program for Individuals Convicted of Driving Under the Influence*, and *a Program for Individuals Abusing Psychoactive Substances*. Currently, no studies have been conducted to assess the effectiveness of these programs, leaving their impact unclear.

The resocialisation process in Lithuanian prisons includes various programs and activities aimed at developing inmates' social skills, education, and vocational training. However, academic research (Aleknevičienė, Kalinauskaitė, 2023) highlights practical challenges related to limited resources, staff shortages, and other systemic factors. Many unapproved programs and positive engagement activities are still being implemented in Lithuanian prisons, with no scientific evaluation of their effectiveness.

Statistics on resocialisation program participation indicate that in 2024 (Lithuanian Prison Service, 2021–2024), sixty-four social rehabilitation programs were conducted in Lithuanian correctional institutions. 1591 inmates completed approved resocialisation programs (compared to 1196 in 2023). This information was not available in previous years. Only the number of participants of approved resocialisation programs was published: 981 in 2022 and 1186 in 2021. These data indicate a significant increase in inmate participation in approved resocialisation programs. However, there is currently insufficient empirical data to assess the quality of the resocialisation process and its long-term effects. Academic research views unapproved programs as lacking explicit content and proven effectiveness.

While the legal framework and strategic documents provide a foundation for the resocialisation process, significant challenges persist in practice, including insufficient funding, which limits resocialisation measures' expansion and specialists' training; a shortage of qualified professionals makes ensuring program consistency and quality difficult. Negative public attitudes towards inmates complicate their reintegration after release (Lithuanian Centre for Social Sciences, 2022). So, resocialisation, as the primary goal of incarceration, is clearly stated in legal acts and strategic documents. However, the practical implementation of this system faces substantial obstacles that hinder the achievement of set objectives.

The significance of resocialisation in Lithuania's penitentiary system was also revealed almost twenty-five years ago. A survey of inmates posed the question: "*Do you believe that the reformed Lithuanian prison system is capable of restoring an incarcerated person's ability to live freely in society?*" The responses were as follows: 16% answered "yes," 18% "partially," 11% "no," and 55% stated "no, but it could be possible in the future" (Piliponytė, 2000). After a quarter of a century, this question remains relevant within the context of ongoing prison reform. Despite the growing academic interest in resocialisation, Lithuania still lacks comprehensive studies on the effectiveness of resocialisation measures.

In response to these challenges and priorities, in 2024, the Lithuanian Prison Service identified the following strategic goals—enhancing the resocialisation process to reduce recidivism and promoting the reintegration of inmates into society by ensuring post-release support, developing new resocialisation measures and adapting them to international best practices, implementing a team-based resocialisation model to improve coordination among institutions and specialists.

This chapter reveals that while Lithuania has made significant strides in aligning its penal enforcement system with international standards, particularly by institutionalising resocialisation as the core objective of incarceration, substantial implementation challenges remain. The transition from a punitive to a rehabilitative model is evident in strategic documents and legal frameworks. However, persistent issues such as inadequate funding, staff shortages, and limited program evaluation hinder the practical realisation of reform goals. Despite measurable increases in inmate participation in resocialisation programs, the absence of empirical data on their effectiveness underscores the need for evidence-based practice and long-term strategic planning.

Critical Criminology Reflections on Lithuania's Penal Enforcement System Reform

Whether the current reform of Lithuania's penitentiary system could lead to more profound systemic and social changes in the penal enforcement system and potentially in public attitudes remains open and timely. To explore this question, we employ a critical perspective, drawing on the dominant ideas of critical criminology from the second half of the twentieth century (Christie, 1999; Hulsman, 1997; Mathiesen, 2006). It is important to note that the emergence of critical criminology was influenced by research conducted in the United States during the 1970s and 1980s, which reported the ineffectiveness of resocialisation programs. These studies indicated that rehabilitation efforts had only a minimal impact on reducing recidivism. Neither education and vocational training, medical treatment, individual or group counselling, nor group therapy produced the expected effects in rehabilitating offenders or reducing the rate of reoffending (Martinson, 1974).

Furthermore, based on findings from late twentieth-century studies on the effectiveness of resocialisation, significant reforms were implemented in the penitentiary systems of Norway, Denmark, Germany, France, the United Kingdom, Italy, and Spain. The implementation of these reforms was driven not only by state-level criminal justice policies but also by active organisations and movements advocating for radical changes in prison conditions and crime prevention strategies. Some of these organisations were established by academics and researchers, such as the Norwegian Association of Penal Reform (KROM), co-founded by T. Mathiesen in Norway, and the Information Group on Prisons (GIP), co-founded by M. Foucault in France, seeking systemic changes through legal reform and public discourse. Other organisations were initiated by inmates, organising collective resistance against prison regimes and penal policies. Their common goal was to reform criminal justice policies to minimise harm to inmates and incorporate humane and resocialisation-focused sanctions.

Critical criminology highlights the inherently political nature of crime and criminal justice. Scholars in this field argue that correctional institutions are inherently painful and desocialising environments. Prisons were historically designed to isolate and punish individuals rather than to rehabilitate them (Christie, 1999; Mathiesen, 2006; Sykes, 2007). According to T. Mathiesen (2006), despite the declared goal of rehabilitation, what occurs in prisons is *prisonisation*—a process in which inmates adjust to the prevailing prison culture, customs, and norms. Mathiesen (2006) referred to prisons as "schools of crime." N. Christie (1999) further argued that for many years, the infliction of pain through punishment was legitimised and justified but also subtly concealed.

According to G. Sykes (2007), although the declared purpose of prisons has not been to inflict suffering for some time, the psychological pain of incarceration can be as crushing as the physical suffering caused by cruel treatment. The issue of the pains of imprisonment is also examined by B. Crewe (2011), who highlights the psychological burden experienced by inmates. The scholar draws attention to the challenges inmates face when seeking psychological support. Since prison staff conduct risk assessments, disclosing personal struggles and emotions can be perceived as a sign of increased risk, potentially delaying an inmate's release. B. Crewe (2011) also identifies the pains of self-regulation. Inmates are expected to take responsibility for their resocialisation process while being regarded as individuals requiring strict control. Consequently, the critical criminological perspective, which views prison as an institution masking retribution and control, raises an essential question: are changes within prisons possible, and if so, what kind of changes?

T. Mathiesen observed that reforms often create the impression that changes occur while the fundamental structures remain unchanged. In Lithuania, this is evident in the emphasis placed on infrastructure modernisation. In contrast, social aspects—such as the effectiveness of resocialisation programs and the limited expansion of alternative sanctions—receive relatively little attention. D. Garland (2001), one of the most prominent contemporary criminologists specialising in punishment policy, social control, and the state's penal power, argues that modern democratic states increasingly rely on criminal justice to manage social problems.

From a critical criminology perspective, the ongoing reform of Lithuania's penal enforcement system faces fundamental challenges that may limit its potential to bring about more profound systemic changes. The following aspects are noteworthy:

- *Discrepancy between declared goals and practical implementation.* Although the stated objectives of custodial sentences are to protect society and reduce recidivism, in practice, resocialisation remains fragmented. Critical criminologists such as N. Christie and L. Hulsman emphasise that penal systems often serve as mechanisms of social control rather than instruments of offender reintegration. In Lithuania, resocialisation concepts may be "imprisoned" within political discourse, lacking critical analysis and concrete implementation mechanisms (Aleknevičienė et al., 2022).
- *Structural deficiencies and staff challenges.* The success of the reform is hindered by inadequate funding and personnel shortages, which may be interpreted as systemic problems. The lack of staff also poses a significant risk to the proper implementation of resocialisation programs.
- *Challenges in infrastructure modernisation.* Slow infrastructure modernisation and non-compliance with international standards suggest that the reform may focus more on symbolic than substantive changes. From a critical perspective, symbolic reforms are often used to legitimise the existing system without altering its fundamental principles.
- *Dependence on external funding.* The reform has relied mainly on Norwegian financial mechanisms, which expired in 2024, raising concerns about its long-term sustainability.
- *Unclear long-term objectives.* For instance, while the goal is to reduce the prison population to 3000 by 2030, there is no clear strategy or plan.
- *Lack of long-term monitoring indicators.* According to Ramakers et al. (2024), successful reintegration of inmates should not be assessed solely by their employment status but also by their long-term social trajectories. In Lithuania, resocialisation is still evaluated superficially, based on the number of program participants or immediate post-release employment rates, without a deeper analysis of long-term life outcomes.

Thus, while reforming Lithuania's penal enforcement system has some positive aspects, the critical criminology perspective reveals underlying problems that may limit its progress and sustainability. The reform risks remaining inertial and fragmented, failing to achieve its declared objectives.

V. Morris (2023) states that reforms can be harm-reducing, system-reorienting, or fundamentally transformative—"imaginable reforms that reduce the harms and use of carceral spaces and practices, semi-imaginable reforms that work to divert and decarcerate people from custody, and unimaginable reforms that replace oppressive structures with caring and compassionate ones." Analysis shows that Lithuania's reform currently aligns with the first category—harm reduction (imaginable reform). Modernising prison infrastructure and optimising personnel are important, but the development of alternative sentencing and a fundamental shift in approach remains weak. Penal policy formation requires comprehensive and ongoing scientific research. There should be a broader discussion on systemic social issues—poverty, social exclusion, education, and addiction—as well as alternative measures to punishment that address public safety and recidivism, given that crime has social roots. Prison reforms remain slow and ineffective without political, institutional, and cultural changes (Sliva & Lin, 2024).

While Lithuania's penal enforcement reform could improve the infrastructure of imprisonment, administrative management, and some aspects of resocialisation in the long run, profound systemic and social changes are only possible if the entire criminal justice system is reshaped on a broader basis. This would require a shift towards more humane correctional practices, the development of alternative sentencing, community engagement, and education about the ineffectiveness of long and harsh sentences in reducing crime and recidivism.

Concluding Remarks

Lithuania continues to maintain one of the highest incarceration rates in the European Union, with long-term imprisonment dominating the sentencing structure and limited application of alternative sanctions. Although the total number of prisoners has decreased over the past decade, the penitentiary system still faces significant systemic, organisational, and individual-level challenges. These include insufficient infrastructure, underfunding, staff shortages, and a lack of effective post-release support.

The resocialisation of inmates remains largely declarative, while prison conditions and negative public attitudes further hinder reintegration. The reorganisation of the penal enforcement system, including establishing the Lithuanian Prison Service and separating Probation Services, reflects efforts to improve administrative efficiency and align the system with international standards. However, the practical implementation of reform measures remains fragmented. From a critical criminology perspective, it is unclear whether the reform will substantially change, as structural problems and symbolic implementation continue to prevail in Lithuanian prisons.

References

Aebi, M. F., & Cocco, E. (2024). *Prisons and prisoners in Europe 2023: Key findings of the SPACE I report* [Online]. Available at: https://wp.unil.ch/space/files/2024/12/SPACE_I_2023_Key_Findings.pdf. Accessed September 26, 2024.

Aleknevičienė, J., & Kalinauskaitė, I. (2023). Resocializacijos įgyvendinimo problemos ir galimybės Lietuvos kalėjimuose. *Socialinė teorija, empirija, politika ir praktika, 26*, 88–104 [Online]. Available at: https://www.zurnalai.vu.lt/STEPP/article/view/33768. Accessed August 25, 2024.

Aleknevičienė, J., Kalinauskaitė, I., & Matačiūtė, L. (2022). Laisvės atėmimo bausmės konstravimo prielaidos Lietuvoje kritinės kriminologijos požiūriu: įkalinimo tikslų analizė. *Kriminologijos studijos, 9*, 232–253 [Online].

Available at: https://www.zurnalai.vu.lt/kriminologijos-studijos/article/view/29630/28706. Accessed August 25, 2024.
Christie, N. (1999). *Nusikaltimų kontrolė kaip pramonė*. Eugrimas.
Council of Europe. (2020). *Recommendation Rec(2006)2-rev of the Committee of Ministers to member States on the European Prison Rules* [Online]. Available at: https://rm.coe.int/09000016809ee581. Accessed October 10, 2024.
Crewe, B. (2011). Depth, weight, tightness: Revisiting the pains of imprisonment. *Punishment & Society, 13*(5), 509–529.
Garland, D. (2001). *The culture of control*. Oxford University Press.
Government of the Republic of Lithuania. (2020a). *National progress plan for 2021–2030* [Online]. Available at: https://e-seimas.lrs.lt/portal/legalAct/lt/TAD/c1259440f7dd11eab72ddb4a109da1b5?jfwid. Accessed October 10, 2024.
Government of the Republic of Lithuania. (2020b). *Programme of the eighteenth government of the Republic of Lithuania* [Online]. Available at: https://e-seimas.lrs.lt/portal/legalAct/lt/TAD/973c87403bc311eb8c97e01ffe050e1c. Accessed October 10, 2024.
Government of the Republic of Lithuania. (2021). *Justice system development programme for 2021–2030* [Online]. Available at: https://tm.lrv.lt/lt/administracine-informacija/planavimo-dokumentai/pletros-programos/teisingumo-sistemos-pletros-programa/. Accessed October 16, 2024.
Hulsman, L. (1997). *Themes and concepts in an Abolitionist approach to criminal justice* [Online]. Available at: https://hulsmanfoundation.org/wp-content/uploads/2014/07/abolitionistapproach.pdf. Accessed August 28, 2024.
Lithuanian Centre for Social Sciences, Institute of Sociology, Department of Ethnic Research. (2022). *Survey results on public attitudes* [Online]. Available at: http://ets.lstc.lt/. Accessed March 1, 2025.
Lithuanian Prison Service. (2021–2024). *Statistical report on the activities of prison resocialization divisions in 2021–2024* [Online]. Available at: https://kalejimai.lrv.lt/lt/administracine-informacija/ataskaitos/metu/. Accessed March 11, 2025.
Lithuanian Prison Service. (2022). *Strategic operational guidelines for 2022–2030* [Online]. Available at: https://kalejimai.lrv.lt/lt/administracine-informacija/strateginiai-dokumentai/. Accessed October 10, 2025.
Lithuanian Prison Service. (2024a). *Regulation on operation resocialization divisions in Lithuanian prisons* [Online]. Available at: https://e-seimasx.lrs.lt/portal/legalAct/lt/TAD/32da9170243b11efb121d2fe3a0eff27. Accessed October 10, 2025.

Lithuanian Prison Service. (2024b). *The resocialization standard for convicted persons* [Online]. Available at: https://e-seimas.lrs.lt/portal/legalAct/lt/TAD/185b3ea2243e11efb121d2fe3a0eff27?jfwid=-vaidom3cm. Accessed October 10, 2025.

Martinson, R. (1974). What works? Questions and answers about prison reform. *The Public Interest, 35*, 22–54.

Mathiesen, T. (2006). *Prison on trial*. Waterside Press.

Ministry of Justice of the Republic of Lithuania. (2021). *Justice system development programme for 2021–2030* [Online]. Available at: https://tm.lrv.lt/lt/administracine-informacija/planavimo-dokumentai/pletros-programos/teisingumo-sistemos-pletros-programa/. Accessed October 28, 2024.

Ministry of Justice of the Republic of Lithuania. (2021b). *E. Dobrovolska: The reform of the penal enforcement system is necessary—We are waiting for proposals from trade unions* [Online]. Available at: https://tm.lrv.lt/lt/naujienos/teisingumo-ministerija-pradeda-bausmiu-vykdymo-sistemos-pertvarka/. Accessed October 28, 2024.

Morris, V. (2023). The role of reform in revolutionary struggles: Advancing imaginable, semi-imaginable, and unimaginable reforms to work towards prison abolition. *Contemporary Justice Review, 26*(2), 200–223 [Online]. Available at: https://doi.org/10.1080/10282580.2023.2284424. Accessed January 28, 2025.

Piliponytė, J. (2000). Resocializacijos galimybės Lietuvos įkalinimo įstaigose. *Sociologija. Mintis ir veiksmas, 1*, 98–114.

Prakapas, R., & Katinaitė, R. (2008). Nuteistų asmenų resocializacija: socialinė komunikacija ir edukacinių realizavimas. *Socialinis ugdymas, 5*(16), 81–92, 155–167.

Prison Department Under the Ministry of Justice of the Republic of Lithuania. (2021a). *Concept of resocialization reform of convicted persons*. Available at: https://kalejimai.lrv.lt/lt/resocializacija-ir-reintegracija-i-visuomene/nuteistuju-laisves-atemimo-bausme-resocializacija/. Accessed October 10, 2024.

Prison Department Under the Ministry of Justice of the Republic of Lithuania. (2021b). *Concept implementation plan for the resocialisation of convicted persons*. Available at: https://kalejimai.lrv.lt/lt/resocializacija-ir-reintegracija-i-visuomene/nuteistuju-laisves-atemimo-bausme-resocializacija/. Accessed October 10, 2024.

Ramakers, A., Aaltonen, M., Nieuwbeerta, P., & Dirkzwager, A. (2024). Realistic reintegration after imprisonment: A sequence analysis of the labour market paths of recently incarcerated individuals. *The British Journal of Criminology*. https://doi.org/10.1093/bjc/azae052. Accessed January 28, 2025.

Sakalauskas, G. (2012). Baudžiamosios politikos įgyvendinimo indikatoriai Lietuvoje. In G. Sakalauskas, S. Bikelis, V. Kalpokas, & A. Pocienė (Eds.), *Baudžiamoji politika Lietuvoje: tendencijos ir lyginamieji aspektai* (pp. 139–167). Teisės institutas.

Sakalauskas, G. (2015). Kalinimo sąlygos ir kalinių resocializacijos prielaidos. *Teisės problemos, 88*(2), 5–53.

Sakalauskas, G. (2024). Issues in implementing penal enforcement policy and the protection of prisoners' rights. In Seimas Ombudspersons' Office. *2023 human rights monitoring report in Lithuania.* Available at: https://www.lrski.lt/wp-content/uploads/2024/09/ZmogausTeises_2024_web-new.pdf. Accessed January 28, 2025.

Sakalauskas, G., Jarutienė, L., Kalpokas, V., et al. (Eds.). (2020). *Kalinimo sąlygos ir kalinių socialinės integracijos prielaidos.* Žara, Lietuvos teisės institutas.

Seimas of the Republic of Lithuania. (2002). *Penal enforcement code of the Republic of Lithuania.* No. 73-3084. Available at: https://e-seimas.lrs.lt/portal/legalAct/lt/TAD/TAIS.171368/asr. Accessed October 10, 2024.

Slade, G., & Vaičiūnienė, R. (2018). In comparative perspective: The effects of incarceration abroad on penal subjectivity among prisoners in Lithuania. *European Journal of Criminology, 15*(2), 217–234. Available at: https://journals.scholarsportal.info/browse/14773708/v15i0002. Accessed October 28, 2024.

Sliva, S. M., & Lin, J. (2024). The wall has no name: The persistence of the prison in the face of change. *Journal of Contemporary Criminal Justice, 40*(4), 576–600. Available at: https://doi.org/10.1177/10439862241272336. Accessed January 28, 2025.

Sykes, G. M. (1972). The purposes of imprisonment. In *Readings in Criminology and Penology* (pp. 578–581). Columbia University Press.

Sykes, G. M. (2007). *The society of captives: A study of a maximum security prison.* Princeton University Press.

The National Audit Office. (2024). *Assessment of the implementation of the government's project "A New Generation of Penal Institutions"*. Available at: https://www.valstybeskontrole.lt/LT/Product/24229. Accessed January 30, 2025.

United Nations (2015). *United nations standard minimum rules for the treatment of prisoners (the Nelson Mandela Rules).* Available at: https://www.unodc.org/documents/justice-and-prison-reform/Nelson_Mandela_Rules-E-ebook.pdf. Accessed October 10, 2024.

Uscila, R. (2022). Lietuvos bausmių vykdymo sistemos įgalinimas. In *Lietuvos teisė 2022: esminiai pokyčiai*. Mykolo Romerio universitetas. https://doi.org/10.13165/LT-22-01-04. Accessed January 31, 2024.

Vaičiūnienė, R., & Viršilas, V. (2017). *Laisvės atėmimo vietose taikomų socialinės reabilitacijos priemonių sistemos analizė, probleminiai taikymo aspektai.* Lietuvos teisės institutas.

Vaičiūnienė, R., & Viršilas, V. (2018). *Socialinės reabilitacijos priemonių taikymo laisvės atėmimo vietose analizė, esamos praktikos tobulinimo perspektyvos.* Lietuvos teisės institutas.

Žilinskienė, L., & Tumilaitė, R. (2011). Resocializacijos modeliai ir jų taikymas. *Sociologija. Mintis ir veiksmas, 29*(2), 285–313.

12

A Prison Without Bars: Prisonisation of Probation Through Intensive Supervision in Lithuania

Simonas Nikartas, Loreta Matačiūtė, and Neila Sventickytė

Introduction

The origins of probation[1] in the mid-nineteenth century are associated with the act of benevolence from citizens such as John Augustus who sought to 'rescue' individuals convicted of relatively minor offences from imprisonment, thereby freeing them from the suffering caused by incarceration and granting them a second chance. It may be asserted that probation, by its very nature, stands in contrast to—and substitutes for—imprisonment, functioning as an anti-prison measure.

[1] In this chapter, we follow a broader concept of probation, as presented in the Council of Europe Probation Rules (2010), where probation is associated with 'the implementation in the community of sanctions and measures, defined by law and imposed on an offender. It includes a range of activities and interventions, which involve supervision, guidance and assistance aiming at the social inclusion of an offender, as well as at contributing to community safety'.

S. Nikartas (✉) · L. Matačiūtė · N. Sventickytė
Faculty of Philosophy, Institute of Sociology and Social Work, Department of Criminology, Vilnius University, Vilnius, Lithuania
e-mail: simonas.nikartas@fsf.vu.lt

A. Dobryninas and S. Nikartas (eds.), *Understanding Crime Control and Punishment in Lithuania*, Crime Prevention and Security Management,
https://doi.org/10.1007/978-3-032-05538-5_12

On the other hand, probation remains a form of punishment that encompasses not only assistance but also the surveillance and disciplining of the individual. This tension between 'mercy and punishment' is an inherent feature of probation, manifesting in both the 'soft' (resocialisation and assistance) and 'hard' (control and punishment) functions of probation agencies, as well as in the professional role conflicts experienced by probation officers in carrying out these contrasting functions vis-à-vis their clients (Allard et al., 2003; Clear & Latessa, 1993; Nikartas & Paliauka, 2024).

This contradiction is likewise observable in deploying probation practices within national criminal justice policies. In international legislation, national statutes, and public discourses, probation and other non-custodial sanctions are presented as tools expected to reduce the prison population and/or lessen the reliance on custodial sentences.[2]

However, research (predominantly conducted in the United States) has shown that probation and other non-custodial measures have not met these expectations. For instance, studies in the 1990s demonstrated that the prison populations in the United States and Canada continued to rise despite expanding community measures (Blomberg et al., 1993; Mainprize, 1992; Petersilia & Turner, 1990). Research by M. S. Phelps indicates that, from 1980 to 2010, both the incarcerated population and the number of individuals under probation supervision in the United States increased, even as recorded crime rates declined (Phelps, 2017). Phelps concludes that, rather than reducing

L. Matačiūtė
e-mail: loreta.mataciute@fsf.stud.vu.lt

[2] The development of probation and other non-custodial sanctions and measures aimed at reducing the use of imprisonment is encouraged by the United Nations' Standard Minimum Rules for Non-Custodial Measures (the Tokyo Rules), which stipulate that member states must develop non-custodial measures within their legal systems in order to reduce the application of imprisonment (see United Nations Standard Minimum Rules for Non-Custodial Measures (the Tokyo Rules), 1990). Similar provisions are found in documents from the Council of Europe, such as the Council of Europe Committee of Ministers' Recommendation No. R (99) 22 of September 30, 1999, 'Concerning prison overcrowding and prison population inflation', which directly encourages member states of the Council of Europe to establish and expand the practice of applying non-custodial sanctions and measures, using imprisonment as a last resort within national criminal justice systems (Council of Europe, 1999).

incarceration, the United States pursued an aggressive expansion of penal control, encompassing both imprisonment and community sanctions, with probationary measures applied in conjunction with mass incarceration rather than as its substitute (Phelps, 2015). These trends have been corroborated by other scholars, including Doherty (2016), DeMichele (2014), and Nellis and Bungerfeldt (2013).

In the European context, Aebi et al. (2015) questioned whether community sanctions in European countries function as alternatives to imprisonment or as complementary measures expanding custodial control. They found that, over 20 years (1990–2010), both the number of probationers and the prison population steadily increased, irrespective of crime rate trends, leading to the conclusion that community sanctions contributed to the expansion of the penal control network.[3] Rather than serving as true alternatives to custody in the European criminal justice systems (see Aebi et al., 2015).

A further observation is that countries with the highest incarceration rates often extensively use community sanctions (see Nikartas, 2018). Such tendencies may be explained by the influence of each society's penal culture, tradition, and severity of criminal justice policies—or what Polish criminologist K. Krajewski terms the 'penal climate' (2014)—on the scale of imprisonment and probation.

Penal climate in some criminological perspectives is also interpreted within the framework of neoliberal penality (Feeley & Simon, 1992; Garland, 2001), a concept reflecting the modern trend to shape penal policy according to economic market models. Punishment and justice become subjects of cost–benefit analyses, focusing on the management of 'dangerous' groups by reducing social issues to quantifiable risk scores and treating justice as a commodity, with offenders and victims as

[3] J. Muncie describes the expansion of the control network as a process by which, in the pursuit of crime prevention and the development of individual correction in communities, the criminal justice system is expanded to include more individuals (see Muncie, 2013). The term 'expansion of the control network' was first introduced by S. Cohen several decades ago to illustrate the risks associated with new sentencing policy reforms. This term signals the danger that, in the process of implementing penal system reforms, social control may be extended to individuals who were not previously subject to it. Such reforms may aim to reduce incarceration by applying them to individuals at risk of imprisonment, but in practice, they are de facto applied to low-risk individuals who, prior to the reforms, would have received less severe sanctions or would not have been punished at all (see Cohen, 1985, 41–42).

its consumers. Community sanctions are no exception: their perceived 'leniency' (the aspect of freedom they afford) is often equated to the objective of reintegration, even though in practice they can be equally considered as products of neoliberal penal logic.

While probation and other community sanctions are of lower intensity than imprisonment, they nonetheless intervene in an individual's life and restrict their liberty. As Doherty (2016) argues, probation is frequently presented as a solution to the problem of high incarceration rates, but should instead be analysed as a continuation of excessive penal control. Accordingly, particularly in national contexts characterised by strict penal policies, imprisonment and community sanctions do not stand in opposition but operate interdependently, ensuring that ever larger numbers of offenders enter the penal control network.

This chapter examines how, within the interplay between probation and prison control, probation and its measures—especially in the case of more stringent forms of supervision such as electronic monitoring (EM)—officially promoted as alternatives to imprisonment in fact acquire carceral characteristics, or, in other words, become 'prisonised'. By analysing the Lithuanian case and drawing on the experiences of those sentenced, the aim is to reveal how intensive supervision (IS) gives rise to forms of social control typical of the prison setting.

Virtual Imprisonment and Probation Prisonisation

In jurisdictions with more stringent criminal-justice policies (e.g., in Eastern Europe or the Anglo-Saxon countries), community sanctions of intensive offender control, such as community custody, IS with EM, or home arrest, have become increasingly popular. These sanctions and measures, by virtue of their degree of control (e.g., strict adherence to daily schedules; restrictions on movement; communication with certain individuals; restriction of psychoactive substances), closely approximate the regime and surveillance characteristic of imprisonment. For this reason, some scholars refer to them as forms of a 'virtual prison' (Roberts, 2004). IS employing EM may also be interpreted as an instrument of neoliberal goals to optimise penal systems, simultaneously answering contemporary society's drive to address social and communal problems through technological means. EM functions as a 'techno-fix' tool that can control offenders remotely, imposing a fictive normality—a rigid routine which is meant to help with the reintegration process—while paradoxically inhibiting genuine community participation, since the individual must remain at home. As some scholars observe, such 'functionality' calls into question whether it is appropriate to present EM as the sole alternative to incarceration when EM itself already constitutes a form of imprisonment (Laurie & Maglione, 2020, 697).

These tendencies suggest that, in both objective and substance, community sanctions and measures are becoming analogous to custodial sentences. It may therefore be argued that we are witnessing a process of the 'prisonisation' of community sanctions.

Prisonisation, a concept introduced by D. Clemmer, refers to a process by which 'prison culture can be absorbed by some of its people' (1950, 315). Clemmer conceptualised the process of prisonisation as analogous to assimilation, suggesting that over a prolonged incarceration period, individuals gradually adopt and internalise a shared set of values and behaviours which are commonplace in prison culture. These aspects (referred to as 'universal factors') include the acceptance of an inferior role, development of somewhat new habits, adoption of local language, recognition that nothing is owed to the environment for the supplying of needs, accumulation of facts concerning the organisation of the prison, and the eventual desire for a good job. Clemmer identified certain factors as having a more significant influence on the transformative process of prisonisation, mainly an individual's personality traits, the readiness to accept the dogmas and rules of the general prison population, and, most importantly, a long sentence and thus a longer subjection to the universal factors. Over time, these shared experiences foster a collective identity among inmates, aligning them with the values, sentiments, and traditions of those who were incarcerated before them (1950, 314–316).

At the institutional level, the term 'prisonisation' is rarely employed in scholarly literature. Nonetheless, considering that probation systems are not inert, formal structures but encompass living communities of both employees and probationers—each with distinct values, behavioural norms, and interpersonal relationships—it is reasonable to assert that prisonisation processes may also occur within probation systems, particularly in those closely integrated with prison institutions. Lithuania serves as an example of such integration, where the probation system has historically been institutionally intertwined with the prison system.

Following Lithuania's independence in 1990, the correctional system retained a management structure inherited from the Soviet period, operating under the jurisdiction of the Ministry of Internal Affairs of the Republic of Lithuania. Non-custodial punishments were managed by the police until 2000, focusing primarily on behavioural control and supervision, with no emphasis on resocialisation measures. On September 1, 2000, a legal reform transferred the management of the correctional system from the Ministry of Internal Affairs to the Ministry of Justice. However, even after these reforms, an independent probation institution was not established. Instead, the management of the probation system was entrusted to the Prison Department, and probation services were only separated from the prison system in 2022.

It can be hypothesised that this two-decade-long integration with the prison system may have led to a form of prisonisation within the probation institution and its community, manifesting as the internalisation of punitive and control-oriented values prevalent in the prison system. For instance, a study by Nikartas and Paliauka (2024) on the experiences of Lithuanian probation officers revealed that during their daily professional activities, they perceived pressure from the Prison Department's leadership to prioritise control and punishment. This punitive culture, transmitted from the top, was particularly troubling for probation officers who prioritised individualised work with clients and resocialisation. These officers reported feeling penalised and undermined for dedicating excessive time to resocialisation measures (e.g., conducting correctional programmes) rather than focusing on offender supervision and control (see Nikartas & Paliauka, 2024).

A similar issue was highlighted in an ethnographic study conducted in the United States by Kras et al. (2017), which found that internal tensions among probation officers concerning their professional roles intensified after their management unit was merged with a prison division characterised by a hierarchical, militaristic structure and a control-focused ethos. In Lithuania, the internalisation of such a culture is further reinforced by the fact that most probation staff and managers are statutory officers. This means career transitions often occur within other statutory institutions, which are still predominantly considered as part of a 'strict', punitive, and control-oriented culture, such as the police, prisons, or criminal investigation bodies. Consequently, the internal values of the probation system are partially influenced by the broader cultural context of Lithuanian institutions, as the personnel carry over these values.

The processes of prisonisation can also be observed within the practice of community sanctions. Lithuania has long been distinguished in Europe for its stringent penal policy. For instance 2024, the country reported an imprisonment rate of 156 per 100,000 inhabitants (World Prison Brief, 2024). While this rate reflects a decline from earlier years (e.g., 330 in 2012), it remains among the highest in Europe. One of the primary contributors to this high rate is the lengthy average duration of imprisonment, which stands at approximately three years (Sakalauskas et al., 2020). In 2024, over half of all incarcerated individuals (2041 out of 3730) served custodial sentences exceeding five years (Prison Service, 2025). Lithuania also ranks high regarding the number of individuals under community sanctions. In 2023, there were 215.2 persons under probation supervision per 100,000 inhabitants—significantly higher than the European average of 174.9 provided in the SPACE II report (Aebi & Molnar, 2024).[4]

Additionally, among the various forms of community sanctions, Lithuania predominantly employs probation and restriction of liberty penalties, both characterised by intensive control of individuals. In contrast, community service is notably underutilised compared to other community sanctions. For instance, only 4.5% of all individuals under the supervision of the Lithuanian Probation Service, which oversees all non-custodial sanctions (excluding fines), were serving a community service sentence (Lithuanian Probation Service, 2024).

[4] Both provided statistics are for January 1st.

The enforcement of community sanctions was further tightened in 2019 with amendments to the Criminal Code, which introduced IS through EM for most individuals subject to community sanctions (Seimas of the Republic of Lithuania, 2000). These measures apply to individuals serving suspended custodial sentences and suspended short-term imprisonment (arrest),[5] and a substantial number of those sentenced to restriction of liberty[6] or granted parole from correctional institutions.[7] The new provisions also restricted judicial discretion in granting IS for probation cases.[8]

IS is imposed for a minimum period of three months and can be extended, usually in cases of non-compliance with sentence conditions or probation violations. However, the total duration of IS may not exceed

---

[5] Suspension of the sentence is regulated in Article 75 of the Criminal Code. This norm determines that persons subject to arrest (short-term imprisonment up to 3 months) or custodial sentence suspension are subject to IS. Such formulation suggests that IS must be applied to all or at least most of these individuals (see Seimas of the Republic of Lithuania, 2000).

[6] The restriction of freedom is a criminal penalty encompassing obligations imposed by the court on a sentenced individual. These obligations resemble probation conditions, including prohibitions on changing residence without notifying the Probation Service, refraining from visiting specific locations, avoiding communication with certain individuals or groups, and participating in programmes aimed at correcting violent behaviour, among others (Nikartas & Jarutiene, 2022). Article 48 of the Criminal Code stipulates that the court shall 'typically' assign IS when imposing this penalty (see Seimas of the Republic of Lithuania, 2000).

[7] The conditions for imposing IS in cases of parole depend on two forms of this measure established in the Penalties Enforcement Code of the Republic of Lithuania (Seimas of the Republic of Lithuania, 2002). The first form is automatic parole, which applies to inmates who have served three-fourths of their imposed prison sentence and are released without involvement from prison parole commissions or a court decision. Exceptions include individuals with revoked probation, considered high-risk, or serving sentences for very serious crimes or specific offences such as sex offences, bodily harm, crimes against human freedom, and public safety. Another group of offenders may seek conditional release through commissions, with eligibility based on sentence length and crime severity. For instance, those sentenced for minor offences, carelessness, or minors whose sentences do not exceed four years can apply after serving one-third of their sentence. Offenders with sentences of four to ten years can apply after serving half their sentence, while those with sentences of ten to twenty-five years can apply after serving two-thirds. The first group requires commission approval, while the second and third groups need court approval. Commissions and courts evaluate behaviour, risk reduction progress, and social integration potential when deciding on conditional release. The imposition of IS is discretionary for this group. Inmates who agree to be subject to IS may also apply for conditional release up to nine months earlier than the abovementioned terms.

[8] In 2024, amendments were made granting courts the discretion to decide on the application of IS.

the length of the sentence suspension or the remaining unserved sentence (Seimas of the Republic of Lithuania, 2012).[9]

As of January 1, 2025, the Lithuanian Probation Service supervised a stock of 1967 individuals serving suspended sentences, 2072 individuals sentenced to restriction of liberty, and 699 individuals on conditional release (Lithuanian Probation Service, 2025). These figures provide an indication of the potential diffusion and expansiveness of EM within the Lithuanian probation system.

Since the enactment of legislative amendments, there has been a significant rise in the use of IS (see Fig. 12.1). It is worth noting that between 2019 and 2020, the Lithuanian Probation Service faced limitations in terms of EM equipment. They relied on 125 devices purchased in 2016, which often led to the implementation of IS without using EM due to insufficient equipment. However, in 2022, the Lithuanian Probation Service acquired 765 units of EM devices through a Norwegian financial support mechanism (Lithuanian Probation Service, 2022). As a result, this investment enabled a progressive rise in the number of individuals subject to EM from 2021 to 2024.

IS, by its nature, is a measure that significantly restricts personal freedom while allowing individuals to reside within the community. Under IS, a strict schedule is imposed, delineating where a person must be and what activities they must engage in at specific hours. The intensity of this control closely mirrors the regulation of daily routines in prison and may be regarded as a form of prisonisation of probation practice. In this context, prisonisation refers to the transfer of institutional mechanisms of control and certain value systems from the prison environment to community supervision, maintaining strict practices of surveillance, social control, and restrictions. We make a supposition that these practices influence individuals' experiences, producing social and emotional effects similar to those caused by incarceration. This analysis of individuals' experiences is grounded in the theoretical frameworks of Sykes'

[9] It is important to note that IS is not an independent form of punishment but rather a measure designed to control the behaviour of individuals sentenced to probation and liberty restriction. IS is implemented in combination with other supervision and resocialisation measures imposed by the court as probation conditions (see Nikartas & Tereškinas, 2022).

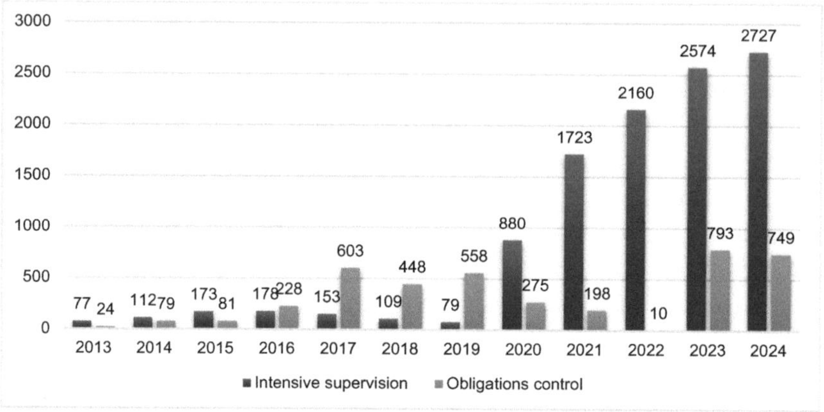

Fig. 12.1 Persons under probation-EM supervision in 2013–2024. New entries (Lithuanian Prison Service, 2013–2021; Lithuanian Probation Service, 2023, 2024)

(1958/2007) concept of the 'pains of imprisonment' and Goffman's (1961/2017) theory of the prison as a total institution.

Sykes identifies five fundamental deprivations experienced by incarcerated individuals: the loss of liberty, goods and services, heterosexual relationships, autonomy, and security. These deprivations function as intrinsic 'pains' of imprisonment, constituting an additional layer of punishment that requires continuous adaptation. Within the context of probation and IS, although the sentence is served in freedom, the spectrum of these pains expands, taking on different and additional forms. IS, much like incarceration, has the capacity to impact the same domains of life identified by Sykes, extending its reach into areas traditionally associated with imprisonment.

Goffman's concept of the total institution describes places characterised by a strict structure where individuals spend their entire time ('sleep, play, work'), with limited contact to the outside world. The totality of an institution arises from the distinct roles and social statuses between the institution's inmates and staff, which leads to variation in the degree of totality. For instance, in prisons, staff occupy managerial roles and maintain substantial contact with the external world, which leads these two distinct groups to a deeper conflict and enhances the control exerted over inmates. However, as Goffman notes, 'total institutions do not really look for cultural victory'. They create and sustain a particular kind of tension between the home world and the institutional world and use this persistent tension as strategic leverage in the management of men (1961/2017, 13). In the context of probation and IS, the totality may be less pronounced compared to prisons, as probationers retain regular contact with the outside world and the conflict with staff is less severe. Nevertheless, the spatial and temporal management inherent in IS generates a persistent tension and community sanctions may take on characteristics of totality.

Further in this chapter, drawing on our qualitative research conducted on the experiences of individuals under IS, we will aim to analyse how IS impacts the lives of probationers.

Imprisoned in a Schedule: Experiences of Individuals Under Intensive Supervision

About Research

Seeking to uncover the individual experiences of EM, a qualitative study was conducted in 2024 using semi-structured interviews with 15 probationers under EM who were serving probation and restriction of liberty sentences. The participants were drawn from the then Vilnius office of the Lithuanian Probation Service. A qualitative approach was selected due to its methodological strength in providing rich, contextual, and relational data. The data was gathered as part of a master's thesis in the Applied and Theoretical Criminology programme at Vilnius University's Faculty of Philosophy. The thesis advisor, Simonas Nikartas, who also co-authored this chapter, oversaw the research. Given the challenges in accessing this specific group, only a few additional selection criteria were applied: participation was voluntary, participants were legally adults (over 18), and all had experience serving their sentences under EM. Participants were recruited as they attended scheduled appointments with probation officers. The interview questions were explicitly tailored to explore the participants' experiences with EM. These questions sought to identify the challenges they faced, their adaptation strategies, and how wearing the electronic device affected various aspects of their lives.

Results

The Start of Intensive Supervision: Shock and Anxiety Stemming from Uncertainty and Lack of Information

Some study participants, who had no prior experience of incarceration and were sentenced to serve their punishment in the community by court decision, generally described their initial impressions negatively. A portion of the sentenced individuals had not encountered such control before and were unaware of what to expect. They were not psychologically prepared for it. The initial reactions of the sentenced individuals were marked by shock, stress, fear, and a sense of uncertainty:

> It was a shock; even my voice changed. I didn't know this <…> it was total stress, you know, I couldn't recover for about a month, and even now I can't recover. Life was spiralling out of control. You feel like a slave.' (Mantas[10])

Accompanying the emotional response was a pervasive sense of uncertainty—the individuals did not know the principles by which EM operated, nor did they understand on what basis a measure not stipulated in the court decision was being applied to them:

> Well, at first, it was a mild shock and a flood of questions, honestly. What, how, and even really, why. There were so many of those questions in my head. Well, and the whole principle of it, how it works, so I started researching online a lot, about how this works, what it looks like, what types there are, and all the rules for wearing it. (Edgaras)

These experiences can be linked to the shock and complex initial adaptation faced by individuals incarcerated for the first time. According

[10] The names of participants have been changed to preserve confidentiality.

to Schmid and Jones (1993), the way prisoners perceive the world of incarceration prior to the punishment directly informs their experiences and survival strategies. At the beginning of their sentence, individuals perceive the process from an outsider perspective, forming an anticipatory image of the punishment process—their initial experiences are shaped by societal perceptions and descriptions of prison. Often, this image is associated with the anticipation of violence, uncertainty, and fear, paralleling the experiences reflected in our results. This initial perception informs their survival strategy, as the incarcerated individual relies on available information to create a plan of action, select important initial contacts, and adapt their behaviour. Only later, as their perspective evolves into that of an insider during the actual adaptive period of serving the sentence, does their understanding change. This shift is influenced by prison subcultures, events, relationships, and partnerships developed with other inmates and staff members.

The characteristics of probationers' initial adaptation may appear similar to those of incarcerated individuals, but it is also important to note the key differences. The shock and uncertainty experienced by first-time offenders under IS reflect, in part, the fact that probation lacks the clear societal symbol that prison represents, making it more difficult to form an anticipatory image. Before incarceration, an individual can craft a survival strategy based on stories, media articles, or films; in the case of probation, they are typically faced only with uncertainty. Furthermore, IS can be more isolating from the perspective of relatability, as there are often no 'like-minded' individuals in the immediate environment who are undergoing or have undergone the same experience. In such cases, it can be harder to share the experience of punishment, and there is limited assistance in crafting survival strategies. Information must be actively sought and is typically obtained from formal and official sources, such as probation officers. This places a greater individual responsibility on the probationer to understand the minutiae of the process, and the adaptation period may be accompanied by a prolonged sense of uncertainty.

Parallel to this theory, individuals with prior experience of serving a sentence, such as the conditionally released probationers interviewed in the study, usually did not experience the same shock or anxiety about IS while serving their sentence in the community:

> *Well, I was glad. <...> because I was released from the correctional facility after three and a half years. And I was truly happy to be out with an ankle tag, to be free, with my family and everything, rather than in prison.* (Viltė)

> *In general, I had already come to terms with it, and it had been used for quite some time. <…> I didn't really have many of those questions. I was already mentally prepared for such a thing.* (Laimonas)

It is undeniable that IS in community, following imprisonment, is often perceived as a privilege and a positive change. However, an important distinguishing feature may be the possession of prior knowledge—information within the prison about better conditions is valuable and garners significant interest. Such information may come from both official sources and personalised accounts of other inmates' experiences. This facilitates preparation and the creation of a strategy for a different form of sentence execution—a new anticipatory image.

Deprivations of Freedom

Under IS, an individual's movement is restricted by a strict schedule. The person is required to be at designated locations at specified times. It can be argued that these restrictions, much like in prison, impose a deprivation of freedom by constraining the autonomy to choose one's whereabouts. Study participants reported feeling as though they were 'imprisoned in their own homes' and unable to participate in social life, despite being formally free:

> *The hardest part for me was coming home at ten and knowing I couldn't go anywhere because I wasn't allowed to go to bars, entertainment venues, or drink or anything like that. They put it [ankle tag] on me at the end of spring, I think, just as summer, festivals, the seaside, and all that were happening, and I was at home.* (Gintaras)

The restrictions felt particularly severe for those who did not have employment. For instance, Nedas had to spend the majority of the day at home, and the few hours allocated for time outside the home were often used for job searches and errands:

> *There's nothing to do because you can't go out. I would use that time to work out somewhere, or something like that. But now I've got leisure time from two to five, and that's the best time to look for a job, go to meetings. But otherwise, that's it - you sit at home, can't do anything.* (Nedas)

Vadimas' situation was even more complex, as he was living in a homeless shelter where staying in his room during the day was prohibited. During the day, he would remain in the shelter's lobby because, according to his schedule, he was required to be at his registered place of residence and was not allowed to leave:

> *I lived in a homeless shelter with an ankle tag, and it turned out that during the day, you couldn't stay in your room because, according to the 'Caritas' rules, you had to leave during the day. But I couldn't leave because I have the ankle tag. So, I used to spend half the day sitting downstairs in the lobby. When there was a court hearing, both the prosecutor and the judge were sceptical and criticised the probation. They said, 'How can you not ensure that the person can stay in their room if they're not allowed to go outside.' Now I can't be in my room, and I can't go outside. I just have to sit in the foyer, and that's it.* (Vadimas)

It can be argued that such experiences closely resemble actual physical imprisonment—the invisible shackles of IS tether the individual to their private 'cell', whether that be an apartment, a room, or the lobby of a homeless shelter.

Even participants with prior incarceration experience found it challenging to adapt to the restrictions of IS. For example, Viltė emphasised that while control in prison is strict, the pace is slower, and she struggled to cope with the demands of the schedule:

> *For the first month, even more than a month, I was constantly running. I was running and rushing. I couldn't keep up, and I was getting frustrated -*

truly. After about a month or two, it was only then that I came to terms with the fact that I had the ankle tag. (Viltė)

Some sentenced individuals, like Julija and Rapolas, perceived IS as more restrictive of their freedom than actual imprisonment, even preferring it to EM:

> Well, I was quietly thinking, you know, maybe it would be better to serve some time - those forty, ninety days, than one and a half years with an ankle tag. No, I'd really rather serve time. (Julija)

> *This is such a restriction, I'm telling you, I'm even angry - I'd rather just serve the time but not wear this for two years. It's both laughable and infuriating. The ankle tag is worse than actual imprisonment. It's such tension. Restriction.* (Rapolas)

Drawing on Goffman's ideas, these experiences reveal that IS, much like imprisonment, establishes 'segregated spaces', where an individual is formally free but confined to a strictly defined 'perimeter of permitted movement (locations)'.

Participants also spoke about the restriction of freedom of self-expression. EM not only limits a person's movement but also their ability to choose clothing and leisure activities, which can be analysed as an extension of true liberty. Experienced deprivation led individuals to adapt their desires and forms of expression during the period of the sentence: '<…> *And I say, so how am I supposed to work out, how am I supposed to dance, how am I…* <…>' (Mantas).

This aspect can be particularly sensitive for women participants in the study, like Alicija, for whom EM constrained her expression of femininity in terms of clothing:

> <…> *I can't wear what I want to; my freedom is restricted, truly. Not the physical freedom to go somewhere or do something, but the freedom to express myself as a woman. I can't wear high heels, I can't wear tights, skirts, dresses, or anything like that* <…>. (Alicija)

Physical Discomfort and Pain

Imprisonment imposes not only a deprivation of freedom but also a restriction of comfort, causing inconvenience in living conditions (accommodation, washing facilities, sleeping arrangements, etc.), daily life, and basic needs like nutrition and hygiene. Prisoners must accept the conditions provided by the prison. Similarly, IS creates physical discomfort and, at times, physical pain. Participants reported that the ankle tag was uncomfortable, restrictive, painful, and interfered with sleeping, washing, and wearing certain clothing:

> <...> *it's a thick, large plastic ring that moves around your leg, and it's in the spot where all the tendons are near the heel. That's the most painful place, and it's always rubbing.* (Alicija)

> *I even ended up in the hospital. It was supposed to stay with the tag until July, but they removed it because I was getting wounds. I mean, it's uncomfortable; I work in construction, and if I hit it anywhere, wounds appear immediately. It's extremely uncomfortable. I can't imagine - this is torture for people.* (Pavelas)

Deprivation of Material Goods and Services

Drawing on Sykes' concept of the pains of punishment, imprisonment involves not only the loss of material goods but also the deprivation of access to common services that were previously part of daily life. IS imposed similar restrictions on the study participants—they were not allowed to visit certain places or were required to adhere to strict schedules that eliminated social life and opportunities to access various services, especially those related to leisure and movement: *'Daily activities, well, I had to stop playing football, which I used to play. It was impossible to play with [an ankle tag], because if someone kicks you, that's it'* (Pavelas).

The strict requirement to follow the schedule also removed the opportunity to choose certain services, such as public transport, because using them took up too much time. For example, in Viltė's case, to ensure she adhered to the schedule, she had to use a taxi, which required spending more money: '<…> *and, you know, I spent a lot of money on taxis, because, naturally, I couldn't keep up. For example, a bus journey would count as part of my free time*' (Viltė).

The deprivation of material goods can also be linked to the impact of wearing an ankle tag on a person's clothing and footwear choices. As mentioned earlier, this aspect was particularly sensitive for female participants in the study.

The loss of material value can further be associated with the challenges faced by individuals wearing an ankle tag in securing employment and ensuring sufficient income to obtain goods and services. The study revealed that offenders encounter negative attitudes from employers, who are reluctant to hire individuals wearing an ankle tag due to concerns over the company's reputation or insurance, even if the applicant's qualifications meet the job requirements: *'Job interviews basically progress until the point where you have to say you need documents for probation and so on, and so on, and so on. That you have an ankle tag, and then that's it' (Nedas).*

Additionally, employers are further deterred from hiring individuals wearing an ankle tag due to the inflexibility of IS conditions. These restrictions require adjustments that employers may be unwilling to accommodate, making it harder for offenders to compete in the job market: '<…> *I got a job in the beginning, worked for a week, but when I found out that I'll wear an ankle tag, I was immediately fired*' (Pavelas). Others are forced to change jobs or face chronic lateness if their work hours conflict with the supervision schedule. This is particularly challenging for jobs that require night shifts or very early mornings. For instance, Vytas had to give up his work as a DJ in nightclubs, and Julija's job starts at 5 a.m., but her schedule does not allow her to leave home until 6 a.m.

In prisons, offenders who lack income are at least provided with basic necessities such as food, accommodation, and other essential services. However, offenders serving sentences in the community under IS are not afforded this safety net. They are required to secure their own housing and cover all necessary living expenses independently. The deprivation of employment opportunities can significantly impact the ability to meet even basic needs. Nedas' experience reflects this challenge. Unable to secure formal employment, he faces severe financial difficulties. The restrictions of IS also limit opportunities for informal work that could alleviate his dire economic circumstances: *'The worst part was that it's really hard to make ends meet, to survive. I had nothing to live on. And I still don't. I have thirty euros in my pocket until the tenth of next month. And yeah, try to figure it out and make do however you can. You can't do anything extra, not even earn a bit under the table or anything. I've only got three hours for myself'* (Nedas).

Deprivation of Autonomy ('Loss of Life Control')

Prison eliminates personal agency, initiative, and decision-making, compelling inmates to adhere to strictly defined institutional order. This principle is equally applicable to EM in probation, which fosters a similar experience of 'loss of life control' despite the offender being formally free.

One of the key aspects of this deprivation is the loss of control over time and daily planning. According to Sykes, inmates in prison lose the ability to decide how to organise their daily routines—every action is strictly regulated. Similarly, IS restricts an individual's autonomy, making their choices contingent on a pre-determined schedule: 'I haven't worked out in three months. <...> Three hours is just not enough for me. Because, if I go and work out, well, that's an hour, an hour and a half. I need to go back home. < ...> You know, doctors, everything that is connected to social stuff, all that doesn't count, it adds up to the free time' (Nedas).

The strict schedule imposed by IS removes any freedom for self-determined time management, compelling individuals to plan their lives rigidly within the constraints of their designated daily timetable. This lack of autonomy is acutely felt when fulfilling essential familial duties, such as parenting or caregiving. The timetable constraints are particularly distressing during unforeseen critical emergencies, such as a family member's sudden illness, and the inability to accommodate: '<...> a teacher called, grandson has a fever. The parents are at work, the school is far away, and you can't go there' (Marija). Similarly, Laimonas is unable to visit elderly and ill relatives as often as he feels necessary.

The constant stress caused by technical malfunctions or inaccuracies of EM forces individuals to impose self-control on themselves. This enforced self-regulation and self-restraint once again deprives them of the freedom to make decisions in their daily activities:

> *The main thing is you keep thinking how it shouldn't run out of battery or that you don't breach the boundary. Because, you know, in my house, I walk to the very edge, it already starts vibrating, and then you rush back.* (Marija)

Bureaucratic Filter

The loss of autonomy is linked to the bureaucratic nature of sentence enforcement. In prison, inmates encounter bureaucracy in daily life, even when trying to meet basic needs (e.g., obtaining certain items like medications, a mattress, hygiene products), for communication (e.g., phone calls, visits), movement within the prison, or participation in various activities—they must continuously obtain permission from the administration and/or prison staff. This deprives individuals of the autonomy to make even simple household decisions that people are accustomed to making freely outside prison.

Research participants faced similar autonomy deprivations due to the bureaucratic nature of sentence enforcement. For instance, individuals had to seek probation officers' permission for work or schedule adjustments. Sometimes, the approval process took too long, causing the person to lose job opportunities or preventing them from responding quickly to emergencies (e.g., critical situations, family illnesses).

Thus, IS functions not only as a means of monitoring and controlling an individual but also as a structural barrier to the reintegration of offenders into society. It becomes a 'bureaucratic filter' that preemptively reduces an individual's ability to compete in the labour market, even though the person is not physically imprisoned. This aligns with

Goffman's ideas that, through bureaucratic regulation, total institutions restrict individual autonomy and entangle them in a system of dependency on control mechanisms.

Deprivation of Security: Constant Anxiety

In Sykes' theory of the pains of imprisonment, deprivation of security refers to the constant threat of being attacked in prison. While such threats are less pronounced under probation supervision, the experiences of offenders subject to EM reveal a strong sense of insecurity about potential punishments for violating probation conditions. For instance, participants in the study reported feeling constant tension about potential EM malfunctions, the ankle tag running out of charge, or failing to return to their designated location on time, and the resulting penalties:

> You wake up in the morning and think, hell, I have to remember to charge the ankle tag. Okay, I will do it while brushing my teeth, and of course, you still forget <...> and then you have to go somewhere. I am frustrated because it always brings some tension. (Alicija)

These experiences align with Goffman's ideas that in total control institutions such as prisons or psychiatric hospitals, individuals are constantly monitored and evaluated according to rules they must unconditionally obey. This situation creates a state of constant tension, as any slight deviation in behaviour can lead to sanctions. According to Goffman, institutional life compels individuals to constantly reflect on their actions, as any deviation may be interpreted as disloyalty or a threat to discipline. The fear of potential sanctions fosters the development of an internal self-control mechanism, which becomes even more effective than direct supervision by authorities (Goffman, 1961/2017).

IS operates according to the same principle—offenders are forced to remain constantly alert and monitor themselves to avoid penalties or stricter sanctions. Interview participants emphasised that they live in a state of constant anxiety, as any technical malfunction or slight delay could be interpreted as a violation. This was illustrated by Viltė: 'You think it [the battery life] will not stretch, it will be down, and again another penalty, two penalties, it goes like this, you know...'. In this way, IS functions as a social disciplinary mechanism, forcing individuals to live in a constant state of alertness.

Deprivation of Relationships

Sykes' original theory discusses the restriction of heterosexual relationships in prison, but in contemporary analysis, this can be expanded to a broader limitation of social connections. EM might indeed restrict romantic relationships (or the potential of them), like in the case of Vadimas: 'And let us say if I want to go meet a woman somewhere, invite her for a coffee, I cannot, or go somewhere further away'. However, it may restrict not only romantic relationships but also communication with family and friends.

As EM use is partly encouraged as a tool to help people integrate into communities better and maintain social ties, it is important to note the lived-in experiences which deny this claim. Due to limited free time in some offenders' schedules, being social sometimes comes at a cost of different, important activities to the offender: '<...> they make me choose, do I want to work out, or do I want to develop relationships' *(Vadimas)*. Vytas noted, that it was his immediate family, who noticed a significant negative shift in his life, which a visible ankle tag has exacerbated due to his feelings of embarrassment while wearing it and being seen by others: 'Maybe you would not notice it yourself as strongly, but my sister really noticed, that I started being more closed-off, I went out less, only to my job. I stayed closed off. I did not even see my family as often as usual'.

Additionally, it can hinder fulfilling family obligations and constrain communication, which is sometimes already negatively affected due to previous interpersonal issues. The limitations to free movement can inadvertently impact family members: 'I can go anywhere in Lithuania if I ask for a permit. No problem. <...> I want to go to Germany, to visit my son, but I cannot' (Rapolas). The effect of restrictions caused by EM on people close to offenders was experienced in multiple ways. For example, Edgaras' mother worried about his psychological well-being, and his partner felt uncomfortable with physical contact during sleep, and Marija's daughter quit her job and moved back from another country in order to temporarily stay with and support her mother.

These experiences demonstrate that individuals wearing ankle monitoring devices may lose the ability to have fully functional relationships during the monitoring period, as EM negatively impacts the offender's family life and other relationships.

Loss of Status, Damaged Identity, and Stigmatisation

Goffman observed that 'prisoners not only live by the set rules, but also adopt the institution's imposed identity as second-class or untrustworthy members of society'. Goffman calls this spoiled identity, where individuals are stigmatised not for their own identity (personality), but because of an imposed label (Goffman, 1961). In the case of EM, this label is visual—individuals wear ankle tags, which provoke stigmatising reactions from others. As a result, offenders feel watched and socially degraded by being labelled as criminals:

> People in the store stared at my leg, whispering. I felt like a criminal, even though I was free. <...> So, the first thing was, 'criminal.' Right away. In the store, on the bus, everywhere. Even children on the bus, I saw how they whispered and pointed fingers, and, you know, it was really unpleasant. (Julija)

> I need to go to a massage, I need to go to a sauna for my health... I feel much discomfort because there are thousands of questions, from the masseuse, from people who are in the same room, and from strangers in the sauna. (Alicija)

This 'spoiled identity' leads individuals to begin seeing themselves through the lens of the stigmatised group. According to Goffman's ideas, in such situations, a person can either try to hide their degraded status (hide the ankle tag) or accept the identity imposed by the institution. Similarly, the participants in the study behaved in this way—some tried to conceal the ankle tags under their clothes or avoid situations where people might notice them:

> Like, if it were found out that I was wearing the ankle tag, I simply would not work there. I had to hide it, and hiding it is really difficult. I always have to answer calls, and if they [probation officers] came to check, it would be a complete disaster. (Viltė)

> It is better not to go to places where I could be recognised. If no one knows, no one says anything. (Vytas)

Others applied neutralisation techniques by attempting to explain the ankle tag as a 'medical device' or a 'technological experiment'. The third group submit to social stigmatisation isolates itself isolate themselves. They stop resisting stigmatisation and accept it as an inevitable element of their daily lives: 'What is the point of explaining? They think you are a criminal anyway. It is better not to leave the house because there are fewer questions' (Marija).

The visual label of a criminal follows them and prevents the person from rehabilitating and creating a positive image through voluntary activities:

> I engage in helping, like grandmas, we go to the store, pay for them, and so on. But I had to stop a little because they no longer saw me as someone who helps, but as a kind of bandit. I would come, pay for something, and they would think I wanted to steal something, to that level. (Vytas)

Some of the study participants, like Jonas, experienced insults and bullying because they were wearing the ankle tag: 'They said, well, you are a cop. No, you are a snitch, how is that?' (Jonas)

Concluding Remarks

This chapter aimed to reveal that community sanctions and measures do not always fulfil the original 'anti-prison' idea of probation and community sanctions, and often transform into an additional penal tool that expands the control network. In the context of a strict 'penal climate' and particularly in close interaction with the prison system, it can experience processes of prisonisation and become a certain form of virtual prison while in the community. The prisonisation of community sanctions was analysed based on the example of IS in Lithuania, particularly noting the experiences of those sentenced to this measure.

Interviews with offenders wearing electronic ankle tags reveal that despite the sentence being formally served in the community, it inflicts experiences akin to the 'pains of imprisonment'—from limited autonomy, strict schedules, social stigmatisation, to imposed excessive self-regulation. Such constraints can hinder offenders' ability to reintegrate into society, particularly in terms of securing employment and maintaining social relationships, while simultaneously exacerbating feelings of anxiety, insecurity, isolation, and stigmatisation. Consequently, it can be posited that, in these experiences, community sanctions deviate from their professed objective of resocialisation and, similarly to incarceration, become a desocialising tool. Drawing on Goffman's theoretical framework, individuals subjected to IS undergo a form of social mortification of selfhood, wherein their social ties, employment opportunities, and competitive standing in the labour market are constrained, ultimately eroding their social status and identity. At the same time, their bodily autonomy and temporal agency are rigorously controlled.

Based on the ideas of Sykes (1958/2007) and Goffman (1961/2017), it is evident that the elements of 'totality' and 'pains of imprisonment', characteristic of prisons, also permeate community-based IS. This creates a paradoxical situation, wherein community sanctions, which are fundamentally designed to mitigate the penal impact and reduce the scale of incarceration, may evolve into a form of 'virtual imprisonment'. The Lithuanian case—where probation has remained an integral part of the prison system throughout an extended period—demonstrates that institutional and cultural elements of punishment and control have successfully 'migrated' into community-based measures, ultimately giving rise to the phenomenon of prisonisation within probation.

In light of this situation, it is crucial to raise the question of what measures could be employed to avoid excessive control and ensure a more favourable and humane environment for the reintegration of offenders.

First, there is a need for greater flexibility in organising IS, allowing sufficient time and opportunities to meet everyday needs (such as work, family obligations, health, etc.).

Second, as mentioned, IS can have a desocialising effect, and the empirical study revealed that offenders intensely experience control and restrictions, with the effects and benefits of 'softer' resocialisation measures being much less emphasised in their experiences. This highlights the need for both policymakers and practitioners to reassess current practices in implementing resocialisation and support measures.

Third, in order to avoid excessive control and intervention in individuals' lives without leading to the prisonisation of their lives, it is important to implement individualised selection when assigning IS, taking into account criteria such as the risk of criminal behaviour related to the individual's movement, presence in specific locations, or the potential threat posed to certain individuals.

In order to gain a deeper understanding of the phenomenon of EM, it would be beneficial to conduct further research within the contexts of various countries. As referenced in our research, different intersections of legal and cultural particularities may provide distinct insights into the experiences of punishment and the presumed effectiveness of such measures. Alongside social aspects, it is also relevant to study EM through the lens of it being a commodifiable and marketable product. In many cases, the implementation of EM directly depends on the private sector, its innovations, and the products it offers. It is crucial to conduct a more thorough analysis of the relationship between the public and private sectors in the context of IS and the level of influence exerted on the execution of sentences. Since the functionality and limitations of ankle tags can vary depending on different equipment manufacturers, it would be valuable to consider how the experiences of those under supervision and the strategies of the supervising institutions may change as a result.

References

Aebi, M. F., & Molnar, L. (2024). *SPACE II—2023—Council of Europe annual penal statistics: Persons under supervision of probation agencies*. Council of Europe & University of Lausanne.

Aebi, M. F., Delgrande, N., & Marguet, Y. (2015). Have community sanctions and measures widened the net of the European criminal justice systems? *Punishment & Society, 17*(5), 575–597.

Allard, T. J., Wortley, R. K., & Stewart, A. L. (2003). Role conflict in community corrections. *Psychology, Crime and Law, 9*(3), 279–289.

Blomberg, T. G., Bales, W., & Reed, K. (1993). Intermediate punishment: Redistributing or extending social control? *Crime, Law and Social Change, 19*(2), 187–201.

Clear, T. R., & Latessa, E. J. (1993). Probation officers' roles in intensive supervision: Surveillance versus treatment. *Justice Quarterly, 10*(3), 441–462.

Clemmer, D. (1950). Observations on Imprisonment as a source of criminality. *Journal of Criminal Law and Criminology, 41*(3), 311–319.

Cohen, S. (1985). *Visions of social control*. Polity Press.

Council of Europe. (2010). *Recommendation CM/Rec(2010) 1 of the committee of ministers to member states on the council of Europe probation rules*. Council of Europe.

Council of Europe Committee of Ministers. (1999). *Recommendation No. R (99) 22 concerning prison overcrowding and prison population inflation* [Online]. Available at: https://rm.coe.int/168070c8ad. Accessed May 11, 2025.

DeMichele, M. (2014). Studying the community corrections field: Applying neo-institutional theories to a hidden element of mass social control. *Theoretical Criminology, 18*(4), 546–564.

Doherty, F. (2016). Obey all laws and be good: Probation and the meaning of recidivism. *Georgetown Law Journal, 104*(2), 291–354.

Feeley, S., & Simon, J. (1992). The new penology: Notes on the emerging strategy of corrections and its implications. *Criminology, 30*(4), 449–474.

Garland, D. (2001). *The culture of control: Crime and social order in contemporary society*. Oxford University Press.

Goffman, E. (1961/2017). *Asylums: Essays on the social situation of mental patients and other inmates*. Routledge.

Krajewski, K. (2014). Different penal climates in Europe. *Kriminologijos studijos, 1*(1). Available at: http://www.zurnalai.vu.lt/kriminologijos-studijos/article/view/3678/2637. Accessed March 10, 2025.

Kras, K. R., Rudes, D. S., & Taxman, F. S. (2017). Managing up and down: Community corrections middle managers' role conflict and ambiguity during organisational change. *Journal of Crime and Justice, 40*(2), 173–187.

Laurie, E., & Maglione, G. (2020). The electronic monitoring of offenders in context: From policy to political logics. *Critical Criminology, 28*, 685–702.

Lithuanian Prison Service. (2013–2021). *Reports on the number of persons under the supervision of the Lithuanian Probation Service*. Available at: http://kaldep.lt/lt/kalejimu-departamentas/administracine_informacija/ataskaitos/metu.html. Accessed April 17, 2025.

Lithuanian Prison Service. (2025). *Annual report for 2024*. Available at: https://kalejimai.lrv.lt/lt/administracine-informacija/ataskaitos/metu/. Accessed May 11, 2025.

Lithuanian Probation Service. (2022). *Annual report for 2022*. Available at: https://probacija.lrv.lt/lt/apie-lietuvos-probacijos-tarnyba/statistika/metines-ataskaitos/. Accessed May 11, 2025.

Lithuanian Probation Service. (2023). *Report on the number of persons under the supervision of the Lithuanian Probation Service.* Available at: https://probacija.lrv.lt/uploads/probacija/documents/files/Darbo%20su%20asmenimis%2C%20esan%C4%8Diais%20LPT%20prie%C5%BEi%C5%ABroje%2C%202022%20m_%20statistin%C4%97%20ataskaita. Accessed April 10, 2020.

Lithuanian Probation Service. (2024). *Annual report for 2024*. Available at: https://probacija.lrv.lt/lt/apie-lietuvos-probacijos-tarnyba/statistika/metines-ataskaitos/. Accessed April 10, 2025.

Lithuanian Probation Service. (2025). *Quarterly report for 2025*. Available at: https://probacija.lrv.lt/lt/apie-lietuvos-probacijos-tarnyba/statistika/metines-ataskaitos/. Accessed April 10, 2025.

Mainprize, S. (1992). Electronic monitoring in corrections: Assessing cost effectiveness and the potential for widening the net of social control. *Canadian Journal of Criminology, 34*(2), 161–180.

Muncie, J. (2013). *Net Widening*. In E. Mclaughlin & J. Muncie (Eds.), *The SAGE dictionary of criminology* (3rd ed.). SAGE.

Nellis, M., & Bungerfeldt, J. (2013). Electronic monitoring and probation in Sweden and England and wales: Comparative policy developments. *Probation Journal, 60*(3), 278–301.

Nikartas, S. (2018). Daugiau probacijos, mažiau kalinių? Ar pagrįstas kalinių skaičiaus mažinimo lūkestis?. *Jurisprudencija: mokslo darbai, 25*(2), 380–401.

Nikartas, S., & Jarutienė, L. (2022). Individualising probation conditions in cases of domestic violence: The study of sentencing practice in Lithuania. *European Journal of Probation*, 1–20.

Nikartas, S., & Paliauka, J. (2024). "I would work with a client, but I have to fill out papers": Understanding professional roles and role conflicts experienced by Lithuanian probation officers. *Probation Journal*. Available at: https://doi.org/10.1177/02645505241267120

Nikartas, S., & Tereškinas, A. (2022). Women's pains of punishment: Experiences of female offenders serving community sentences in Lithuania. *Probation Journal, 69*(1), 66–85.

Petersilia, J., & Turner, S. (1990). Comparing intensive and regular supervision for high-risk probationers: Early results from an experiment in California. *Crime & Delinquency, 36*(1), 87–111.

Phelps, M. S. (2015). The curious disappearance of sociological research on probation supervision. *Criminal Justice and Law Enforcement Annual, 7*(2), 1–30.

Phelps, M. S. (2017). Mass probation: Toward a more Robust theory of state variation in punishment. *Punishment & Society, 19*(1), 53–73.

Roberts, J. V. (2004). *The virtual prison: Community custody and the evolution of imprisonment*. Cambridge University Press.

Sakalauskas, G., Jarutienė, L., Kalpokas, V., Vaičiūnienė, R., et al. (Eds.). (2020). *Kalinimo sąlygos ir kalinių socialinės integracijos prielaidos*. Žara, Lietuvos teisės institutas.

Schmid, T. J., & Jones, R. S. (1993). Ambivalent actions: Prison adaptation strategies of first-time, short-term inmates. *Journal of Contemporary Ethnography, 21*(3), 439–463.

Seimas of the Republic of Lithuania. (2000). *Criminal code of the Republic of Lithuania* [Online]. Available at: https://e-seimas.lrs.lt/portal/legalAct/lt/TAD/TAIS.111555. Accessed May 11, 2025.

Seimas of the Republic of Lithuania. (2002). *Penalties enforcement code of the Republic of Lithuania* [Online]. Available at: https://e-seimas.lrs.lt/portal/legalAct/lt/TAD/TAIS.171368/asr. Accessed May 11, 2025.

Seimas of the Republic of Lithuania. (2012). *Probation law of the Republic of Lithuania* [Online]. Available at: https://e-seimas.lrs.lt/portal/legalAct/lt/TAD/TAIS.415894/asr. Accessed May 11, 2025.

Sykes, G. (1958/2007). *The society of captives: A study of maximum security prison.* Princeton University Press.

United Nations. (1990). *Standard minimum rules for non-custodial measures (the Tokyo Rules). General Assembly Resolution 45/110* [Online]. Available at: http://www.un.org/documents/ga/res/45/a45r110.htm. Accessed March 10, 2025.

World Prison Brief. (2024). *Lithuania, prison population rate (per 100,000 of national population)* [Online]. Available at: https://www.prisonstudies.org/country/lithuania. Accessed May 11, 2025.

13

Crime Prevention and Victim Support: New Actors in the Field of Criminal Justice

Algimantas Čepas

Introduction

Crime prevention and victim support are both new actors in Lithuania's criminal justice scene, but they are emerging at different stages. While the crime prevention system has been in a state of development for 30 years, victim support, apart from the services provided for domestic violence victims, is just beginning to take its first steps.

Although crime prevention and victim support are different policy fields, analysing them together offers valuable insights. A comparative analysis is helpful for these issues because punitiveness in both areas comes from different sources but leads to similar outcomes. Such a comparison helps better understand how conceptual factors influence real-world practices in both fields. Moreover, it may delve even deeper.

A. Čepas (✉)
Faculty of Philosophy, Institute of Sociology and Social Work, Department of Criminology, Vilnius University, Vilnius, Lithuania
e-mail: algimantas.cepas@fsf.vu.lt

A. Dobryninas and S. Nikartas (eds.), *Understanding Crime Control and Punishment in Lithuania*, Crime Prevention and Security Management,
https://doi.org/10.1007/978-3-032-05538-5_13

Examining both domains could uncover the underlying social mindsets and emotions that drive punitiveness—deep inclinations that go beyond the explicit sources of individual domains.

Despite the progress in Lithuanian crime prevention strategies, the influence of the Soviet-era conceptual framework remains a subtle but important factor. This legacy, characterised by a tendency towards centralised control and repression, often hinders community-based and restorative initiatives. Recognising this subtle influence does not mean diminishing Lithuania's efforts but acknowledging the complex challenges of post-Soviet transition.

The development of victim support in Lithuania differs significantly from that of crime prevention. While some progress has been made, certain notions regarding victims' rights and interests remain deeply rooted in Soviet-era thinking. In this framework, victim support is still limited primarily to the criminal justice system, where the prevailing state view is that the main interest of a victim lies in the punishment of the offender. Compensation for the harm suffered is treated as a secondary concern, while the recognition of victim support as a social service is only gradually gaining ground and becoming better understood.

However, the development of a victim support system in Lithuania was driven primarily by external influences rather than internal policy initiatives. Support services for victims of domestic violence were introduced as early as 2011, mainly thanks to the efforts of national human rights organisations advocating for victims' rights (Seimas of the Republic of Lithuania, 2011). However, more comprehensive support services for all victims of crime only became available after the adoption of the Law on Victim Support in 2021. And the law was only drafted after the European Commission found in 2019, as part of an infringement procedure, that Lithuania had not fully implemented the EU provisions of the Victims' Rights Directive (European Commission, 2019). The fact that significant progress was only triggered by external legal pressure and not by internal initiatives has shaped attitudes towards victim support. Instead of being seen as a natural part of the Lithuanian justice and social system, victim support is viewed as an obligation imposed by external standards. This externally driven nature of the reforms has contributed to a sense of detachment, where victim support is often viewed through a bureaucratic lens rather than as an intrinsic, rights-based commitment. The establishment of support services is often seen as a technical requirement necessary for regulatory compliance, rather than a moral and social responsibility to ensure justice and dignity for victims.

Although the introduction has already outlined obstacles such as the lingering influence of a negative legacy and the complexity of externally driven reforms, it is important to recognise the tangible progress made in Lithuania in both crime prevention and victim support. The following analysis considers these developments separately to provide a clear and balanced perspective. This separate consideration allows for a nuanced understanding of both the progress and results achieved in each area and the remaining obstacles. At the end of this chapter, these different processes are generalised to draw conclusions about their common characteristics and identify the underlying drivers common to both.

The Development of Crime Prevention in Lithuania After 1990: From Fighting Crime to Preventing It?

Crime prevention has been a priority in Lithuania and has been emphasised in almost every government program since the country regained its independence in the 1990s. The program of the first Lithuanian government, adopted on 11 October 1990, already outlined the state's commitment to crime prevention. It stated: "The government will, within its competences, take stricter measures to fight against crime and other law violations, develop and implement legal measures to protect the market, the Lithuanian state and the property of its citizens. To this end, a new state program against crime and law violations will be formulated, including preventive measures and various forms of liability" (Government of the Republic of Lithuania, 1990).

As can be seen from this historical statement, crime prevention in Lithuania was traditionally closely linked to a broader emphasis on "the fight against crime", which in later government programs was reframed as "crime control" (later in this text we will analyse these terminological changes in more detail and examine how they reflect general changes in Lithuanian perspectives and approaches to crime prevention and control).

The first decade after the restoration of Lithuania's independence was characterised by a significant tightening of repressive criminal policy. The Criminal Code was revised more than fifty times, with most of these amendments introducing new offences and increasing the severity of existing penalties. As a result, the prison population increased from 9,175 in 1991, corresponding to 248 inmates per 100,000 inhabitants, to 14,412 in 1999, equivalent to 410 inmates per 100,000 inhabitants (Sakalauskas, 2020).

During this period, crime prevention initiatives were largely marginalised, and even those measures nominally labelled as crime prevention were essentially repressive in nature. A particularly concerning case of this repressiveness occurred in 1993 when the Law on Operational Activities was amended to authorise prosecutors to impose preventive detention. This allowed for the detention of individuals for up to two months based on an abstract legal criterion—a sufficient basis for believing that a person might commit a dangerous act—the formation or participation in a criminal association or the terrorisation of a person (Seimas of the Republic of Lithuania, 1993). Despite its introduction as a "temporary law", which was only intended to apply for a few months, the provision on preventive detention was quickly incorporated into the Code of Criminal Procedure in 1993, with the only change being that the decision-making power was transferred from the public prosecutors to the courts (Seimas of the Republic of Lithuania, 1993). Although the Code of Criminal Procedure amendment was initially presented as temporary, it was extended twice, allowing preventive detention to remain in the Lithuanian legal system until 1997.

A limited, albeit remarkable, shift away from repressive rhetoric occurred in the 2000s and coincided with Lithuania's efforts to join the European Union. The European Council invited Lithuania to open accession negotiations in December 1999, and the country officially became a member of the EU on 1 May 2004. As Lithuania approached

EU accession, its crime prevention policies began to reflect broader European trends that emphasised not only deterrence but also social prevention measures and the principles of restorative justice. The European influence towards more liberal policies was evident. Some accession reports even explicitly stated that "given that the present institutional set-up prioritises repressive measures, more attention should be paid to prevention" (Commission of the European Communities, 2002).

The emphasis on the inevitability of punishment, which is rooted in repressive ideologies, remained in government rhetoric even after EU accession. Nevertheless, in the 2000s and well into the twenty-first century, the emphasis has shifted, at least in part, to rehabilitation, crime prevention through social intervention and alternative justice models. However, there are some signs that a return to the policies of earlier decades is on the horizon. Some recent policy changes point to a resurgence of punitive approaches. While the nineteenth government of the Republic of Lithuania acknowledges the importance of crime prevention in its 2024 program, it simultaneously reintroduces deterrence-based policies. This is reflected in the renewed emphasis on "shaping penal enforcement policy focused on ensuring the inevitability of accountability", "ensuring accountability for corruption-related offences by tightening responsibility and penalties" and "tightening liability for shadow economic activities" and similar affirmations (Seimas of the Republic of Lithuania, 2024). Remarkably, this renewed focus on deterrence comes when recorded crime rates in Lithuania have been falling. Over the last ten years, the number of recorded offences has fallen dramatically, from 82,872 in 2014 to 47,126 in 2024 (Information Technology and Communications Department, 2025a, 2025b).

The Soviet Legacy in Crime Prevention: Collectivism, Medicalised Thinking, and a Tool to Combat "Internal Threats"

It has already been mentioned that this deep-rooted tendency to emphasise deterrence in Lithuanian criminal policy has historical roots in the ideologies of the Soviet era. A central principle of the Soviet worldview was that social life could be organised scientifically. The concept of deterrence embodies a mechanistic view of crime, which is seen as a predictable outcome of certain stimuli and reactions (Sutherland et al., 1992). But the Soviet worldview went beyond purely mechanistic calculations. It was based on a deeply collectivist ontology in which the individual was subsumed under the grand narrative of the state (O 'Rourke, 2012). This collectivist ethos, coupled with the imposition of a monolithic ideology and a homogenised way of life, fostered an anthropomorphic notion of society. The state was no longer perceived as a mere collection of individuals, but as a living organism, a singular, unified entity. Deviance could therefore be equated with a pathological condition, a disease that threatened the integrity and vitality of this social organism. Therefore, the very term "crime prevention" was replaced by the term "crime prophylaxis" (Galinaitytė, 1975). This linguistic shift was not merely semantic. It signalled a fundamental conceptualisation of crime as a social "disease", a pathological condition that needed to be diagnosed and treated. In this framework, people who committed crimes were seen as "individuals living a parasitic lifestyle" (Vaisieta, 2012), a dehumanising label that deprived them of agency and justified their marginalisation. This parasitic characterisation turned them into carriers of pathogens that threatened the health and stability of the collective body. This medicalised view logically culminated in the conclusion that the only effective means of preventing crime, or rather the spread of this social disease, was the rigorous isolation of these "parasites".

A vivid example of such thinking from Soviet-era Estonia: "crime can be likened to a deep-rooted disease that can only be treated by a decisive intervention requiring the removal of the afflicted part and the eradication of its source" (Книге, 1985). Prisons and psychiatric institutions were turned into quarantine zones to contain and neutralise these perceived threats. The aim was to prevent the "disease" from infecting the "healthy cells" of society. Furthermore, the actual effect of this harsh punitive approach on crime remains unclear. This ambiguity is largely due to the classification of crime statistics in the Soviet era, which prevented an objective assessment. Crime statistics from before the 1970s are still not available to the public. Although the officially reported crime rates were remarkably low, they had to be presented that way due to communist ideology, which considered crime to be a temporary and vanishing bourgeois relic. As a result, many crimes were not recorded and the overall crime rate was artificially suppressed (Dobryninas et al., 2012).

After its independence, Lithuania attempted to break free from the Soviet-era medical crime prevention model. In particular, psychiatric institutions in Lithuania were never used for punishment, and the terminology changed from "prophylaxis of crime" to "crime prevention". Nevertheless, remnants of the medicalised perspective remain in the current approach. The persistence of this medicalised perspective is evident in several key aspects of the contemporary Lithuanian approach to social issues. For example, the persistent practice of categorising crime prevention into primary, secondary, and tertiary levels (Government of the Republic of Lithuania, 2005c) reflects the focus of a medical model on levels of intervention reminiscent of preventive medicine and treatment.

The language used in discussions of social problems also shows a continued reliance on medical metaphors. The term "social rehabilitation", which was recognised in the previous Code of the Execution of Penalties as one of the main objectives of penal institutions (Seimas of the Republic of Lithuania, 2002) and was only abandoned with the adoption of the new code in 2022 (Seimas of the Republic of Lithuania, 2022a), suggests that criminal behaviour is a condition that requires therapeutic intervention. Similarly, the description of drug use as a "social ulcer" in government rhetoric (Ministry of the Interior of the Republic of Lithuania, 2024) describes it as a festering sore on the body of society and implies the need for treatment rather than a complex social problem that requires nuanced solutions. Establishing "immunity departments" within state institutions to fight corruption (Lithuanian Police, 2025) is another example of how corruption is portrayed as a disease to be tackled by the body politic rather than a systemic problem that requires structural reform. These linguistic choices illustrate how a medicalised understanding of social problems continues to shape Lithuania's approach despite the formal departure from Soviet-era practices.

Objectivism, Statistics, and the Myth of a Crime-Free Society

Another consequence of this objectivist, "scientific" perspective on crime was the tendency to treat crime as an objective reality. A legacy of the Soviet era is the inclination to view crime as a broad social phenomenon, which is reflected in the use of the term *nusikalstamumo prevencija* (prevention of criminality) instead of *nusikaltimų prevencija* (crime prevention). This view has led the state to overlook that not all crimes are registered. Thus, the concept of "latent crime" only appeared in government documents in 2014 (Government of the Republic of Lithuania, 2014). At the same time, official crime statistics were considered an irrefutable reflection of reality. As a result, law enforcement agencies tend not to open investigations into certain offences to prevent crime statistics from deteriorating. For example, although more than 50,000 reports of domestic violence are reported annually in Lithuania, only around 6,000 such crimes are officially registered (Bylaitė, 2024). While academics have suggested using the term "deviance" instead of "criminality" to more accurately describe the social and legal realities (Dobryninas, 2001, Dobryninas, 2007), official rhetoric has continued to favour the term "criminality" (for simplicity, this term is translated as "crime" in this chapter).

The concept of crime as a social phenomenon was difficult to reconcile with the Soviet depiction of society as an ideal system. The solution was to redefine crime (criminality) not as a social but as an "anti-social", "antagonistic" phenomenon. The working definition of crime (criminality) was "a historically changing, massively widespread social phenomenon of an antagonistic, legal and criminal nature, comprising the totality of crimes committed in a given state or part of a state in a given time" (Abramavičius & Čepas, 1996).

These ideas established crime as something that was fundamentally incompatible with society and that had to disappear. The prevailing view regarded crime as a remnant of the bourgeois past that had already faded and should be completely eradicated (Misiūnas, 1972). This perspective explains why the "fight against crime" became the only acceptable way to conceptualise crime. This was not just a question of semantics, but had real implications for the functioning of law enforcement. The "militia"—a paramilitary body rather than a civilian police force—reflected and reinforced the hostile relationship between the state and those it regarded as threatening elements of society. Moreover, the Soviet militia actively suppressed armed resistance in Lithuania, and its ranks, especially its leadership, were largely filled with poorly educated individuals from Russia and other Soviet territories. As a result, the law enforcement agencies were perceived very negatively, and public confidence was practically non-existent (Dobryninas et al., 2012). As will be discussed later, strengthening trust in the police became one of the most important goals of subsequent crime prevention initiatives in Lithuania.

After regaining independence, Lithuania endeavoured to dissolve this adversarial framework. The rapid transition from "militia" to "police" in the first months of independence (Seimas of the Republic of Lithuania, 1990) symbolised a shift to a more community-oriented approach to law enforcement (although the specific term "community policing" has yet to be coined in the Lithuanian language). The aspiration for a crime-free society disappeared from political rhetoric and public discourse almost immediately after the restoration of independence (although, as will be shown later, it reappeared in some altered forms). Nevertheless, subtle indications suggest that a dichotomous approach persists beneath the surface of crime prevention policies. The "fight against crime" has recurred in government programs and legislative initiatives throughout the thirty years of statehood, in some periods with more emphasis, in others with less. For example, the 2012 Law on Criminal Intelligence introduced the term "intelligence" into the realm of civilian law enforcement, a term previously reserved for military applications, subtly emphasising a combative stance (Seimas of the Republic of Lithuania, 2012). Furthermore, the frequency of phrases such as "to crush criminal groups" in the media and political rhetoric, as well as the frequent invocation of a monolithic "criminal world" to be fought against (Seimas of the Republic of Lithuania, 2023b), maintains a hard division between "us" and "them".

The "scientific" approach to crime was part of a broader effort to apply a similarly rigid, systematic framework to all aspects of social life, rooted in the legacy of the planned economy. This influence persisted despite Lithuania's explicit constitutional guarantee of economic freedom (Constitution of the Republic of Lithuania, 1992). In the early years of independence, crime prevention largely took the form of government programs and action plans targeting specific types of crime. More than 20 such programs have been adopted since 1992. The sheer volume of these documents reflected the enduring Soviet tradition of meticulous state planning. However, this bureaucratic approach obscured the reality that crime prevention efforts were severely constrained by limited resources—insufficient funding, a shortage of qualified personnel, and restricted access to empirical data and criminological expertise. As a result, these programs often functioned more as symbolic affirmations of the government's commitment to crime prevention than as actionable strategies.

Some of these documents still contained traces of the "fight against crime" rhetoric from the Soviet era, but its intensity had noticeably diminished. Nevertheless, the core approach remained unchanged and took on a different form. Situational crime prevention dominated these strategies, while social prevention efforts were largely limited to educational lectures warning the younger generation against crime. This preference for situational measures—rather than tackling the social causes of criminal behaviour—was driven, at least in part, by a militaristic "us versus them" mentality. In contrast to social crime prevention, which aims to mitigate the structural factors that lead to the intention to commit a crime, situational strategies only intervene at the final stage, after these structural factors have already done their work and the intention to commit a crime has already emerged. Therefore, situational crime prevention can be seen from a militaristic perspective as an endeavour to detect and fight a crime just before it happens.

At first glance, the extensive range of programmatic documents reflects a sustained government commitment to crime prevention. However, a comprehensive analysis reveals significant inconsistencies in the scope, methods, and fundamental concepts underpinning these initiatives (Government of the Republic of Lithuania, 1999), while others are limited to 11 (Government of the Republic of Lithuania, 1995), indicating a lack of consistency in addressing crime-related issues. While some programs provide detailed assessments of the current state of play that span several pages (Government of the Republic of Lithuania, 2009), others are limited to a few short paragraphs (Government of the Republic of Lithuania, 2005a), raising questions about the depth of understanding of the problems they seek to address. These discrepancies go beyond mere numbers. Many programs were based on different philosophies, contributing to confusion about their implementation and overall effectiveness. For example, some programs emphasised restorative and reintegrative (Government of the Republic of Lithuania, 2004a), while others focused exclusively on punitive measures (Government of the Republic of Lithuania, 2005a). This divergence not only reflects different conceptualisations of crime prevention but has sometimes even led to inherent contradictions within the same documents, making their implementation difficult. The National Program for Drug Control and Prevention of Drug Addiction 2004–2008 is an example of a contradictory approach, as it simultaneously commits to enforce the principle of the inevitability of punishment fully and to prioritise the rehabilitation and social reintegration of people who use narcotics and psychotropic substances (Seimas of the Republic of Lithuania, 2004).

The fragmented approach can primarily be attributed to the fact that evidence-based crime prevention was hardly considered in earlier programs and has only recently gained importance as part of government initiatives (Seimas of the Republic of Lithuania, 2022b). However, it entered research articles significantly earlier (Justickaja, 2011). As a result, most programs were developed without empirical underpinning and often relied on conventional wisdom or ad hoc strategies rather than data-driven methods.

To make matters worse, the focus was on activities rather than outcomes—a flaw deeply rooted in a disjointed drafting process. Each drafting process typically began with the Ministry of the Interior or other institution tasked with developing the program asking for input from the various agencies, with no indication of key priorities or strategic objectives. Without a defined framework, each agency interpreted the request in its way, resulting in a wide and often divergent range of responses. Rather than being guided by a set of principles and priorities, input was largely influenced by agencies' individual mandates and perspectives. The lack of a unified vision meant the proposals reflected isolated operational preferences rather than a coordinated strategy. The final review process further exacerbated the problem. Representatives of the lead ministry—or occasionally another coordinating institution—made only a superficial assessment of the compiled document and merely fulfilled the bureaucratic requirements for government approval. Even the program objectives were often defined only after the measures had been compiled, to classify the measures proposed by other agencies, rather than as a basis for finding the most appropriate measures to achieve the objectives. The result was a patchwork of measures that did little to create a coherent plan to achieve the desired results.

Another notable limitation of these programs was the lack of connection between the drafting process and budgeting. The programs were often adopted in the middle of the year, while the budget for the following financial year was not set until the end of the current period. As a result, budgetary considerations were rarely included in program design. Instead of the program coordinators managing the funds, the individual institutions were authorised to apply separately to the Ministry of Finance for additional funds to implement certain measures. Although such requests were occasionally granted, the institutions knew that if an action requiring additional funds was included in a program. Still, the necessary funds were not subsequently allocated. They would have to finance the action using their internal budgets. This fact discouraged them from proposing ambitious measures that required significant financial support, as the institutions were reluctant to embark on major new initiatives without secured funding. As a result, many of the proposed measures were never implemented, and the lack of additional funding was often cited as the sole reason for their failure.

A key factor in the overall ineffectiveness was also the lack of monitoring and evaluation. Even when monitoring mechanisms were in place, implementation was often superficial and reduced to mere formalities. The lack of clear objectives made meaningful evaluation virtually impossible, leaving policymakers without the necessary insights to refine and improve future initiatives.

The understanding that crime prevention requires a common ground emerged in the first decade of independence. In 1997, a public institution (i.e., not subordinate to any government agency) was established under the name "Centre for Crime Prevention in Lithuania". The founders included the President of the Republic of Lithuania, the Lithuanian Parliament (Seimas), the Lithuanian Government, the Supreme Court of Lithuania, Vilnius Municipality, and the Association of Lithuanian Municipalities. The Centre's statute sets out its main tasks, including the development of an effective crime prevention system in Lithuania, the development of a scientifically based crime prevention policy, and the coordination of crime prevention programs (Crime Prevention Centre of Lithuania, 1997). In 1998, the Government recognised that the Centre was equivalent to a National Crime Prevention Council (Government of the Republic of Lithuania, 1998). This suggests that there were early efforts to establish a Scandinavian-style crime prevention model in Lithuania.

However, the centre's activities soon proved ineffective. Although it was involved in several government programs on crime prevention and even coordinated one (Government of the Republic of Lithuania, 2004b), it did not achieve significant results. In 2009, state budget funding for the Centre was discontinued due to legal changes that eliminated institutional funding for public institutions in general. The Centre survived a few more years by participating in national and international research and applied projects. However, in 2023, it was closed.

Another attempt to create a uniform basis for crime prevention in Lithuania took place in 2001, when the Lithuanian Government's program implementation plan included the development of a National Crime Control Concept for Lithuania (Government of the Republic of

Lithuania, 2001). The draft concept was prepared by the Institute of Law, an academic institution under the Ministry of Justice, which at the time was primarily involved in criminological research. However, when the government received the draft, the approach changed, and it was decided to turn the concept into a program. Based on this concept, the draft National Crime Prevention and Control Program was developed and approved by the Seimas of the Republic of Lithuania on 20 March 2003 (Seimas of the Republic of Lithuania, 2003). The coordination of the program was entrusted to the Inter-institutional Commission for the Implementation of the National Crime Prevention and Control Program, the composition of which was approved by the Lithuanian Government. The Minister of the Interior acted as chairman of the commission and the Minister of Justice as deputy chairman (Government of the Republic of Lithuania, 2003). Therefore, the development of the Lithuanian prevention system leaned towards the French model of a centralised prevention system. The program was implemented through action plans. The first of these plans was approved in 2005 (Government of the Republic of Lithuania, 2005b). Subsequently, plans were approved for the years 2007–2009 (Government of the Republic of Lithuania, 2007) and 2010–2012 (Government of the Republic of Lithuania, 2012). However, these plans became shorter and shorter, and fewer institutions were involved in their implementation. The plan for 2013–2015 was not approved, and in 2015, the National Crime Prevention and Control Program was abolished following the adoption of the Public Security Development Program for 2015–2025 (Seimas of the Republic of Lithuania, 2015).

Although the National Crime Prevention and Control Program was in force for 12 years, it ultimately failed to achieve its objectives. Since its adoption, its effectiveness was questionable, and in its final years, it was largely neglected. The fundamental weaknesses of the program were embedded from the outset and stemmed from a lack of clarity about its purpose and structure. It was originally conceived as a conceptual framework to serve as a basis for sector-specific initiatives to prevent crime. However, during the drafting process, a shift in approach led to its transformation into a program. The result was an ambiguous hybrid: neither a clearly defined strategic concept nor a functional, results-oriented initiative.

One of the greatest weaknesses of the program was the extent of institutional involvement. It comprised an extensive network of institutions—some directly subordinate to the government, others independent or only loosely connected to the state authorities. While recognising the role of independent institutions within a high-level strategic concept approved by parliament is logical, their inclusion in the government's operational implementation plans led to practical difficulties, as the government could not involve the non-subordinate institutions in the action plans for implementing the national program.

Another major shortcoming was the rigid and overly broad definition of priorities in crime prevention. When the Seimas approved the program, it set fixed priorities that were difficult to adjust. This approach deviated from the original concept, which envisaged a more flexible framework in which priorities could evolve based on developing and adopting sector-specific programs. Instead of focusing efforts on a limited number of high-risk areas, almost all conceivable crime areas were prioritised. These included violent crime, property crime, crime in public places, organised crime, human trafficking, illegal migration, arms trafficking, corruption, economic and financial crime, drug offences, and juvenile delinquency. The sheer breadth of this list diluted the importance of the individual categories.

The lack of leadership exacerbated these structural and operational problems. Crime prevention was not assigned to a specific ministry, nor was the government given a clearly defined role in overseeing its implementation. It was merely recognised as an entity responsible, along with the President and Parliament, for managing crime prevention at the national level.

The National Crime Prevention and Control Program outlined, but did not emphasise, the role of municipal administrations in crime prevention. The program stated that municipalities should develop and implement crime prevention and control programs and measures at the municipal level and participate in developing crime prevention and control strategies in their area. Later, however, more attention was paid to crime prevention initiatives at the municipal level. In 2011, the

Government of the Republic of Lithuania adopted the Safe Municipality Concept (Government of the Republic of Lithuania, 2011), which set out the basic principles that must be followed for municipalities to play a greater role in ensuring public safety. Unfortunately, the provisions of the concept were only laid down in the form of recommendations. Any other arrangement would not have been possible, as local self-government is enshrined in the Constitution as a local public administration system that operates based on autonomy and is not directly subordinate to the state authorities. Therefore, the laws enacted by the government are binding on local self-government bodies only in cases where the applicable laws expressly state that the government must regulate certain relations concerning the implementation of the laws. There are no provisions within the existing legal framework that designate the Government as the regulatory authority for issues at the municipal level related to crime prevention. Consequently, many of the concept's fine-sounding provisions have only been partially implemented. For example, the concept stipulated that municipalities should develop programs to strengthen public safety. However, such programs have been developed in less than a third of all municipalities. And even where they were developed, they were usually only intended for a period of two years and were not updated thereafter. Furthermore, a closer examination of these programs at the municipal level clearly shows that the municipalities lack the necessary capacity to develop such documents effectively. These programs contain hardly any analyses based on empirical data. Even readily available statistical information on crime in the municipality has not been used. They also tend to identify crime-related factors beyond municipal control, making them ineffective in addressing local problems. There appears to be a heavy reliance on situational tactics to prevent crime. Still, even these measures tend to be limited to initiatives such as encouraging public participation in voluntary police support groups and the introduction of neighbourhood watch initiatives. Furthermore, many municipal programs contain identical, standardised statements about how crime problems should be tackled, which are repeated verbatim in a number of documents. This suggests that there has been no significant effort to develop crime prevention strategies tailored to individual municipalities' specific needs and circumstances. Few municipalities have implemented another recommendation of the Safe Municipality Concept, namely, establishing a dedicated structural unit or position in the municipal administration responsible for organising activities to strengthen public safety. Less than half of the municipalities have established public order departments, and only one-tenth of all municipalities have created specialised crime prevention commissions. Moreover, even in the cases where such commissions have been established, they were composed only of representatives of the municipal and state institutions operating in the municipality. In contrast, representatives of local communities and non-governmental organisations are practically absent from their composition. Last but not least, criminological research has shown that attitudes remained unchanged even in municipalities that claimed to participate in implementing the Safe Municipality Concept. Even municipal institutions continued to see the police as solely responsible for their execution. Without real commitment to the concept, its failure was hardly unexpected (Nikartas, 2014).

The Rise and Fall of National Crime Prevention Programs

The role of municipalities in crime prevention was further emphasised in subsequent policy discussions. The Public Safety Development Program for 2015–2025 even included a provision advocating a gradual decentralisation of crime prevention, to transfer the functions of coordinating crime prevention to the municipalities (Seimas of the Republic of Lithuania, 2015). To facilitate the implementation of this program provision, in 2020, the Ministry of Interior initiated, and the Centre for Crime Prevention in Lithuania developed the "Concept for the Crime Prevention and Control System Model in Lithuania" (Crime Prevention Centre of Lithuania, 2020). This was followed by the "Proposals of the Working Group of the Ministry of the Interior of the Republic of Lithuania Regarding the Improvement of the System for Organising Crime and Other Legal Violation Prevention in the Republic of Lithuania" (Ministry of the Interior of the Republic of Lithuania, 2023a).

However, this approach to decentralisation was subsequently abandoned. The Program to Strengthen and Develop Public Safety, which was adopted in 2023, no longer mentions any concentration of crime prevention at the municipal level. Instead, it merely acknowledges that the role and responsibility of the municipalities in the organisation and implementation of crime prevention are inadequate. Despite this policy change, part of the crime prevention model presented in the proposals of the Ministry of Interior working group from 2022 was piloted by the Ministry of Interior in the municipalities of Kalvarija and Kelmė in 2024. However, this pilot project was characterised by significant shortcomings: lack of resources, insufficient criminological expertise, insufficient empirical data, and the lack of a clear monitoring protocol. As a result, the pilot project could not provide conclusive results regarding the model's effectiveness.

As mentioned above, the National Crime Prevention and Control Program was abolished in 2015 following the adoption of the Public Security Development Program for 2015–2025. In 2023, this program was in turn replaced by the Public Security Strengthening and Development Program (Seimas of the Republic of Lithuania, 2023b). Although crime prevention is mentioned in these documents, it remains a secondary focus. While the 2015 program acknowledged continuing the National Crime Prevention and Control Program, crime prevention was only linked to one of the five objectives. Not all tasks under this objective were directly related to it. In the 2023 program, improving the effectiveness of crime prevention is listed as one of five priorities for program implementation, alongside strengthening preparedness for hybrid threats and emergency situations, improving the protection of the EU's external border, improving the human resources of public security institutions, and increasing the efficiency of fire protection. Little attention is paid to crime prevention, and even when it is, it is mainly about organised crime, cybercrime, financial crime, and terrorism. The 2023 program indeed envisages the creation of an effective system for organising and implementing the prevention of crime as one of its 34 strategic directions. Still, no concrete steps have yet been taken towards this goal. Last but not least, the only crime prevention-related objective in the 2015 program was titled "creation of a living environment safe from crime", a concept criticised in criminological literature as a revival of long-forgotten Soviet-era claims about the total eradication of crime (Sakalauskas, 2016). Another contentious aspect of the program was its reliance on public perception as a measure of crime prevention effectiveness, with success assessed (among other indicators) by the percentage of crime victims who viewed police work positively, effectively equating the police's image with public safety. Ultimately, the role of perceptions was further reinforced by recognising residents' subjective sense of security as a key criterion for evaluating the success of crime prevention efforts. The latter criterion was carried over into the 2023 program, where the subjective sense of security is used to measure how successfully the foundations for effective crime prevention and control, as well as the reduction of terrorist threats, are being established (Ministry of the Interior of the Republic of Lithuania, 2023b).

Summarising the development of crime prevention in Lithuania since 1990, it is clear that the gap between rhetoric and tangible progress is considerable. Despite the frequent use of the language of crime prevention in official discourse, it has not been possible to create a uniform and effective crime prevention system. An important factor contributing to this stagnation is the lack of clear leadership. No single institution has emerged to take ownership of the crime prevention agenda and drive systematic change. This has led to fragmented policies rather than coherent strategies. Furthermore, the development of the Lithuanian crime prevention framework is still strongly influenced by the legacy of the Soviet era. Even 30 years after the restoration of independence, these historical remnants still characterise the approach to crime prevention, particularly in the form of a punitive mindset. The emphasis remains on situational crime prevention and a focus on police powers, with criminal justice often seen as the primary solution to crime.

Victim Support as Bureaucratic Compliance: The Limits of Formal Harmonisation

In this chapter, victim support in Lithuania is given less importance than crime prevention for two main reasons. Firstly, generic victim support services are still in the early stages of development. Secondly, although victim support services for victims of domestic violence have existed since 2011, they do not have any noticeable punitive tendencies and therefore remain somewhat outside the central topic of this discussion.

On 14 January 2021, the Parliament of the Republic of Lithuania adopted the Law on Victim Support (Seimas of the Republic of Lithuania, 2021). This law transposes the European Union (EU) Victims' Rights Directive into Lithuanian law, and aligns national regulations with EU standards to improve rights and support for victims of crime. At least for the moment, there do not appear to be any significant contradictions between the provisions of the law and the directive, which indicates a smooth integration of EU principles into the Lithuanian legal system.

However, the timeline for transposition has been significantly delayed. The Directive stipulated that EU Member States should have transposed it into their national legal frameworks by 16 November 2015. Despite this, Lithuania only began drafting the Law on Victim Support after the European Commission issued a reasoned opinion in 2019, pointing out that Lithuania had not fully transposed the provisions of the Directive. The fact that Lithuania only began developing generic victim support in response to the European Commission's infringement procedures has influenced the overall approach to this field. Rather than demonstrating a proactive commitment to strengthening victim support mechanisms, the process appears to have been driven by a need to comply with external legal requirements rather than a genuine recognition of the importance of victim assistance. As a result, the field has often been approached somewhat dismissively or perfunctorily, lacking the depth of engagement and institutional commitment.

First and foremost, it cannot be said that Lithuania has finally created a unified victim support system. In reality, the country has three different and largely disjointed systems, revealing a fragmented approach to victim support. The first system, dedicated to providing support to victims of domestic violence, has been in operation since 2011 (Seimas of the Republic of Lithuania 2011). The second, which focuses on supporting victims of human trafficking, was introduced in 2015 (Prosecutor General of the Republic of Lithuania, Minister of the Interior of the Republic of Lithuania & Minister of Social Security and Labour of the Republic of Lithuania, 2015). Finally, a third system was set up in 2021 to provide generic victim support. The problem is further complicated by the diversity of organisations involved in these three different legal frameworks. Some organisations, often non-governmental organisations, participate in all three schemes, while other organisations are only active in one specific area, resulting in a fragmented service landscape. Crucially, no concerted effort has been made to harmonise or at least to coordinate the functioning of these three systems.

The fact that the elements of victim support are scattered across at least three different systems leads to a lack of human and other essential resources. As a result, it can be difficult for victims to receive comprehensive and timely support, as the scope and availability of services vary widely. Yet despite these obvious shortcomings, the state has not taken any significant steps to address the problem. Instead of taking targeted measures to strengthen victim support services, the legal framework assumes that stronger human and other resources are unnecessary for victim support services to function.

The legal framework for victim support services places relatively low demands on the organisations that provide assistance. For example, the Law on Victim Support regulates that staff working directly with victims only need a university degree in a social science field or even no training at all if they have at least one year's professional experience in a field relevant to victim support. This minimum requirement does not necessarily ensure that staff have specialised knowledge or adequate training in dealing with victims of crime, which can affect the quality of support provided. Furthermore, organisations that provide victim support must limit themselves to lower-level support services. For example, they are not obliged to offer psychological counselling; emotional support is considered sufficient, although victims of crime often face severe psychological consequences that require professional intervention. The law stipulates that organisations must have premises where victims can access confidential counselling from specialists such as legal advisors, psychologists, or social workers; it does not explicitly state that these services must be offered in-house. This means that while victims may have access to physical spaces for consultations, the actual availability of specialised professionals remains uncertain, leading to potential gaps in essential services.

Although the legal framework stipulates that only organisations that can fulfil all legally assigned tasks can be accredited, this requirement is effectively diluted by the existing accreditation procedure (Minister of Social Security & Labour of the Republic of Lithuania, 2024). The procedure allows organisations to subcontract services or work with other institutions to meet the accreditation criteria. This means that organisations do not necessarily have to have the internal capacity to provide all the required services. Accreditation thus becomes more of a procedural formality than a guarantee of quality or performance.

To summarise, Lithuania's legal harmonisation with EU victim-support standards conceals poor implementation. Despite the adoption of the necessary legislation, the lack of real commitment has led to a fragmented victim support landscape consisting of three uncoordinated victim support systems. This confusion, resulting from delayed implementation and reactive compliance, hinders the efficiency of resources and victims' access to comprehensive support. Minimal staffing requirements and a watered-down accreditation process further compromise the quality of services. The emphasis on basic support makes it clear that the focus is on bureaucratic compliance with formal requirements rather than on the welfare of victims. As a result, while victim support in Lithuania is legally compliant, it lacks the cohesion and depth to help those in need effectively.

Concluding Remarks

What conclusions can be drawn from this overview of the processes involved in building crime prevention and victim support systems in Lithuania? Both processes have faced significant obstacles, and neither has successfully overcome them. External factors have influenced each process, yet these influences stem from very different ideological and political systems. On one hand, crime prevention has been shaped by the lingering effects of a 50-year-long Soviet occupation, while the imposition of European legal standards has influenced victim support. Despite the vastly different sources of influence, both processes have ultimately resulted in similar outcomes: Lithuania's crime prevention and victim support systems have been developed in a fragmented, disjointed, and somewhat inefficient manner.

A core issue driving both crime prevention and victim support failures may be the persistent "us versus them" mentality, a deeply ingrained adversarial worldview. In crime prevention, this translates to a persistent Soviet-era perspective in which the state wages a relentless fight against crime. Any reintegrative or restorative approach is viewed with suspicion and dismissed as a concession to the "criminal world". This mentality is also expressed in a dismissive attitude towards victim support. The support mandated by the EU is seen as an "EU fable", a bureaucratic requirement that has nothing to do with actual needs and leads to bare minimum, compliance-focused implementation rather than a genuine commitment to the well-being of victims. In both cases, the punitive approach functions as a defensive barrier, resisting any push for progressive change. This resistance is rooted in the perception that change is being imposed from the outside (them) onto the inside (us). Is this tension unavoidable, and will punitiveness persist even after future reforms? It could be, but it's also possible that it won't.

References

Abramavičius, A., & Čepas, A. (1996). Nusikaltimas ir nusikalstamumas. In A. Abramavičius, A. Čepas, A. Drakšienė, J. Nocius, V. Pavilonis, J. Prapiestis, & G. Švedas (Eds.), *Baudžiamoji teisė. Bendroji dalis* (pp. 113–140). Eugrimas.

Bylaitė, G. (2024). *Apsauga nuo smurto artimoje aplinkoje ir seksualinių nusikaltimų*. In E. Leonaitė (Ed.), *2023 m. žmogaus teisių padėties Lietuvoje stebėsenos ataskaita* (pp. 27–52). Ombudspersons' Office of the Republic of Lithuania.

Commission of the European Communities. (2002, October 9). *2002 Regular report on Lithuania's progress towards accession {COM(2002) 700 final} SEC(2002) 1406*. [online]. https://www.europarl.europa.eu/meetdocs/committees/empl/20021021/02-1406EN.pdf [Accessed 23 Marrch 2025].

Constitution of the Republic of Lithuania. (1992, November 10). *The Constitution of the Republic of Lithuania (adopted by citizens of the Republic of Lithuania in the referendum of 25 October 1992).* Lietuvos aidas, No. 220-0. [online] Available at: https://www.e-tar.lt/rs/legalact/TAR.47BB952431DA/format/MSO2010_DOCX/ [Accessed 24 March 2025].

Crime Prevention Centre in Lithuania. (1997). *Statutes of the Public Institution "Crime Prevention Centre in Lithuania"*. Registered in the Vilnius City Business Register on 8 October 1997, No. V197-193.

Crime Prevention Centre in Lithuania. (2020). *Concept of the crime prevention and control system model in Lithuania.* [online] Available at: https://vrm.lrv.lt/uploads/vrm/documents/files/LT_versija/Viesasis_saugumas/Koncepcijos/Koncepcija%2020201219_galut.pdf [Accessed 24 March 2025].

Dobryninas, A. (2001). Atskiriamasis teisingumas. *Jurisprudencija, 20*(12), 107–112.

Dobryninas, A. (2007). Įvadas. In J. Aleknevičienė (Ed.), *Socialinės deviacijų problemos*. Eugrimas.

Dobryninas, A., Drakšienė, A., Gaidys, A., Viliekienė, E. & Žilinskienė, L. (2012). *Pasitikėjimo Lietuvos teisėsauga profiliai*. Vilnius University Press.

European Commission. (2019, March 7). *March infringements package: Key decisions.* [online]. Available at: https://ec.europa.eu/commission/presscorner/detail/en/memo_19_1472 [Accessed 23 March 2025].

Galinaitytė, J. (1975). *Nepilnamečių nusikaltimų profilaktika*. Mintis.

Government of the Republic of Lithuania. (1990). *Programme of the Government of the Republic of Lithuania.* [online] Available at: https://lrv.lt/uploads/main/documents/files/Apie_vyriausybe/Ankstesnes_vyriausybes/po_1990_1_programa.pdf [Accessed 23 March 2025].

Government of the Republic of Lithuania. (1995, February 24). Programme for the Improvement of Employment and Crime Prevention for Minors. Approved by Government Resolution No. 264 of 20 February 1995. Official Gazette, No. 17-395. [online] Available at: https://www.e-tar.lt/portal/lt/legalAct/TAR.1A44452FE7AD [Accessed 24 March 2025].

Government of the Republic of Lithuania. (1998, November 19). National Programme for the Adoption of the ACQUIS. Approved by Government Resolution No. 1305 of 10 November 1998. Official Gazette, No. 101-2803. [online] Available at: https://www.e-tar.lt/portal/lt/legalAct/TAR.930D2C218FCB [Accessed 24 March 2025].

Government of the Republic of Lithuania. (1999, January 22). Organised Crime and Corruption Prevention Programme. Approved by Government Resolution No. 62 of 15 January 1999. Official Gazette, No. 10-220. [online] Available at: https://www.e-tar.lt/rs/legalact/TAR.03D742ACB6E0/format/MSO2010_DOCX/ [Accessed 24 March 2025].

Government of the Republic of Lithuania. (2001, February 14). Implementation Measures of the 2000–2004 Government Programme of the Republic of Lithuania. Approved by Government Resolution No. 149 of 9 February 2001. Official Gazette, No. 14-437. [online] Available at: https://www.e-tar.lt/rs/legalact/TAR.2BAEDCB677B8/format/MSO2010_DOCX/ [Accessed 24 March 2025].

Government of the Republic of Lithuania. (2003, June 18). Resolution on the Establishment of the Interinstitutional Commission for the Implementation of the National Crime Prevention and Control Programme and on the Approval of its Regulations. Official Gazette, No. 58-2594. [online] Available at: https://www.e-tar.lt/rs/legalact/TAR.F0D609E2BD2E/format/MSO2010_DOCX/ [Accessed 24 March 2025].

Government of the Republic of Lithuania. (2004a, February 26). Programme for the Socialisation of Children and Youth. Approved by Government Resolution No. 209 of 23 February 2004. Official Gazette, No. 30–995. [online] Available at: https://www.e-tar.lt/portal/lt/legalAct/TAR.665078C14E98 [Accessed 24 Mar. 2025].

Government of the Republic of Lithuania. (2004b, May 22). Juvenile Justice Programme for 2004–2008. Approved by Government Resolution No. 600 of 19 May 2004. Official Gazette, No. 83-3008. [online] Available at: https://e-seimas.lrs.lt/portal/legalAct/lt/TAD/TAIS.233765 [Accessed 24 March 2025].

Government of the Republic of Lithuania. (2005a, April 12). Integrated Programme for the Prevention and Control of Motor Vehicle Thefts for 2005–2007. Approved by Government Resolution No. 387 of 7 April 2005. Official Gazette, No. 47-1573. [online] Available at: https://www.e-tar.lt/portal/lt/legalAct/TAR.8B5075A4B4FF [Accessed 24 March 2025].

Government of the Republic of Lithuania. (2005b, January 15). Implementation Plan for the National Crime Prevention and Control

Programme for 2005–2006. Approved by Government Resolution No. 12 of 12 January 2005. Official Gazette, No. 6-158. [online] Available at: https://www.e-tar.lt/rs/legalact/TAR.782B58AC826F/format/MSO2010_DOCX/ [Accessed 24 Mar. 2025].

Government of the Republic of Lithuania. (2005c, May 7). National Programme for the Prevention of Violence Against Children and Assistance to Children for 2005–2007. Approved by Government Resolution No. 491 of 4 May 2005. Official Gazette, No. 58-2021. [online] Available at: https://www.e-tar.lt/rs/legalact/TAR.B06AB4B75338/format/MSO2010_DOCX/ [Accessed 23 March 2025].

Government of the Republic of Lithuania. (2007, August 18). Implementation Plan for the National Crime Prevention and Control Programme for 2007–2009. Approved by Government Resolution No. 806 of 8 August 2007. Official Gazette, No. 90-3575. [online] Available at: https://www.e-tar.lt/rs/legalact/TAR.960B50D28870/format/MSO2010_DOCX/ [Accessed 24 March 2025].

Government of the Republic of Lithuania. (2009, September 19). Programme for the Prevention and Control of Human Trafficking for 2009–2012. Approved by Government Resolution No. 1104 of 9 September 2009. Official Gazette, No. 112-4761. [online] Available at: https://www.e-tar.lt/portal/lt/legalAct/TAR.1BC7B0F0773E [Accessed 24 March 2025].

Government of the Republic of Lithuania. (2011, February 22). Concept of Safe Municipalities. Approved by Government Resolution No. 184 of 17 February 2011. Official Gazette, No. 22-1057, [online] Available at: https://www.e-tar.lt/rs/legalact/TAR.8AF1C8882FDD/format/MSO2010_DOCX/ [Accessed 24 March 2025].

Government of the Republic of Lithuania. (2012). Interinstitutional Action Plan for the Implementation of the National Crime Prevention and Control Programme. Approved by Government Resolution No. 1381 of 14 November 2012. [online] Available at: https://www.e-tar.lt/rs/legalact/TAR.CA1B12D93D73/format/MSO2010_DOCX/ [Accessed 24 March 2025].

Government of the Republic of Lithuania. (2014, June 2). State Programme for the Prevention of Domestic Violence and the Provision of Assistance to Victims for 2014–2020. Approved by Government Resolution No. 485 of 28 May 2014. Register of Legal Acts, No. 5986. [online] Available at: https://www.e-tar.lt/rs/legalact/0ef33c60ea2811e38557d238694e3fc9/format/MSO2010_DOCX/ [Accessed 25 March 2025].

Information and Communications Department under the Ministry of the Interior of the Republic of Lithuania. (2025a). Data on criminal offences committed in the counties of the Republic of Lithuania from January to December 2014. Form_2Ž-APSK. [online] Available at: https://www.ird.lt/lt/reports/view_item_datasource?id=2664&datasource=6850&page=1&export=pdf [Accessed 23 March 2025].

Information and Communications Department under the Ministry of the Interior of the Republic of Lithuania. (2025b, January 9). Data on criminal offences committed in the counties of the Republic of Lithuania from January to December 2024. Form_2Ž-APSK. [online]. Available at: https://www.ird.lt/lt/reports/view_item_datasource?id=11378&datasource=102557&export=pdf [Accessed 23 March 2025].

Justickaja, S. (2011). Nusikaltimų prevencija Lietuvoje: perėjimas nuo intuityvios prie įrodymais grindžiamos. *Teisės problemos, 1*(71), 81–104. Available at: https://teise.org/wp-content/uploads/2016/10/2011-1-justickaja.pdf [Accessed 24 Mar. 2025].

Lithuanian Police. (2025, January 30). Management structure. [online]. Available at: https://policija.lrv.lt/lt/struktura-ir-kontaktai/valdymo-struktura/ [Accessed 23 March 2025].

Minister of Social Security and Labour of the Republic of Lithuania. (2024, June 10). Description of the Accreditation Procedure for Services Provided to Victims of Criminal Acts. Approved by Order No. A1-390 of 10 June 2024 (amending Order No. A1-318 of 21 April 2021). Register of Legal Acts, No. 10572. [online] Available at: https://www.e-tar.lt/rs/actualedition/645f572026e911efbdaea558de59136c/Ktktnpkzqb/format/ISO_PDF/ [Accessed 24 March 2025].

Ministry of the Interior of the Republic of Lithuania. (2023a). Working Group Recommendations for the Improvement of the Crime and Other Offences Prevention System in the Republic of Lithuania. [online] Available at: https://e-seimas.lrs.lt/rs/lasupplement/TAK/0c44a771c6f011ed9b3c9397e1236c2a/2d3ca3de2704cf70ed4230c346af4afe/format/ISO_PDF/ [Accessed 24 March 2025].

Ministry of the Interior of the Republic of Lithuania. (2023b, December 14). Description of the Development Programme Progress Measure No. 07-018-10-07-01 "Create Preconditions for Effective Crime Prevention and Control and Reduction of Terrorist Threats". Approved by Ministerial Order No. 1V-487 of 25 July 2023 (amended by Order No. 1V-693 of 28 November 2024). Register of Legal Acts, No. 24206. [online] Available at: https://www.e-tar.lt/rs/aesupplement/b327a0202ae511ee9de9e7e0fd363afc/QyTiQKnFgO/1009cbe8b25011ef88c08519262548c4/ [Accessed 24 March 2025].

Ministry of the Interior of the Republic of Lithuania. (2024). Reporting Drug Distribution Will Be Possible via a Special Telephone Line. [online] Available at: https://vrm.lrv.lt/lt/naujienos/pranesti-apie-narkotiku-platinima-bus-galima-specialiu-telefonu/ [Accessed 23 March 2025].

Misiūnas, J. (1972). Tarybinės baudžiamosios teisės sąvoka, uždaviniai ir sistema. In Žvirblis, J. (Ed.) *Tarybinė baudžiamoji teisė. Bendroji dalis.* Mintis.

Nikartas, S. (2014). *Gyventojų dalyvavimas užtikrinant saugumą bendruomenėse: kriminologinės ir teisinės prielaidos*. Lietuvos teisės institutas.

O'Rourke, J. J. (2012). *The problem of freedom in marxist thought: An analysis of the treatment of human freedom by Marx, Engels, Lenin and contemporary Soviet philosophy* (Vol. 32). Springer Science & Business Media.

Prosecutor General of the Republic of Lithuania, Minister of the Interior of the Republic of Lithuania, and Minister of Social Security and Labour of the Republic of Lithuania. (2015, December 28). Recommendations for the identification of victims of human trafficking, pre-trial investigation and inter-institutional cooperation. Approved by Joint Order No. I-327/1V-1015/A1-758 of 17 December 2015. Register of Legal Acts, No. 20631, Available at: https://www.e-tar.lt/rs/actualedition/801bbb20ad5311e5b12fbb7dc920ee2c/xQoPgydZBX/format/ISO_PDF/ [Accessed 23 Mar. 2025].

Sakalauskas, G. (2016). Nusikaltimų prevencijos programų Lietuvoje nuostatos: Tarp absurdo ir kokybės. *Kriminologijos Studijos, 2016*(4), 72–97.

Sakalauskas, G. (2020). Įkalinimo praktika Lietuvoje. In G. Sakalauskas, L. Jarutienė, V. Kalpokas, & R. Vaičiūnienė (Eds.), *Kalinimo sąlygos ir kalinių socialinės integracijos prielaidos* (pp. 15–26). Lietuvos teisės institutas.

Seimas of the Republic of Lithuania. (1990, December 20). Law on the Police of the Republic of Lithuania. Lietuvos aidas, No. 148-0. [online] Available at: https://www.e-tar.lt/rs/legalact/TAR.7B82276223C5/format/MSO2010_DOCX/ [Accessed 25 Mar. 2025].

Seimas of the Republic of Lithuania. (1993a, December 18). Law on the Supplement to the Code of Criminal Procedure of the Republic of Lithuania. Official Gazette, No. 70-1310. [online] Available at: https://www.e-tar.lt/rs/legalact/TAR.1B266F2EB841/format/MSO2010_DOCX/ [Accessed 23 March 2025].

Seimas of the Republic of Lithuania. (1993b, July 21). Provisional Law on the Supplement to the Law on Operational Activities of the

Republic of Lithuania. Official Gazette, No. 30-679. [online] Available at: https://www.e-tar.lt/rs/legalact/TAR.56EC096968B4/format/MSO2010_DOCX/ [Accessed 23 March 2025].

Seimas of the Republic of Lithuania. (2002, 19 July). Penitentiary Code of the Republic of Lithuania. Approved by Law No. IX-994 of 27 June 2002. Official Gazette, No. 73-3084. [online] Available at: https://www.e-tar.lt/rs/actualedition/TAR.A0A0CCC6B997/USgpCdgdfr/format/ISO_PDF/ [Accessed 23 Mar. 2025].

Seimas of the Republic of Lithuania. (2003, April 2). National Crime Prevention and Control Programme. Approved by Seimas Resolution No. IX-1383 of 20 March 2003. Official Gazette, No. 32-1318. [online] Available at: https://www.e-tar.lt/rs/legalact/TAR.03398C5173D8/format/MSO2010_DOCX/ [Accessed 24 March 2025].

Seimas of the Republic of Lithuania. (2004, April 21). National Drug Control and Drug Addiction Prevention Programme for 2004–2008. Approved by Seimas Resolution No. IX-2110 of 8 April 2004. Official Gazette, No. 58-2041. [online] Available at: https://www.e-tar.lt/portal/lt/legalAct/TAR.08751FC4B149 [Accessed 24 March 2025].

Seimas of the Republic of Lithuania. (2011, June 14). Law on Protection Against Domestic Violence of the Republic of Lithuania. Official Gazette, No. 72-3475. [online] Available at: https://www.e-tar.lt/rs/actualedition/TAR.E14E65020CCC/WvKlznCIJc/format/ISO_PDF/ [Accessed 24 March 2025].

Seimas of the Republic of Lithuania. (2012, October 20). Law on Criminal Intelligence of the Republic of Lithuania. Official Gazette, No. 122-6093. [online] Available at: https://www.e-tar.lt/rs/actualedition/TAR.3B8E4F16C815/ROkgXKUfTV/format/ISO_PDF/ [Accessed 23 March 2025].

Seimas of the Republic of Lithuania. (2015, 13 May). Public Security Development Programme for 2015–2025. Approved by Seimas Resolution No. XII-1682 of 7 May 2015. Register of Legal Acts, No. 7293. [online] Available at: https://www.e-tar.lt/rs/lasupplement/ea944da0f95d11e4927fda1d051299fb/740954b0f96111e4927fda1d051299fb/ [Accessed 24 Mar. 2025].

Seimas of the Republic of Lithuania. (2021). Law on Assistance to Victims of Criminal Acts of the Republic of Lithuania. Register of Legal Acts, No. 908, 20 January. [online] Available at: https://www.e-tar.lt/rs/lasupplement/599af1605b2b11eb9dc7b575f08e8bea/65b3f1a000f211ec9f09e7df20500045/ [Accessed 24 Mar. 2025].

Seimas of the Republic of Lithuania. (2022a, July 14). Amendment to the Penal Enforcement Code of the Republic of Lithuania. Register of Legal Acts, No. 15495. [online] Available at: https://www.e-tar.lt/rs/lasupplement/6d3310b0037a11edb32c9f9d8ba206f8/74c575100e7a11edb4cae1b158f98ea5/ [Accessed 24 Mar. 2025].

Seimas of the Republic of Lithuania. (2022b, July 7). National Anti-Corruption Agenda for 2022–2033. Approved by Seimas Resolution No. XIV-1178 of 28 June 2022. Register of Legal Acts, No. 14816. [online] Available at: https://www.e-tar.lt/portal/lt/legalAct/2b958160fdbc11ec8fa7d02a65c371ad [Accessed 24 March 2025].

Seimas of the Republic of Lithuania. (2023a, May 25). National Agenda for the Control, Prevention of Use, and Harm Reduction of Narcotics, Tobacco, and Alcohol until 2035. Approved by Seimas Resolution No. XIV-1982 of 23 May 2023. Register of Legal Acts, No. 9953. [online] Available at: https://www.e-tar.lt/portal/lt/legalAct/bb3f7080faf211ed9978886e85107ab2 [Accessed 24 Mar. 2025].

Seimas of the Republic of Lithuania. (2023b, June 23). Programme for the Strengthening and Development of Public Security. Approved by Seimas Resolution No. XIV-2088 of 22 June 2023. Register of Legal Acts, No. 12562. [online] Available at: https://www.e-tar.lt/rs/lasupplement/2628ef40118a11ee9f7ec2ffce8b47bc/5fbde3e0119a11ee9f7ec2ffce8b47bc/ [Accessed 24 March 2025].

Seimas of the Republic of Lithuania. (2024). Programme of the 19th Government of the Republic of Lithuania. Approved by Seimas Resolution No. XV-54 of 12 December 2024. [online] Available at: https://e-seimas.lrs.lt/rs/lasupplement/TAD/d4b57910b89711efbb3fe9794b4a33e2/f628f3f4b89d11efa6bcd8fd37368776/ [Accessed 23 March 2025].

State Border Guard Service under the Ministry of the Interior of the Republic of Lithuania. (2025, February 10). Organizational structure of the State Border Guard Service under the Ministry of the Interior of the Republic of Lithuania. Approved by Order No. 4-259 of the Head of the State Border Guard Service, 11 August 2022. [online]. Available at: https://vsat.lrv.lt/lt/struktura-ir-kontaktine-informacija/struktura/ [Accessed 23 March 2025].

Sutherland, E. H., Cressey, D. R., & Luckenbill, D. F. (1992). *Principles of criminology* (11th ed.). AltaMira Press.

The European Parliament and the Council. (2012, October 25). Directive 2012/29/EU of the European Parliament and of the Council of 25 October 2012 establishing minimum standards on the rights, support and protection of victims of crime, and replacing Council Framework Decision 2001/220/JHA. *Official Journal of the European Union,* L 315/57, 14 November. [online] Available at: https://eur-lex.europa.eu/legal-content/EN/TXT/PDF/?uri=CELEX:32012L0029 [Accessed 24 March 2025].

Vaisieta, T. (2012). Sovietinio veltėdžiavimo fenomenas kasdienybės praktikų ir jų trajektorijų požiūriu. *Lietuvos Istorijos Studijos, 29*, 111–126.

Книге, И. И. (1985). К вопросу о понятии "образ жизни" и о некоторых аспектах его изучения. In Спиридонов, Л., Гилинский, Я., & Раска, Э. (Eds.), *Теоретические проблемы изучения территориальных различий преступности. Труды по криминологии.* Tartu.

Correction to: Punitive Attitudes Towards Difference: Bullying Perception in the 1980–2000 Generation

Goda Damaševičiūtė and Jovita Žėkaitė-Maconko

Correction to:
Chapter 6 in: A. Dobryninas and S. Nikartas (eds.),
***Understanding Crime Control and Punishment in Lithuania*,**
Crime Prevention and Security Management,
https://doi.org/10.1007/978-3-032-05538-5_6

The original version of the book was inadvertently published with the incorrect subheading of section 2 in chapter 6 which has been updated to "Reintegrative Shaming: Conditions for Bullying Emergence, The Bullying Process, and its Participants". The book has been updated with the changes.

The updated version of this chapter can be found at
https://doi.org/10.1007/978-3-032-05538-5_6

A. Dobryninas and S. Nikartas (eds.), *Understanding Crime Control and Punishment in Lithuania*, Crime Prevention and Security Management,
https://doi.org/10.1007/978-3-032-05538-5_14

Index

A. Dobryninas and S. Nikartas (eds.), *Understanding Crime Control and Punishment in Lithuania*, Crime Prevention and Security Management,
https://doi.org/10.1007/978-3-032-05538-5

FSC
www.fsc.org
MIX
Papier | Fördert gute Waldnutzung
FSC® C083411

Kolibri 360 GmbH
Ferdinand-Jühlke-Straße 7
99095 Erfurt, Deutschland
produktsicherheit@kolibri360.de